ROYAL HISTORICAL SOCIETY
STUDIES IN HISTORY
SERIES
No. 28

MONEY, PRICES AND POLITICS IN FIFTEENTH-CENTURY CASTILE

Recent volumes published in this series include

For a complete list of the series please see pp. 185-6

MONEY, PRICES AND POLITICS IN FIFTEENTH-CENTURY CASTILE

Angus MacKay

LONDON
ROYAL HISTORICAL SOCIETY
1981

© Angus MacKay 1981
ISBN 0 901050 82 2

The Society records its gratitude to the following, whose generosity made possible the initiation of this series: The British Academy; The Pilgrim Trust; The Twenty-Seven Foundation; The United States Embassy bicentennial funds; The Wolfson Trust; several private donors.

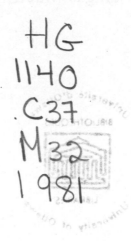
Printed in England
by Swift Printers (Sales) Ltd
London E.C.1.

To my parents

CONTENTS

MAPS

ACKNOWLEDGEMENTS

Most of the data in this book have been extracted from the cathedral archive of Burgos, the municipal archives of Burgos and Seville, and the *Biblioteca Nacional* in Madrid, and I would like to thank the staff of these institutions for their unfailing help and generosity. In particular I would like to express my warmest thanks to Don Constantino Juez Cerezo, Don Atanasio Megido García, and Don Matías Vicario: when, during the long days spent in the cathedral archive, it seemed as if the analysis of the *Libros Redondos* of Burgos would never be completed, their friendship, eccentric humour, and enchanting conversations and recollections dispelled many a period of despondency.

I am grateful to the The British Academy and to the University of Edinburgh for contributing to the expenses of those periods of study in Spain during which I collected most of the material contained in this book.

Among those who patiently listened to some of my wilder ideas or helped me with some of the technical problems which I inevitably encountered, I am particularly indebted to Professor F.C. Spooner and Dr. Wray Vamplew.

Finally — and despite the fact that this is emphatically not his kind of history — I wish once more to record my special debt of gratitude to Professor Denys Hay: *i Cada loco con su tema!*

ABBREVIATIONS

A.C. Burgos	Archivo de la Catedral, Burgos.
ADM	Archivo de los Duques de Medinaceli, Seville.
AGS	Archivo General de Simancas.
D. de C.	Diversos de Castilla
EMR	Escribanía Mayor de Rentas
Exp. Hac.	Expedientes de Hacienda
AHN	Archivo Histórico Nacional, Madrid.
AM	Archivo Municipal (of Burgos, Carmona, Seville etc.).
BN, MS	Biblioteca Nacional, Madrid; Sección de Manuscritos.
Carp.	Carpeta.
Escorial	Archivo del Real Monasterio del Escorial.
Leg.	Legajo.
Mrs.	*Maravedíes.*
Pergs.	Pergaminos.

INTRODUCTION

Although I was not trained as an economic historian, the importance of the problems which this book attempts to solve persuaded me to embark on the study of prices. I soon became convinced of the intrinsic fascination of this area of historical analysis, but at the outset my reasons for embarking on the venture were eminently practical and perhaps even pedestrian. Nearly all historians working on late medieval Castilian history are convinced of the importance of the quantitative information which they extract from the archives and cite in their studies; but all these historians are also fully aware of the upheavals in the Castilian monetary system and the chronic instability of the money of account, the *maravedí*. Until these upheavals and instabilities can be properly described, therefore, there is no way of knowing what the quantitative information really means. Basically the problem is one of an inability to 'measure' the data. I hope that this book provides the necessary descriptions as well as the basic information which will allow such measurements to be made.

In this connexion I would like to use the preface to draw attention to the equation which I occasionally use during the course of this study. If we are to analyse subtle changes in the scale of monetary disturbances, a method of calculation must be devised and applied which allows us to 'weigh' and 'compare' different data. In particular, in order to analyse the interactions between different coin changes, determine the intentions of royal monetary policies, and calculate bimetallic ratios, it is necessary to reduce the various data on the finenesses and weights of coins to comprehensible common denominators. To do this, I have constructed an equation which allows for the calculation of the price in *maravedíes* of a mark of fine silver or gold by using the data available for the intrinsic content of coins. Thus $P = xy/z$ where 'P' is the price of one mark of gold or silver in *maravedíes*, 'x' is the value of the coin in *maravedíes*, 'y' is the number of these coins minted from one mark, and 'z' is the fineness of the coin relative to the maximum degree of purity of gold or silver. The equation, of course, contains an in-built margin of error, since it fails to take into account the value of the alloy of coins, but the value of these approximate calculations clearly outweighs the limitations.

Of course, I do not confine myself to problems of mere measurement. On the contrary, I use the quantitative data I have accumulated in order to examine the supply of precious metals, royal monetary policies, and the relationships between monetary disturbances and the political and social tensions of the period. In doing so I hope to persuade the reader who is more interested in these latter aspects that it is well worthwhile persevering with the discussions of the more technical monetary problems.

Angus MacKay
Edinburgh.

1

THE 'KINGDOM' AND THE SUPPLY
OF PRECIOUS METALS

As the title suggests, this book is concerned with a particular kind of history in which monetary factors receive close attention. In geographical terms the area studied is the fifteenth-century kingdom of Castile. At the outset, therefore, two fundamental questions must claim the attention of both reader and writer alike. Firstly, in concentrating on this kind of history, what causal role is being ascribed to monetary factors? Secondly, was the kingdom of Castile a cohesive economic and political unit or was it in reality an uneasy combination of varied regions?

Because of the polemics arising from Hamilton's studies on the monetary and price history of early modern Spain,[1] it is not easy to formulate an answer to the first question. In general terms, of course, the tendency in modern economic analysis has been to move away from monetary explanations, but in the case of Spanish historiography discussions of such problems may cover several centuries at a time and also present the unwary historian with some uncomfortable pitfalls of a methodological and ideological nature. In 1956, for example, Pierre Vilar published a fascinating article in which, as well as devoting a great deal of critical attention to the Spanish example and the works of Hamilton, he launched a biting attack on Keynesian interpretations and theories, and argued forcefully in favour of an 'explicit' return to Marx. 'Statistical information has accumulated', argued Vilar, 'but our understanding has not always advanced. The crisis of economic thought, not unconnected with the general difficulties of capitalism since 1929, has led some historians into theoretical oversimplifications which are necessarily unhistorical. Their models are not based on reality.'[2] Hamilton's work, of course, was regarded as displaying many of these 'theoretical oversimplifications'. Discussion, however, was not confined merely to arguments about theories and models. In an important book published in 1970,

---

[1] Earl J. Hamilton, *American Treasure and the Price Revolution in Spain, 1501-1650* (Cambridge, Mass. 1934); *War and Prices in Spain, 1651-1800* (Cambridge, Mass. 1947); *El florecimiento del capitalismo y otros ensayos de historia económica* (Madrid, 1948).

[2] Pierre Vilar, 'Problems of the Formation of Capitalism', *Past and Present,* no. 10 (1956), 15-38. Vilar repeats some of the arguments in the introduction to his *Oro y moneda en la historia (1450-1920)* (3rd ed., Barcelona, 1974).

4

Gonzalo Anes worked out the implications of his discovery that modern Spain, like France, had its local market prices or *mercuriales*.[3] Did not these sources provide much better information than the rather dubious type of documentation used by Hamilton? In any case, the general result seems to have been that the study of price, wage and monetary data for periods prior to the eighteenth century in Spain declined in vigour.[4]

Since most of the polemics have centred on the sixteenth and seventeenth centuries, it is not difficult to justify studies dealing with earlier periods which have been relatively ignored. In fact in the histories of the prices, wages and monetary systems of later medieval Europe, the kingdom of Castile, despite its intrinsic interest and potential importance, remains a largely unexplored area. Studies exist on aspects of the earlier history of Castilian prices and coins, numismatists have introduced some order into the classification of later medieval moneys, and Hamilton published an account of prices and wages in the neighbouring kingdoms of Valencia, Aragon and Navarre.[5] Hamilton's valuable study, however, is of little use for an examination of the Castilian scene, and as a result historians have been forced to fall back on outdated and confusing works, such as those by Sáez.[6] As far as the sources are concerned, the matter is simpler — for the centuries prior to the *mercuriales* historians, like beggars, cannot be choosers. Thus, if the documentation used in the present study may seem 'imperfect', I can only plead that the historian has to make the best of the material at his disposal.

The detailed role ascribed to monetary factors will emerge during the course of the book. In general terms, however, the point of view adopted is that, although money and precious metals could play a creative and dynamic role in economic and political activity, they were just as likely to become a function of economic activity. In other words, given the proposition that there was no change in economic

[3] G. Anes Alvarez, *Las crisis agrarias en la España moderna* (Madrid, 1970).

[4] For further data on price histories see Angus MacKay, 'Recent Literature on Spanish Economic History', *Economic History Review,* 2nd ser. xxxi (1978), 129-45.

[5] Earl J. Hamilton, *Money, Prices and Wages in Valencia, Aragon and Navarre, 1351-1500* (Cambridge, Mass., 1936). Two recent and stimulating studies on earlier periods are J. Gautier-Dalché, 'L'histoire monetaire de l'Espagne septentrionale et centrale du IXe au XIIe siècles: quelques réflexions sur diverses problèmes', *Anuario de Estudios Medievales* vi (1969), 43-95, and J. Valdeón Baruque, 'Las reformas monetarias de Enrique II de Castilla', in *Homenaje al Prof. Alarcos* (Valladolid, 1966), II, 829-45.

[6] The most frequently used of these is Liciniano Sáez, *Demostración histórcia del verdadero valor de todas las monedas que corrian en Castilla durante el reynado del Señor Don Enrique IV, y de su correspondencia con las del Señor Don Carlos IV* (Madrid, 1805).

activity or in prices 'without its accompanying buzz of monetary phenomena of all sorts',[7] then the problem of whether these phenomena *created* or *reflected* such changes is one which cannot be answered in advance but only in terms of the other variables, such as the state of the evolving agrarian and demographic structures, which also played dynamic roles to a greater or lesser extent in each particular case. It need hardly be added that, as far as the case of late medieval Castile is concerned, our knowledge of *all* the variables is so rudimentary that the task of weighting them becomes something of a guessing game. Accordingly, the interpretations and solutions advanced in this book are provisional and tentative. It is possible, for example, that the role of the Crown and of political factors have been exaggerated. Nevertheless, even if the monetary phenomena were to be denied any creativity and were to be reduced to a strictly *reflective* role, it could still be claimed that the information and hypotheses mark a valuable advance on the present state of knowledge. But, although we will be returning to these questions, it is now time to consider the extent to which it makes sense to consider the kingdom of Castile as a cohesive unit. In doing so, it will also be possible to focus the discussion on some of the other variables which played a creative role in economic and political activity.

The 'Kingdom' of Castile:
Co-ordinating factors and regions

Of all the variables during the late medieval period, the area encompassed by the 'kingdom' of Castile was probably the most mercurial, although it must be remembered that changes in the configurations of the frontiers of Castile also implied important demographic consequences. At first sight the problem of the moving frontiers seems irrelevant to the precise period covered in this study: the last dramatic phase in the reconquest had taken place in the thirteenth century, and the Muslim kingdom of Granada was not to fall to the Castilians until 1492. It would, however, be highly misleading to think in terms of either precise dates or precise frontiers. True enough, we can date the fall of particular towns, such as Córdoba (1236) and Seville (1248), to the Castilians. But reconquest implied repopulation and colonisation, and rather than the dates of sieges, battles and capitulations we should concentrate on the continuous problem of the occupation of territories on the frontiers of

[7]The phrase is Vilar's in 'Problems of the Formation of Capitalism', 28.

an expanding society.[8] And even the term 'expanding' is ambiguous! For do we mean that both 'blades' of the Malthusian 'scissors' were involved? In fact at a time when elsewhere in Europe population growth caused pressure on food resources, the kingdom of Castile doubled the size of its territory with the result that even in the century prior to the Black Death there was an abundance or 'saturation' of land and a crisis of manpower. Land, in other words, expanded at a faster rate than population, and the consequences of this 'reversal' of the Malthusian 'scissors' were still being worked out during the period studied here. The study of these consequences would require another book, but the salient features can be briefly sketched in. The abundance of land and shortage of manpower (compounded by the Black Death) implied an almost total absence of demesne exploitation in the arable sector of the economy, pastoralism and transhumance expanded rapidly, the great lay and ecclesiastical lords competed for manpower by offering better conditions and terms of land tenure, and the opportunities of the new frontier society of the south continued to attract colonists and men from the north. Such a bald summary, of course, misses out many important issues such as the changing patterns of 'assimilation' and 'expulsion' which affected the Muslims who remained in Christian territory after the thirteenth-century reconquest. But in essence, and despite the serious absence of good studies on the late medieval demography of Castile, I believe that the summary contains the essential points.[9]

If the 'reconquest' of the thirteenth century continued, so to speak, into the fourteenth and fifteenth centuries, can we be sure that the reverse phenomenon did not occur with the conquest of Granada in 1492? Did Granada perhaps fall at an earlier date? In many ways it did. It should be remembered, for example, that the origins of the Nasrid kingdom of Granada are to a large extent to be explained by the fact that its founder, Muhammad I or Ibn al-Ahmar (1232-73) entered into a vassalage relationship with the Crown of Castile.[10] In theory — and to some extent in practice — the rulers of Granada paid

---

[8]On this problem and related aspects see A. MacKay, *Spain in the Middle Ages: From Frontier to Empire, 1000-1500* (London, 1977), chs. 2, 3, and 8.

[9]A full bibliography covering these points would be enormous. In addition to the studies by Cabrillana, Garcia de Cortázar, González, González Jiménez, Ladero Quesada, Mitre Fernández, Moreta, Pastor de Togneri, and Sobrequés Callicó listed in A. MacKay 'Recent Literature', 137-45, there are excellent contributions on demographic aspects by Cabrera Muñoz and Collantes de Terán in *Andalucia, de la Edad Media a la Moderna,* ed. M.A. Ladero Quesada *(Anexos de la revista 'Hispania',* 7: Madrid, 1977).

[10]For a summary of the details of this relationship and of Muhammad I's service in Ferdinand III's campaigns in the Seville region, see MacKay, *Spain in the Middle Ages,* pp. 63-4.

tribute (*parias*), made war and peace for the kings of Castile, and were even supposed to attend the Castilian *cortes*. Naturally enough, changing fortunes in the real world of politics imposed themselves on these theoretical relationships, but it would not be entirely wrong to regard the late medieval kingdom of Granada as a 'client' state of Castile.[11] In due course we will return to the monetary implications of this dependence, as symbolised by the payment of tribute or *parias*.[12]

The Granadan example is also useful for examining the concept of the 'frontier' more closely. Even during the static phases of the reconquest there was no such thing as a clear geographical frontier. Indeed the ease with which men strayed across the 'frontiers' was proverbial, and the authorities of both sides were kept busy showing lost travellers the right way back; as one Moorish castellan put it, 'this, after all, is what neighbours are for'.[13] And just as men strayed across the frontier, so too did ideas, culture, merchandise and money. In fact elsewhere I have argued that frontiers unite as well as divide and that they demand socio-geographical definitions in terms of sub-cultures. Thus the frontier world of Andalusia-Granada developed its own styles of fighting, an elaborate set of peace-keeping mechanisms, and a marked degree of acculturation. Well before 1492, for example, Franco-Gothic art had established itself in the Alhambra, and the royal *alcázar* built in Christian Seville was to all intents and purposes a Moorish palace.[14]

These random reflections and rather odd examples should be sufficient to indicate that, despite legislation, the sea and land frontiers of Castile were 'open'. In theory and in law frontiers were envisaged as areas where one sovereignty ended and another began. Many and interminable were the laws, tax-farming regulations (*cuadernos*), and proceedings of the *cortes* which dealt with the control of trade across the frontiers. In fact, on paper, the royal customs administration in fifteenth-century Castile was remarkably

[11] In general see M.A. Ladero Quesada, *Granada. Historia de un país islámico* (Madrid, 1969): E. Mitre Fernández, 'La frontière de Grenade aux environs de 1400', *Le Moyen Age*, LXXVIII (1972), 489-522; L. Suárez Fernández, *Juan II y la frontera de Granada* (Valladolid, 1954). For a detailed example of the conditions of 'clientage' see the published documentation of the 1439 truce negotiations in J. Amador de los Ríos, *Memoria histórico-crítica sobre las treguas celebradas en 1439 entre los reyes de Castilla y de Granada* (Madrid, n.d.).

[12] Below, pp. 35-6.

[13] Excellent examples of trans-frontier co-operation between Christian and Moorish 'neighbours' are given in J. de Mata Carriazo, 'Los moros de Granada en las actas del concejo de Jaén de 1479', *Miscelánea de estudios árabes y hebraicos*, IV (1955), 81-125, reprinted in *Homenaje al profesor Carriazo* (Seville, 1971), I, 265-310.

[14] See Angus MacKay, 'The ballad and the frontier in late mediaeval Spain', *Bulletin of Hispanic Studies*, LIII (1976), 15-33.

8

sophisticated and detailed. Even something similar to the modern 'sterling allowance', for example, was brought into being with the stipulation that sums of twenty and ten florins could be taken out of the kingdom by nobles and non-nobles respectively for their personal expenditure. The main features of the customs system can perhaps best be studied by referring to the 'zones' outlined on Map 1.[15]

Map 1 – The Customs Organization of Castile

[15]On all these points and also for what follows, see M.A. Ladero Quesada, 'Las aduanas de Castilla en el siglo XV', *Revue internationale d'histoire de la banque,* no. 7 (1973), 83-110.

1. The North. In the ports of this zone trade was subject to the *diezmos de la mar* — that is, *ad valorem* customs duties of ten per cent. For administrative purposes the zone was subdivided into two tax-farming areas, Galicia and Asturias on the one hand and the Basque coast on the other. Apart from Galicia, where the loading and discharging of goods was confined to named ports, merchants could use any of the northern ports provided they returned from abroad to the same port.

2. The East. Although the ordinances bristle with exceptions and differences of detail, customs duties similar to those of the northern zone were levied on the frontiers with the kingdom of Navarre and the Crown of Aragon. Broadly speaking there were two customs areas in the east, one of these was formed by the frontier bishoprics of Calahorra, Osma and Siguenza, and the other was made up of the bishoprics of Cuenca and Cartagena. In this zone both imports and exports were channelled through designated control points or *puertos*: Logroño, Vitoria, Calahorra, Agreda, Soria, Molina, Requena, Moya, Murcia, Almansa, and Yecla.

3. The South. During periods of truce a customs tax known as the *diezmo y medio diezmo de lo morisco* was levied on trade between the kingdoms of Castile and Granada. Here too there were officially designated *puertos:* Antequera, Zahara, Alcalá la Real and Huelma on the frontier itself, and Jerez, Tarifa and Cartagena for seaborne trade. Trade between Castile and Granada, of course, constituted only a fraction of the total volume of imports and exports in this southern zone. Thus, in addition to the *diezmo y medio diezmo de lo morisco* the south was subjected to the much more lucrative customs duty known as the *almojarifazgo*. There were two tax-farming regions for the collection of this duty, the bishopric of Cartagena and kingdom of Murcia in the south-east, and the *almojarifazgo* of Seville. In the south-east the tax-farmers levied the *almojarifazgo* on maritime trade by attempting to register and channel it through Lorca, Murcia and Cartagena. In the south-west the *almojarifazgo* administration was centred on Seville, but the competence of the tax-farmers not only covered the huge archbishopric of Seville itself but the bishopric of Cádiz as well. Here the administration was far more sophisticated and the Seville *almojarifazgo* constituted the most important source of Castilian customs income during the fifteenth century.

4. The West. No customs administration existed along the Portuguese frontier, although there were officials whose duty it was to prevent the export of 'forbidden' merchandise. The absence of a customs system in this zone is easily explained by the fact that trade flowed from Castile to Portugal; consequently Castilian disinterest was balanced by the keen desire of the Portuguese kings to control and tax this one-sided trans-frontier commerce.

It would appear, therefore, that the customs organization of the kingdom of Castile during the fifteenth century was well-regulated and sophisticated. Yet the appearances are deceptive, and despite the detailed regulations, smuggling, fraud and corruption were frequent. The frontiers, in short, were 'open', and it was an easy matter to avoid customs officials. Jerez, for example, had a special privilege which exempted merchandise needed by the town from taxes and customs duties. Goods which arrived at the ports of Cádiz and Puerto de Santa María, therefore, were nominally sent to Jerez in order to avoid payment of duties, and from there they were redistributed further inland. Similarly, further north, cloth was smuggled into Castile across the Aragonese frontier. Frequently, smugglers were actively helped by corrupt officials. There were allegations that customs officers in the bishopric of Calahorra, in Galicia, and in Asturias co-operated with merchants in a scheme to lower the customs duties, and in the Seville region even military and naval officials, including the admiral and his lieutenant, were accused by the Crown of lining their own pockets by protecting exporters from tax officials.[16] Could it be that the many and interminable laws and regulations dealing with customs duties should be interpreted as admissions that practice fell far short of matching theory? If so, then it should be noted that precious metals and money always figured prominently on the lists of forbidden exports along with such other items as grain, horses, iron and weapons. In fact an illegal trade in precious metals and grain was a well-established feature of economic activities in Seville.[17]

But if on examination the kingdom of Castile turns out to have been 'fluid' and 'open' on its frontiers, there is a problem which is still more vexing in the context of the present study. To what 'market' should the data of this study be related? Indeed even if it is granted that the transaction function of money was increasing in range and frequency, how many Castilians actually thought in terms of any

[16]Evidence for these, and other, examples in AM, Jerez, caja l, no. 36 de orden 338; AGS, D. de C., leg. 4, no. 29 and no. 102, fos. 1-10v; *ibid*, leg. 6, no. 38; Escorial, X.11.14., fos. 68-9; Tomás González, *Colección de cédulas, cartas patentes, provisiones, reales ordenes y documentos concernientes a las Provincias Vascongadas* (Madrid, 1829), I, 1-28. See also *Cortes de los antiguos reinos de León y Castilla* (Real Academia de la Historia, Madrid, 1866) (hereafter *Cortes),* II, 10-11, 24-5, 280; *ibid*, III, 149, 411, 684-5.

[17]At one stage it was even suggested that, since so much wheat was smuggled abroad out of Andalusia, the smuggling of grain should be made legal. For Genoese participation in illegal trade in coins, see below p. 40.

'market' outside the confines of their immediate village or town, and how many goods were actually bought or sold with cash? Although he did not use modern terminology, King John II of Castile thought that despite regional variations, most Castilian prices conformed to a quasi-'national' market system with the centre of congruence being the international fairs at Medina del Campo.[18] But of course there was no such 'national' market and there is as yet no firm evidence at all to suggest that data on real prices and wages in Burgos or Seville can tell us anything about prices and wages in Compostela, Toledo or Murcia. Indeed what is badly needed is data for an analysis of the differential geography of markets and prices.[19] It seems obvious that the kingdom of Castile did not constitute an integrated economic unit and the degree of convergence or congruence between its price structures would reveal a great deal about the regional economies.

Although it is impossible to measure the extent of the transaction function of the monetary system of Castile, there are important and obvious indicators which need to be emphasised. In the first place any historian who has worked systematically through various series of Castilian fifteenth-century documents cannot fail to have been impressed by the ubiquity and co-ordinating role of the money of account or *maravedí*. The documentation on royal fiscality presents a special case which needs to be examined in greater detail:[20] but the same impression is to be derived from other types of archival sources, such as the vast holdings of seigneurial documents in the Archivo de los Duques de Medinaceli, the ecclesiastical records of the national and cathedral archives, and the municipal *actas* and accounts of towns like Seville, Burgos and Murcia. Of course, it is tempting to argue that these sources only reveal the transaction function of the monetary system in the upper reaches of society, and that we know little of the extent of this function at social levels specifically below those of the nobility, churchmen, merchants, and urban oligarchs. But if we know nothing about the velocity of circulation of coins, the differential patterns in the monetary system meant that the billon coins were by and large the exchange tokens of the *gente menuda* or 'lesser people'.[21] In this study it is argued that, to some extent, the

[18]I base this conclusion on the ordinance of 1442 in BN, MS., 13107, fos. 181-92, which is discussed in greater detail below, pp. 64-5.

[19]At present only the nineteenth century has been treated in this way: Nicolás Sánchez-Albornoz, 'Congruence among Spanish Economic Regions in the Nineteenth Century', *Journal of European Economic History,* III (1974), 725-45.

[20]Below, pp. 12-15.

[21]See, for example, below, pp. 102-3. Even the 'aristocratic' ordinance of the Infantes of Aragon in 1442 assumes the natural link between billon coins and '*los pueblos*': BN, MS., 13259, fo. 315 (Appendix A-4).

Castilian monarchy debased its coinage for political reasons; but this process took place within the context of a general European bullion famine, and there is no reason why we should summarily reject the evidence of the constant complaints in the *cortes* and royal ordinances to the effect that the billon money supply was failing to meet the demands of the transaction function at the lower social levels.[22] And when royal manipulations of the billon coins did take place, it is hardly surprising that the social consequences spilled out from the town halls and exchanges into the public squares and streets. Were not the popular uprisings and pogroms of 1391 and 1473 directly linked to the fate of the billon coins?[23]

Faute de mieux there is another well-studied body of evidence which can be used to analyse the problems of regional and functional patterns — namely, that relating to the royal fiscality. The coins of the Castilian monetary system were royal coins, and from the Basque mountains to the Granadan frontier they circulated and penetrated in a way that royal writs often failed to do.[24] Moreover, the royal taxes not only bore most heavily on the third estate or *pecheros* but some of the more important taxes were related (however notionally and crudely) to patterns of economic production and the circulation and volume of trade.[25] The efficacy of taxation, of course, was also linked to the regional and chronological variations in the administrative and political powers of the monarchy.

The co-ordinating roles of the monetary system and government rested on two basic foundations — the existence of the money of account, the *maravedí*, and the perpetual drive to increase the income from taxation and administer it more effectively. The *maravedí*, of course, was for most of the period under review a purely imaginary money. It was also, as we shall see, highly unstable and subject to sudden devaluations. Nevertheless as a money of account it performed its co-ordinating role and produced an integrated system from the bewildering variety of gold, silver, copper and even foreign coins

[22] For example, in 1469 Henry IV not only claimed that the resumption of minting had been requested by towns because trade was grinding to a halt, but he also argued that the 'poor' were suffering from a scarcity of small coins: AGS, EMR., Leg. 519, letter of 9 August 1469 (Appendix A-8).

[23] See, for example, the comments of Diego Enriquez del Castillo, below, p. 76, and the discussion on the monetary causes of popular unrest, below, pp. 101-4.

[24] At this stage I am only concerned with stating a theoretical position which more or less corresponded to practice. On counterfeiting and the problems of the proliferation of mints in Henry IV's reign, see below pp. 78-85.

[25] Although I cannot deal with this problem in the monograph, I should like to emphasize here that, in the agrarian sector, the lords' 'surplus-extraction mechanism' in later medieval Castile was also one that functioned almost entirely with money.

which were in circulation. Whatever the variations and regional differences, the people in León, Burgos, Seville and elsewhere calculated in *maravedíes*: in short, the money of account reduced the confusion of coins to something approaching a coherent and unified monetary system. Later in this study the vicissitudes in the fortunes of the *maravedí* will be examined in detail.

To a large extent the role of royal taxation depended on both the theoretical and practical power of the monarchy. Is it too fanciful to link together the French and Castilian patterns of 'absolutism' (or even 'tyranny'), high levels of taxation, debasements, devaluation of the moneys of account, and high rates of nominal inflation, and contrast them with the English and Aragonese-Catalan patterns of constitutional monarchies, powerful representative assemblies, and monetary stability?[26] In any case these associations and contrasts help to give an impression of political and constitutional trends which cannot be analysed here in detail. Early in the fifteenth century the Castilian monarchy attempted to establish a doctrine of 'absolute royal power', and despite the vagaries of practical politics a theoretical 'absolutism' was successfully formulated which was to a large extent supported by the nature of the administration and institutions of government. The king was above the law, held his power directly from God, and the *cortes* were relatively powerless assemblies which were not representative in any meaningful sense. These developments were accompanied — in some cases preceded — by important fiscal innovations. The fourteenth century witnessed the appearance of a new tax, the *alcabala*, which can be aptly compared to the French *taille* in that, although it was a sales-tax and not a tax of repartition, it arose from the demands of war expenditure, became a permanent imposition and accounted for well over half of the regular income of the Crown. At the same time the *cortes* became an assembly which docilely granted those taxes which still needed consent, and financial institutions such as the central *contadurías* were created to deal with the increases in Crown income. These comments have been necessarily brief because what is of interest here is the general picture of the regional variations.[27] That this analysis in differential geography is possible is largely due to the excellent work of Ladero.[28]

For the purposes of taxation, the kingdom of Castile was divided

[26] Some of these points are discussed in detail below, pp. 97-101.

[27] For a more detailed discussion of Castilian 'absolutism', taxes, and institutions see A. MacKay, *Spain in the Middle Ages,* pp. 131-59.

[28] For what follows see in particular M.A. Ladero Quesada, 'Para una imagen de Castilla: 1429-1504', in *Homenaje al Dr. D. Juan Reglà Campistol* (Universidad de Valencia, 1975), I, 201-15.

Map 2 Fiscal Densities in Fifteenth-Century Castile

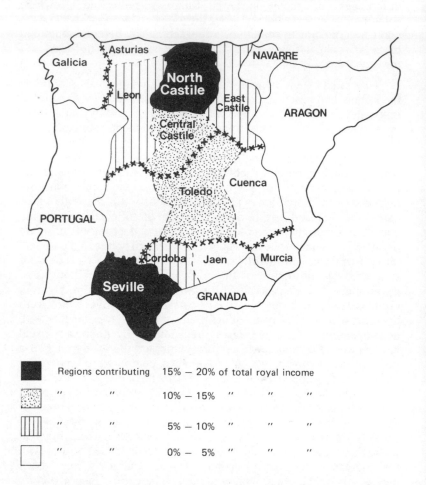

■	Regions contributing	15% – 20% of total royal income
▦	" "	10% – 15% " " "
▥	" "	5% – 10% " " "
□	" "	0% – 5% " " "

Note. The map and statistics on fiscal 'densities' are based on data in M.A. Ladero Quesada, 'Para una imagen de Castilla : 1429 – 1504', in **Homenje al Dr. D. Juan Reglà Campistol** (Universidad de Valencia, 1975), I, 201–15. The figures for total royal income (excluding **cortes** subsidies) which Ladero gives in this study differ from those which he cites in **La Hacienda Real de Castilla en el siglo XV** (La Laguna, 1973), p.43. Apart from the 1465 figures, however, the discrepancies are slight in nature. As far as the major difference for 1465 is concerned, the problem is probably to be resolved by Ladero's comment that in one case his figure is based on the 1463 **arrendamientos** 'pero es seguro que 1465 no fue ya un año de cobro normal' ('Para una imagen ...', 202). In any case, although one set of figures is used at present and the other set later, the differences do not substantially affect the nature of the argument presented here.

into areas which on the whole corresponded to traditional judicial and ecclesiastical regions. Using the abundant documentation on royal fiscality, Ladero has mapped the various divisions and sub-divisions, and he has analysed how much each area was worth in terms of royal taxation, and the extent to which royal power fluctuated from region to region (see Map 2). For the purposes of this study much of the detail is omitted, and where necessary Ladero's analysis is amended.

If it cannot be maintained that the fiscal areas necessarily coincide with the differential geography of the regional economies, it is equally clear that it would be misleading to envisage them as merely geopolitical in nature. The map of fiscal 'densities' shows that the truth lies between these political and economic co-ordinates. From the point of view of political history the map contains few surprises. The regions of the north-west and the south-east were traditionally amongst those where the monarchy found the tasks of government extremely difficult if not at times impossible. For most of the fifteenth century Galicia was in the grip of a widespread anarchy which culminated in the *hermandino* rebellion of the years 1467-70,[29] and in Murcia the Fajardo family 'governed' for long periods of time during which it seemed as if the royal administration had ceased to operate completely. The 1460s, for example, witnessed a complete collapse of royal authority in the latter region and, in the words of the town *actas* of Murcia, the *adelantado* Pedro Fajardo ruled 'almost as a viceroy'.[30] From the point of view of the royal court, the situation was aptly summed up by Fernando del Pulgar when, in 1473, he wrote to the bishop of Coria: 'As far as the kingdom of Murcia is concerned, I swear to you my lord that we regard it as being as foreign to us as the kingdom of Navarre because no letters, messengers, *procuradores,* or quaestors have gone there from here, or come here from there, for over five years . . .'.[31] But while bearing in mind such variations in the fabric of political control, Spooner's observations on the relationship between taxation, the economy and the monetary system are as valid for Castile as they are for France. 'The flow of tax remittances, perfectly or imperfectly achieved, implied also the sale of cash crops, the use of money in commercial transactions, and inevitably the development of monetary institutions. All this imparts a certain cohesion . . . to . . . monetary history. . .'[32]

[29]MacKay, *Spain in the Middle Ages,* pp. 176-7.

[30]For an excellent study on Murcia during this period see Juan Torres Fontes, *Don Pedro Fajardo, adelantado mayor del reino de Murcia* (Madrid, 1953).

[31]*Ibid.,* p. 119.

[32]Frank C. Spooner, *The International Economy and Monetary Movements in France, 1493-1725* (Cambridge, Mass. 1972), p. 6.

FISCAL 'DENSITIES' IN FIFTEENTH-CENTURY CASTILE: REGIONAL PERCENTAGE CONTRIBUTIONS TO TOTAL ROYAL INCOME

Area	Region	1429	1451	1465
North Castile		16.3%	17.8%	17.5%
East Castile		9.3%	9.2%	7.7%
Central Castile		12.1%	9.9%	8.5%
León		9.6%	7.4%	6.6%
Asturias		1.8%	1.5%	1.6%
Total:	León-Castile	**49.1%**	**45.8%**	**42.0%**
	Galicia	4.8%	5.2%	4.2%
Toledo		11.2%	11.5%	11.7%
Cuenca		5.1%	4.4%	4.0%
Extremadura		4.2%	3.9%	5.1%
Servicio-Montazgo		1.3%	2.4%	2.3%
Total:	New Castile-Extremadura	**22.0%**	**22.3%**	**23.1%**
Seville		15.4%	16.2%	19.7%
Córdoba		4.1%	5.8%	7.4%
Jaén		2.8%	3.0%	2.4%
Total:	Andalusia	**22.3%**	**25.0%**	**29.5%**
	Murcia	1.7%	1.7%	1.1%
		100%	100%	100%

The two most important sources of Crown income were the *alcabala* (sales-tax) and the customs duties — the former accounting for about 75% of regular royal income, and the latter for about 12%[33] — and the map reveals this relationship between taxation and trade. The areas of greatest fiscal and commercial activity were without doubt Seville and North Castile. Of these two, Seville was rapidly coming to the forefront during the course of the fifteenth century. The city itself, with some 40,000 inhabitants, was the largest in the kingdom, and in addition to the flourishing *alcabala* revenues this was the zone with the largest volume of customs duties (*almojarifazgo mayor*). The region was at the crossroads not only of the European and African economies but of those of the Mediterranean and the Atlantic as well, and the Genoese established themselves in force in a Seville which, by the fifteenth century, was a financial and banking centre of European importance.[34]

Since the data for this study are derived mainly from Burgos, the area of North Castile will be studied below in more detail, and both it and the Seville region will figure prominently in the discussion on precious metals.[35]

Next in order of importance were the areas of Central Castile and Toledo. The economic centre of the latter region, of course, was the town of Toledo itself which, in fiscal terms, was of the same status as Burgos and more productive than either Santiago de Compostela or Córdoba. The wealth of Central Castile is partly to be explained in terms of its towns — Valladolid, which linked the region to Burgos and North Castile, and Avila and Segovia which linked the mountains and plains and were vital to the transhumance structure. But the international fairs of Medina del Campo also belong geographically to Central Castile and, becoming economically more significant during this century, they provided an alternative, though intermittent, economic capital for the region. These 'active' regions contrasted with areas such as Murcia and Asturias, which were economically stagnant and on the margin of the great trade routes, and where the urban socio-economic structure was not so fully developed.[36]

Nevertheless, it should be stressed that this fiscal geography can be misleading, although once most of the qualifications have been

[33] Ladero, 'Para una imagen', 204-5.

[34] For detailed studies of the Sevillian economy during this period see A. Collantes de Terán, *Sevilla en la baja edad media: la ciudad y sus hombres* (Seville, 1977); R. Pike, *Enterprise and adventure. The Genoese in Seville and the Opening up of the New World* (New York, 1967); J. Heers, *Gênes au XV siècle* (Paris, 1961).

[35] below pp. 18-22 and pp. 23-41.

[36] Ladero, 'Para una imagen', 208-9, 211, 214.

noted the result is to strengthen rather than alter the validity of the overall picture. In the region of León, for example, it was the areas closest to Central Castile (Zamora and Salamanca) which were economically more active than the north-western lands round Astorga and the town of León itself.[37] The region of East Castile had no urban or economic centres to compare with those of North and Central Castile, but it contained some of the kingdom's most important salines and much of its revenue was derived from customs duties. But this region also included the Basque provinces which were as difficult to govern as Galicia or Murcia — here the Crown obtained hardly any revenue, and the so-called *pedidos* merely signified the taxational presence of the monarch in a lawless area which did not even have a customs organization along the frontier with Navarre.[38] In general terms, therefore, the picture is one of 'weak' peripheral areas (especially in the north-west and south-east) and a 'strong' corridor from the central part of the north coast down to the Seville region. It is now time to concentrate on the region most closely related to the data of this study, namely North Castile.

In the terminology of the fiscal geography of the period, Ladero's region of North Castile included the *merindades* of Burgos, Candemuño, Cerrato, Castrojeriz, Villadiego, Asturias de Santillana, Castilla la Vieja, Bureba, Silos, Carrión, Campos, Monzón, Saldaña, Campoo, Liébana and Pernia. Its economic capital was the city of Burgos, but Palencia, on its western limits and close to Valladolid and Medina del Campo, was also of considerable importance. Apart from the *alcabalas,* which were as usual farmed out in conjunction with the *tercias,* this region was important for its coastal salines and for the customs duties, known as the *diezmos de la mar,* which were alienated by Henry IV to his constable, Pedro Fernández de Velasco, in 1467.[39]

Molenat's study of the communications systems at the end of this period helps to support the view that this fiscal region was also an economic one.[40] Such an economic region, of course, is seen as being dominated by Burgos itself: 'Dans le cadre d'une région économique bien individualisée, autour du "pôle de croissance" de Burgos, dans un rayon suffisament vaste pour que les relations soient significatives,

[37]*Ibid*., 208-9.

[38]*Ibid*., 207-8.

[39]*Ibid*., 206-7.

[40]J.-P. Molenat, 'Chemins et ports du nord de la Castille au temps des Rois Catholiques', *Mélanges de la Casa de Velázquez,* VII (1971), 115-62.

il s'agit de rechercher à la fois par quels chemins la ville commandait la région et s'assurait son approvisionnement et la circulation des marchandises. . . .'[41] Moreover because of its relationships with Bilbao and the coast, both Molenat and Pérez see the region as assuming the same configuration as Ladero's North Castile, and they both contrast it with the regional economy of Central Castile 'gravitant autour de Valladolid et Tolède.'[42] In effect the major routes northwards from Burgos lent a coherence to the region which it did not possess in natural geographical terms — due north to Laredo or Bilbao (via Valmaseda), and to Bilbao (via Pancorbo and Orduña) and Vitoria (via Pancorbo and Miranda de Ebro).[43]

But of course one region shaded into another, and the other routes radiating from Burgos were just as important. For example, to the south-west a busy road linked Burgos to Valladolid and to the international fairs at Medina del Campo. Burgos, in other words, also 'belonged' to other regional economies. The point is important in terms of some of the prices cited in this study. The documents, for example, specifically state on occasion that the canons of Burgos bought their wax in bulk at the fairs of Medina del Campo, and the famous wines of Toro and of Madrigal were carted along the same route from Valladolid to Burgos.[44] Indeed, the status of Burgos as a wool capital, as well as the fact that most of the areas of North Castile were *países de acarreo,*[45] means that the region's economic structure was a function of activities which transcended the regional boundaries.

The reasons for Burgos's economic importance at a supraregional level are well known.[46] Situated on the famous Pilgrim Route to Compostela and regarded as the political 'capital' of the kingdom, the town was at the heart of communications to the ports of the north coast and controlled the wool export trade. This latter factor was the most important, and from an early date it led to the rise of a powerful group of native merchants who soon replaced the foreign

[41]*Ibid.*, 115-6.

[42]*Ibid.*, 115 and note 6.

[43]Two of the maps which Molenat appends to his study are invaluable because of their combination of detail with clarity: *'Le chemin de Valladolid à Burgos et le "camino real francès"'*, and *'Les chemins de Burgos à la côte'.*

[44]See below, p. 43.

[45]See in particular Molenat, 'Chemins et ports', 119.

[46]A recent study which contains much useful background and bibliographical information is T.F. Ruiz, 'The Transformation of the Castilian Municipalities: The Case of Burgos, 1248-1350', *Past and Present,* no. 77 (1977), 3-32. On more specifically economic aspects see M. Basas Fernández, *El consulado de Burgos en el siglo XVI* (Madrid, 1963) and R.S. Smith, *The Spanish Guild Merchant. A History of the Consulado,* 1250-1700 (Durham, 1940), ch. 1.

entrepreneurs who had been attracted to Burgos along the *camino francés*. In a very real sense the wool trade was the trade of Burgos, and every year the wool clipped in the *sierra* was collected and exported to Flanders.[47] Yet by the fifteenth century the Burgos merchants had well-developed interests in other economic activities. In Seville, for example, the Burgos men formed the largest colony of native merchants and they dealt in a wide variety of commodities such as Andalusian olive oil, leather, Malaga almonds and dye for the cloth industry.

A *consulado* was created in Burgos in 1494, but the creation of this institution was obviously the confirmation, in a new form, of a merchant guild which had clearly existed for some time. It is certain that an association of merchants, with a prior and consuls, functioned in 1447, and a religious confraternity of merchants, which later became an official merchant guild, probably existed at the beginning of the century. Indeed since Castilian merchants, based in Burgos, possessed a guild in Flanders by at least 1336, an even earlier date seems likely.[48]

The terminology applied to this association of merchants — *gremio, república, hermandad, cofradía* — reveals that it represented a strong mixture of merchant guild and religious confraternity. Its power, however, marked it off from other artisan and merchant guilds. In the first place it was not restricted to Burgos merchants. In 1455, following a dispute between Burgos and Basque merchants, Henry IV created two 'national' associations of merchants. The Burgos association covered towns south of the Ebro river, and hence merchants from Toledo, Segovia, Soria, Medina del Campo, Logroño and other towns could belong to the Burgos guild. It was understood, of course, that the term 'merchant' did not include simple artisans or retailing merchants but only those dealing in imports and exports. Moreover the wool trade ensured that the connexions with other towns were not simply formal, and Burgos also seems to have acted as an economic clearing house when the fairs at Medina del Campo were not in being.[49]

This short digression on the activities of the wealthier and more powerful Burgos merchants is not without its significance for the themes of this book. On a practical level, for example, there was the connexion between wool exports and silver imports. The *consulado*

[47]Basas Fernández, pp. 29-30, 85, 155-6.

[48]Smith, pp. 41-3; Basas, pp. 30-3, 50-1, 186.

[49]Basas, pp. 50-1 and AGS., Exp. Hac., Leg. 2, no. 96 which records a wide variety of transactions and bills of exchange, all of which were drawn up in Burgos.

ordinances of 1494 stated that they confirmed the existing practice whereby the prior and consuls arranged for shipping contracts and insurance on the north coast and notified the merchants of all the towns concerned of the dates of sailing.[50] Indeed the very problem of the sailing dates of the merchant fleets necessitated the existence of an organization inland which would ensure that the arrival of wool at the ports coincided with fleet departures. Thus, as will be seen later, quite apart from fluctuations in the Flanders trade, the patterns of sailing dates for the fleets also affected calculations about silver supplies from Flanders and the organization of the Castilian mints.[51]

In more general terms the activities of the Burgos merchants are important because if they illustrate the role of the town as a 'pôle de croissance' within the regional economy, they also show that the cohesiveness of the region was severely strained. The men of the north coast, who were shippers rather than merchants, never allowed themselves to be dominated by their hinterland.[52] It was Basque ships which carried Burgos wool to Flanders and returned with cloth, silver and other goods to supply the Castilian demand at the fairs of Medina del Campo. Although the success of the Basques as international shippers and the existence of a powerful organization or *hermandad* of north-coast towns lie outside the scope of this discussion, they help to explain the successful resistance against the threat of total domination by Burgos. For example, from the middle of the fifteenth century, it became clear that the Castilian 'nation' at Bruges (which was the terminal point for Castilian exports of wool) was seriously divided by clashes between Castilians and Basques, and it was this situation which led to Henry IV's creation of two 'nations'.[53] Similarly, as against the Bilbao shippers' control over the export arrangements from the north coast, for example, the Burgos merchants attempted in 1453 to contract separately with the port of Santander.[54] In short, while the cohesiveness of the North Castile region was the product of its inter-regional and international relationships, the play of interests (merchants-shippers, wool exports-*países de acarreo*) also led to internal conflict and tensions.

[50]Basas, p. 156.

[51]See below pp. 31-2, 105.

[52]For what follows and on the Basque shippers in general, see J.A. García de Cortázar, *Vizcaya en el siglo XV. Aspectos económicos y sociales* (Bilbao, 1966); L. Suárez Fernández, *Navegación y comercio en el golfo de Vizcaya* (Madrid, 1959); J. Heers, 'Le commerce des basques en Mediterranée', *Bulletin Hispanique*, LVII (1955), 292-324.

[53]Suárez, *Navegación y comercio*, pp. 120-1; Garcia de Cortázar, pp. 212-29; Basas, pp. 37, 155-61.

[54]Smith, ch. V; Basas, pp. 201-2.

A greater degree of attention has been concentrated on the Burgos region not simply because most of the quantitative information has been derived from the town of Burgos itself, but also because there is an important distinction to be made between 'real' and 'nominal' data. As far as the former are concerned, the matter is simple — the evidence of real prices, for example, may tell us something about the Burgos region, but it cannot really tell us anything much about other regions, such as those of the peripheral or 'stagnant' north-west or south-east. But if, in reality, Castile was a series of regions and 'markets' rather than a cohesive economic unit, the monetary, minting, and governmental systems still played a co-ordinating role which imposed a 'nominal' unity on the kingdom. The word 'nominal' is used again because in fact the behaviour of 'nominal' prices was a supra-regional phenomenon which is best related to the 'nominal' entity of the kingdom.[55] Nor should the term 'nominal' be taken to mean something 'unreal' or non-existent; on the contrary, the consequences of contemporary 'nominal' thinking and practice were very real indeed. Thus, for some purposes, the co-ordinating role of the governmental and monetary systems makes it possible to treat the kingdom of Castile as a cohesive unit — for, despite variations, the taxational structure pertained to the kingdom, and minting policies and the mints themselves were constantly being organized on a kingdom-wide basis.

Nor can it be maintained that contemporaries were being naive when they thought in such terms. In the first place, their rather abstract or theologically orientated economic thinking was complex and subtle rather than simple. This was so because Christian theologians and Jewish rabbis were frequently called upon by creditors and debtors to determine how debts should be paid after periods of debasement, and they also had to resolve all the knotty problems arising out of usury and disguised usurious practices. At a more general level, too, there was the problem of the 'just price' which, in Castile, came to be identified in abstract with the market price, thus forming the basis of a scholastic value-theory, which eventually evolved into the surprisingly 'modern' doctrines of the sixteenth-century 'School of Salamanca'.[56]

[55] See below, pp. 23, 59.

[56] This is not the occasion to dwell at length on the general economic and monetary thought of the period, but I should like to emphasise two points. The first one is the obvious fact that, far from being a backwater, Castile by the early sixteenth century had established its reputation for original monetary theories: see, in particular, M. Grice-Hutchinson, *Early Economic Thought in Spain, 1177-1740 (London, 1978)* and the same author's *The School of Salamanca. Readings in Spanish Monetary Theory, 1544-1605* (Oxford, 1952). The second is to relate the abstract thought to royal policies. Fifteenth-century Castile did not have its 'School of Salamanca', but it is

Secondly, at a practical level, royal ordinances on monetary problems catered for the kingdom as a whole and displayed a considerable mastery of detail and remarkably sophisticated touches. Indeed, as might be expected, the inter-relationship between ordinances and monetary problems was so complex that it is frequently difficult to ascertain whether the situation at any given moment determined or reflected royal policies. Above all, both the royal officials and the Crown's opponents were not so naive or ill-informed as to be unaware that debasements affected the fortunes of the money of account and that this in turn had effects on taxes, rents, prices and wages — and not just in Burgos but over the whole kingdom. Of course, no king was going to openly draw attention to his debasements and their effects, and it is consequently fairly predictable that documentary evidence as to sophisticated discussions of monetary affairs usually relates to those periods during which the monarch was in the control of his opponents. Thus, when John II was trapped by his enemies in 1442, he had to shelve his previously naive and simplistic explanations and admit that his debasements had led to a devaluation of one-sixth in the value of fixed incomes.[57] This example illustrates the rather 'uneasy' scope of this study. Given the present state of knowledge, it is impossible to ascertain the regional variations in incomes — indeed, we cannot even say which incomes were 'fixed' or stable. But, on the other hand, John II was absolutely right in that his debasements had led to a devaluation which, whatever the regional variations, was bound to have kingdom-wide effects because of the co-ordinating role of the monetary system.

It is hoped, therefore, that readers will be charitable and remember both the pioneering nature of this study and the pains which I have taken to emphasise its limitations.

The Supply of Precious Metals

The minting capacity of the kingdom of Castile expanded rapidly during the course of the fifteenth century: up to the mid-1430s there were four mints, by 1462 there were six, and by 1470 there were about twenty (see Map 3). Does this growth in the number of mints indicate an abundant supply of gold and silver? In fact the matter is very complex. We will see later that counterfeiting and political factors

56 continued
instructive, for example, to compare men like Saravia de la Calle and Covarrubias on prices with the royal ordinances of John II, or to note that Henry IV and his officials knew all about the practical scarcity of money at the Medina fairs long before Domingo de Soto wrote on the matter. For these particular examples see below, pp. 64-5, and Grice-Hutchinson, *Early Economic Thought*, pp. 99-100, 103.

[57] See below, p. 63.

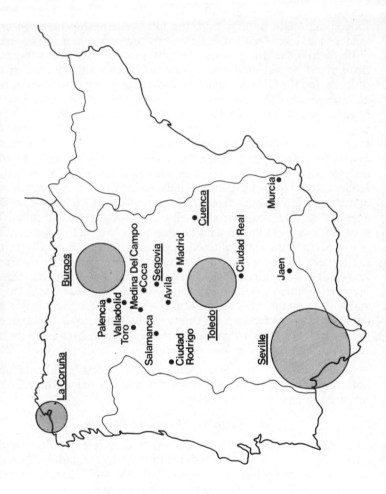

Map 3 – The Castilian Mints in the Fifteenth Century

The names of the six 'regular' minting establishments are underlined : <u>**Segovia**</u>

The circles indicate the approximate capacity of the mints concerned : La Coruña (5–6 furnaces), Burgos (7–9 furnaces), Toledo (9 furnaces), Seville (12 furnaces).

played an important role in the proliferation of mints.[58] Moreover, the mints might have been kept busy because of crises in supplies which prompted debasements, recoinages, and deliberate switches away from gold and silver to copper.

How did Castile fit into the late medieval patterns of bullion movements?[59] Geographically, the kingdom faced out to both the Mediterranean and Atlantic economies. Northwards, the Flanders route implied links which ultimately reached out to the German and central European silver mines. Southwards, trade with the Maghreb, the important Genoese colonies established in Andalusia, and the survival of the Nasrid kingdom of Granada, implied links which ultimately reached out to Sijilmasa, Tuat, Timbuktu, and the sources of gold in the western Sudan and its hinterland. Of course, the strength or stability of these connexions could alter with the passage of time. Thus, while the Castilians consolidated their commercial and naval hold on the Flanders route during and after the Hundred Years War, from the mid-fifteenth century the gold of the trans-Saharan caravan routes began to be tapped by the Portuguese who, following up their earlier success at Ceuta (1415), had reached Arguin and would soon be established at São Jorge da Mina.

The general context into which we must fit the Castilian data is one which Day has described as a bullion famine: 'a major "liquidity crisis" lasting about a generation (*circa* 1395 to *circa* 1415) that affected to a greater or lesser degree the whole of Europe and the Near East, and was destined to cast its shadow over most of the fifteenth century.'[60] This famine was characterised by an inadequate stock of bullion which was depleted by the decline of silver mining centres, interruptions in the trans-Sahara gold trade from the western Sudan, and above all a constant and 'crippling' leakage of precious metals to the Levant because of an unfavourable balance of trade.[61] The famine was particularly acute in the late fourteenth and early fifteenth centuries, beginning during the years 1388-94 and reaching a peak in 1409-10.[62] During this period most states witnessed an abrupt decline

[58] In fact there may well have been more than twenty mints by 1470. For discussion of the proliferation of mints see below pp. 78-85.

[59] A recent and extremely useful overall view of late medieval monetary history is John Day, 'The Great Bullion Famine of the Fifteenth Century', *Past and Present*, no. 79 (1978), 3-54. For what follows see also in particular F.C. Spooner, pp. 9-20; V. Magalhães-Godinho, *L'Economie de l'Empire Portugais aux XVe et XVIe siècles* (Paris, 1969), pp. 97-172; P. Vilar, *Oro y moneda*, pp. 61-82.

[60] Day, 3.

[61] *Ibid.*, 6, 11-12, 35-8.

[62] *Ibid.*, 17-8, 25. Of the dates preferred by Day, I choose 1388 because it is an 'Iberian' or Catalan one. In the case of England we must move back even earlier to the 1370s

in minting, and from the 1390s onwards debased 'black money' tended to invade the markets as rulers tried to counter the bullion famine by resorting to competitive devaluation.[63] Castile's neighbour, Portugal, provides a striking example to illustrate the 'famine' thesis — for if, on the one hand, the Crown could not even mint any gold coins until a late date, on the other hand the Portuguese silver *real* was progressively debased during the period 1383-1433 until it was almost pure copper.[64]

It has been noted that Day argues that the liquidity crisis 'cast its shadow over most of the fifteenth century'. In fact he identifies another period of contraction during the years 1440-60 which 'was characterized to a greater extent than that of half a century earlier by the proliferation of base billon and copper pieces of every type and description'. The period, in fact, coincides more or less with the years 1440-66 which Spufford identified as being those of 'the small change inflation', and this inflation in turn was due to 'inadequate monetary stocks'.[65]

When examined against this background, the Castilian situation appears in some respects to be exceptional, and because of this one or two points need to be stressed at the outset. Firstly, the evidence suggests that Castile did not suffer to the same extent as her European neighbours — certainly any analogy with other Iberian states could be totally misleading.[66] Day argues that the bullion shortage 'affected the gold and silver circulation in varying degrees depending on the structure of trade relations and the minting policies of the individual states'.[67] Although this statement seems to be unexceptional, it is also linked to corollaries which do not quite fit the Castilian case. He argues, for example, that changes in the mint ratios in Catalonia, Valencia, France, and England were insufficient to overcome bullion famine and stimulate bimetallic flows:[68] the evidence will show that the same was probably not true of Castile. Only one state, it would appear, was exceptional as far as Day is concerned: 'Venice seems to be the only case, however, where the shortage of one metal (silver) was very largely compensated for by the abundance of the other and

[63]*Ibid.*, 15-6.

[64]*Ibid.*, 23, 45.

[65]*Ibid.*, 45-6.

[66]For example, none of the other Iberian states were as important as 'markets' for precious metals as Castile: see below pp. 33-4.

[67]Day, 33.

[68]*Ibid.*, 21-3.

where, as a consequence, the crisis was without serious long-term effects."[69] I hope it will become clear that Castile, too, was to some extent a rather exceptional case.

It does not follow from the foregoing comments, however, that Castile escaped the bullion famine. Thus, although the ensuing discussion stresses the importance of bimetallic ratios and the apparently 'abundant' supply of precious metals in Castile, it must be remembered that the terms and the discussion itself are *relative* to the general picture of a 'liquidity crisis'.

In general, Spooner's argument that there was a relative abundance of gold during the period 1450-1550 holds good for the preceding century as well.[70] The century after 1350 witnessed a famine of silver: by 1420-40 none of the German or central European silver mines had an output of more than 10,000 marks per year, and the demands on silver in a war-ravaged Europe led at times to dramatic falls in the bimetallic ratio.[71] In contrast to this, estimates as to the volume of the trans-Saharan supply of gold confirm the picture of a *relative* abundance of gold.[72] The demand for silver itself stimulated an increase in silver production and an improvement in techniques which, starting in about 1450, reached its peak during the second decade of the sixteenth century.[73] Did the growth of silver-supply in turn stimulate the Genoese and Iberian searches for the sources of West African gold? In fact there were many reasons, among them the acute shortage of *all* precious metals, which prompted men such as Ca da Mosto or Columbus to put gold high on their list of priorities.[74] The demand for gold was always present and the only factor that changed, both geographically and timewise, was that of the relative scarcity which prompted the bullion flows. If we simplify the problem of bimetallic ratios to an alarming extent, the way in which relative scarcity (or abundance) prompted these flows becomes clearer. Thus, about the mid-fifteenth century, if we add the evidence of Malfante to the arguments of Magalhães Godinho, the bimetallic ratios of the Sudan (1:1) and the Maghreb (9:1) 'compensated' that of Northern Europe (11:1). The bimetallic ratio of the Iberian peninsula of

[69]*Ibid.*, 33.

[70]Spooner, p. 11.

[71]Magalhães-Godinho, pp. 138-47.

[72]*Ibid.*, p. 119. Day, pp. 36-8 stresses the decline in the trans-Saharan supply; this view may well be correct, but what I am stressing here is the *relative* position of gold.

[73]Spooner, pp. 15-16.

[74]For a good summary of the relative importance of the factors in the case of the Portuguese, see Magalhães-Godinho, pp. 40-1.

approximately 10:1 not only confirms the picture of a relative abundance of gold and a shortage of silver, but also emphasizes a strategic and intermediary position between North Africa and northern Europe.[75]

The Burgos data, royal ordinances on the coinage, and other fragments of evidence enable us to examine the bullion situation in Castile in more detail. Using the equation $P = xy/z$ and the Burgos quotations for silver *reales* and Aragonese gold florins, the approximate bimetallic ratio of minted coins can be calculated for almost the whole period from 1400 to 1474.[76] When these ratios are compared with those which Jacques Heers calculated for Genoa, there can be no doubt as to the relative shortage of silver in Castile.[77] Although fluctuations in the Genoese bimetallic ratio ranged from 10.5:1 to 12.5:1 during the period 1430-80, the ratio remained above 11:1 for virtually four out of the five decades, and after 1462 it stabilized at 11.7:1. In comparison, the lower Castilian ratio, remaining below 10.5:1 for all but sixteen of the years from 1400 to 1475, reflected a higher demand for silver. Despite their approximate nature, the calculations for Castile also reveal clearly defined periods:

	Min.-Max.	Average
1404, 1407, 1412, 1416	10.65-11.08	10.81
1419-1431	9.31- 9.95	9.58
1432-1441	10.13-11.29	10.65
1442-1463	8.3 -10.39	9.39
1464-1469	10.62-12.59	11.51
1470-1474	8.99-11.02	10.04

In short, within an overall context of a relative shortage of silver when compared to Genoa, the data show that while silver appreciated

[72] For Malfante's hear-say evidence, contained in the famous letter of 1447 from Tuat, see G.R. Crone, ed. *The Voyages of Cadamosto and other documents on Western Africa in the second half of the Fifteenth Century* (Hakluyt Soc. 1937), pp. 85-90. See also Magalhães-Godinho, p. 97 and M. Malowist. The Western Sudan in the Middle Ages', *Past and Present*, no. 33 (1966), 8.

[76] See Appendix B-6. Such calculations, of course, give the approximate bimetallic ratio in terms of *fine* silver and gold. On the equation $P = xy/z$ see the Introduction.

[77] J.Heers, *Gênes*, pp. 57-8 and the graph 'Rapport Or-Argent (métal monnayé)', p. 660. Most of the ratios cited in Day, p. 34, only go down to about 1430, but the English example is useful as another comparison.

during the 1420s, 1440s, and 1480s, the demand for gold increased during the 1430s and 1460s.

These calculations, of course, are based on what may be termed the market value of coined money. However, the 'official' ratios, as calculated from the royal ordinances, confirm the preoccupation with silver. Thus the coin values which John II laid down in 1442 give a bimetallic ratio of 9.97:1 and those of Henry IV in an ordinance of 1462 give a ratio as low as 8.53:1.[78] These 'official' ratios, in turn, had a short-term effect on the market ratio since, as will be seen later, price quotations for coins reacted temporarily to the values laid down in the ordinances.

It would be a mistake, however, to assume that fluctuations in the bimetallic ratio were simply caused by royal ordinances or by variations in the pulse of bullion imports. In fact, if we correlate the data on ratios with the main features relating to the debasements and reforming ordinances (discussed later), it seems clear that other factors must be taken into account. In effect, the long periods of relatively high demand for silver (1419-31 and 1442-63) preceded the two main cycles of royal debasements which began in 1429/30 and 1462/3 respectively. Similarly, the appreciations in gold during the 1430s and 1460s appear to have resulted from the debasements, and the reform ordinances of 1442, 1462 and 1471 had the effect of reducing the demand on gold by lowering the bimetallic ratio.[79] In order to explain the connections between these phenomena, of course, it is possible to emphasise the frequent complaints about the shortage of billon coins and argue that this situation put a premium on silver. Similarly, since debasement would tend to ease the strain at the level of the billon coins, the bimetallic ratio would readjust itself in favour of the gold coins. But the effects of debasement were probably more subtle. As the silver content of the smaller billon coins was reduced, so were these coins accepted into circulation with greater reluctance, and despite royal ordinances, the hostility to billon was matched by an increase in the demand for the stable gold coins.[80] Indeed, it was at

---

[78]Ordinance of 29 January 1442, BN, MS. 13259, fos. 312-4 (Appendix A-3), and M.A. Ladero Quesada, 'Moneda y tasa de precios en 1462: Un episodio ignorado en la política económica de Enrique IV de Castilla', *Moneda y Crédito,* no. 129 (1974), 91-115.

[79]The ordinance of 1462 appears exceptional in that it came at the end of more than two decades with an average ratio of 9.39:1. But this ordinance, promulgated on the heels of the debasement of 1461 and followed almost immediately by further debasements, must be viewed within a much narrower chronological context. The 1461 debasement was accompanied by a sharp rise in the ratio (from 8.64:1 to 10:1), the reform of 1462 entailed a reduction (8.23:1), and from 1463 onwards the ratio stood at an average of 11.5:1.

[80]This interpretation suggested itself on reading Spooner, p. 102.

times such as these that the monarchy complained of the appreciation of Aragonese gold florins and Castilian gold *doblas* to values well above those laid down in the ordinances. Thus it was precisely at the height of the monetary anarchy during the 1460s that the bimetallic ratio reached its highest average, and peaks in the ratio in 1440 and 1469 were soon followed by reforming ordinances. In fact, if we were to accept an anonymous account of the monetary situation at the end of Henry IV's reign (1454-74), the flight from billon to gold coins even gave way to a flight from all coins and a relapse into a system of barter![81]

Bimetallic ratios tell us nothing about the volume of precious metals, but there is evidence enough to attempt an outline of bullion movements. The most reliable approach to the problem is provided by a document, dating from the early 1430s, which gives interesting data on silver supplies.[82]

The document, drawn up in a form suitable for deliberation in the royal council, contained both an offer made by a group of Burgos merchants and the reactions of royal officials to the offer. The proposal of the Burgos merchants, none of whom are named in the document, was that they would take over the running of a mint and that:

> they will provide 10,000 marks of silver, or more if necessary, in order to keep the mint fully working for the next ten years. They will mint at the same fineness and manner as at present without the king having to provide any silver or money, and the said silver will be valued at a price of 505 *mrs* per mark for as long a period as should be preferred.

This proposal, it need hardly be pointed out, was extremely vague on matters which were of crucial importance, and in their comments the mint treasurers and the chief royal financial officials (*contadores mayores*) emphasized the obscurities. Did the offer of 10,000 marks of silver in fact mean that this amount would be supplied each year? Was the price of 505 *mrs* per mark envisaged in terms of coined money, and were the merchants promising to maintain this price throughout the ten years? Without further information, the royal officials argued, the proposal could not be properly evaluated.

---

[81] This account is cited extensively below, pp. 79-80. The anonymous author's reference to the Castilian people resorting to barter 'like the Guineans' is not so far-fetched as may at first sight appear. See, for example, Day, 14-5.

[82] For this document, from which the quotations that follow have been translated, see Appendix A-1. From internal evidence — for example, the posts attributed to Diego Romero, the mints listed, and the silver prices quoted — it is evident that this document dates from the first half of the 1430s.

To these comments the merchants replied by making it clear that the price of 505 *mrs* per mark would remain fixed over the ten-year period, and that they would either mint twice as many coins as those currently produced, or would maintain an even higher level of production if this should be desired. On the face of it, this was an extremely generous offer, but in their final comments the royal officials still argued against accepting it. If the price of silver were to rise during the course of the ten years, they argued, 'there is no doubt that they [the merchants] would stop minting in order not to lose money'. Would prices rise during these years? In the view of the royal officials this would be inevitable if a contract involving fixed prices and quantities of silver were to be put into effect:

> Furthermore . . . with regard to their offer to provision the said house with silver at 505 *mrs* per mark, it seems to us . . . that . . . it is not in your service to let it be publicly known that Your Highness stipulated the amount of silver to be worked . . . because, being known, it will cause the price of silver to rise as well as the prices of gold and everything else, since those who possess the silver will know that these amounts will have to be minted each year and prices will perforce increase. It is even doubtful whether [in these circumstances] silver could be obtained, because experience has shown that some rich Genoese merchants in Seville sold a certain quantity of silver [in advance] to your treasurer of the said mint [of Seville], and they promised to deliver it within a certain period and at a certain price. But as soon as the other merchants found out, they wrote to Flanders and elsewhere with the result that silver became more expensive; for this reason these said merchants could not fulfil their undertaking and they are now imprisoned by virtue of your command. The same would now happen if this matter became known . . . It seems to us . . . that it would be much more in Your Majesty's interest if this task were given to your treasurers so that they can buy the said silver secretly. . . .

Although the document contains further quantitative data of great interest, it is worth pausing at this point to consider the light which this information throws on Castilian silver supplies. Were the merchants being too optimistic? Their offer was made shortly after a silver crisis in 1429 during which, as we will see, the Crown had resorted to forced loans and had even contemplated the confiscation of Church plate.[83] Among the victims of the Crown's pressing need for silver were the Burgos merchants, and it may well be that their proposal was designed

---

[83] Below, pp. 95-6.

to prevent further forced loans in the future. But, as the royal officials pointed out, the activities of speculators in Seville had already led to the imprisonment of those Genoese who had offered to supply silver, and they surely had a strong case for arguing that a similar fate might befall the Burgos merchants. Given the European shortage or 'famine' in precious metals, there was a real danger that a declared mint price for silver would be overtaken by the market. In fact the risks were probably greater in Burgos than in Seville, for although the wool route to Flanders can also be envisaged as a silver route to Castile, the relatively inflexible sailing dates of the north-coast fleets would provide additional pressure in the markets. Indeed, when the Burgos merchants first made their offer, they asked that 'they be given a reply before next Thursday because the ships they will have to use will be leaving soon — otherwise they will be able to do nothing until the coming year'.

On the other hand, even when confronted with such problems, the Burgos merchants persisted in offering a steady supply of silver at fixed prices, and it must be admitted that they were in the best possible position to provide expert advice. Burgos, after all, was the wool capital of Castile, and Bruges, where the Castilian merchants were organized into a 'nation' with its own *consulado,* was the terminal point of the wool exports.[84] Moreover, there is additional evidence which enables us to decide whether the offer to supply 10,000 marks of silver per year was realistic.

In their final considerations on the merchants' proposal, the royal officials commented that 10,000 marks per year was not a large quantity and that any offer to double current mint production was too vague unless it was related to the output of a specific mint. Accordingly, in order to assist the royal council, they provided data on the optimum production of each of the royal mints. Allowing for holidays, illnesses, shortages of coal and the inevitable disruptions at seed-time and harvest-time, the *contadores* based their calculations on a working year of 200 days. For these 200 days the furnaces of all the mints, save those at La Coruña which were smaller, had a production capacity of 1,000 marks of silver each. The relative importance of the various mints and the total potential production each year, therefore, was as follows:

---

[84] See above p. 20. In 1348 the Castilians at Bruges received a statute which gave them a status equivalent to that of the Hansa, and the subsequent emergence of a 'nation' and *consulado* received official recognition from Philip the Good in 1428. See L. Suárez Fernández, *Navegación y comercio,* pp. 15-6; J.A. Garcia de Cortázar.' p 213.

	Mint	Marks of silver
Seville:	12 furnaces	12,000
Toledo:	9 furnaces	9,000
Burgos:	7'furnaces 'and 2 more which could be added'	9,000
La Coruña:	6 small furnaces	5,000
		Total 35,000

The calculations of the royal officials are of great interest for several reasons. In the first place they support the contention that the merchants' offer of 10,000 marks was modest in terms of total minting capacity. But although the merchants had not designated any mint in particular, they did refer in their petition to *la casa* in the singular, and being Burgos men it is obvious that they meant their proposal to apply to the mint at Burgos. Thus in terms of this particular mint the offer of 10,000 marks per year was a good one, and this explains why the royal officials were anxious to stress that the Burgos capacity could be raised to 9,000 marks by the addition of two more furnaces.

Even more interesting, however, is the light which the figures throw on Castilian silver supplies. Whichever way we look at the data, the projected output of silver coins over this period of ten years was high. Clearly a maximum output of 350,000 marks of silver is unlikely — one must allow for the suspicion that the calculations of the *contadores* were optimistic, and it would be foolhardy to assume that all the mints would maintain uninterrupted production for ten years at full capacity. On the other hand, the merchants were guaranteeing 100,000 marks of silver for the Burgos mint alone. Does a figure of 200,000 marks of silver for these ten years represent a reasonable compromise? Yet even if we were to reduce this estimate, it is still clear that Castilian output must have been much higher than that of its Iberian neighbours and that the kingdom's mints must have been among the busiest in Europe.[85] Hamilton, for example, calculated Valencian output over 21 years at just under 24,000 marks while the Navarrese mints only had an output of just over 100,000 marks during a period of 110 years.[86]

[85] See, for example Day, pp. 16, 31.
[86] For the precise figures see Hamilton, *Money, Prices and Wages,* pp. 210-12.

Before accepting these arguments, however, one problem remains to be considered. If there were relatively abundant supplies of silver, how is a shortage of silver in 1429/30 to be explained? It may be that in Castile the major European 'liquidity crisis' lasted somewhat longer than elsewhere, but more important at this specific stage was the Crown's decision to wage a foreign war in 1429. The implications of this decision will be discussed later.[87] At this point I wish to emphasize that disruptions in the Flanders trade during the 1420s must also be taken into account. From 1421 complicated issues, arising from international relations and naval hostilities, had bedevilled relations between Philip the Good, allied to the English, and John II of Castile, who was nominally allied to the French.[88] The results, as far as trade is concerned, may be surmised from the following extract from a letter which John II sent to the Burgos oligarchy in 1429:

> You know that I was informed that in the county of Flanders new taxes had been imposed and levied on all the goods which my subjects and peoples bought and sold [there], although it was never the custom for these [taxes] to be demanded or levied. Wherefore I, understanding that it was in my service to do so, ordered and commanded that no persons from my kingdoms or lordships, or from outside them, should go to the county of Flanders or the kingdom of England, and that no merchandise from my realms and lordships should be taken there and no goods should be brought from there to these my realms and lordships. . . . And inasmuch as during this embargo certain compromises were offered to me by the county of Flanders, I ordered Sancho Ezquerra de Angulo . . . to go there and negotiate over certain matters which I understood to be in my service. And he went there, and according to his report, those of the said county of Flanders have lifted and removed the new tax and have agreed to other matters which are to my benefit and to the common good of my kingdoms and lordships. Therefore it is my wish to order the cessation . . . of the said embargo and prohibitions . . . as far as the county of Flanders is concerned. . . [89]

Although the date of the imposition of the embargo is unknown, the new taxes to which the king referred were first levied in Flanders in

[87] Below, pp. 95-6.

[85] For an account of these problems see Suárez Fernández, *Navegación y comercio,* pp. 98-102. Suárez, however, appears to have been unaware of the embargo which is discussed in what follows.

[89] AM, Burgos, *Actas capitulares,* 1429-30, fo. 33, royal letter, dated 13 April 1429, recorded at the council meeting of 21 April 1429.

1421.[90] Of course, it would have been impossible to ensure that the subsequent embargo was fully implemented; but it is equally unlikely that the volume of trade would not have been considerably reduced, and silver would have been among the commodities affected. In 1429, however, the embargo was lifted and Castilian privileges in Flanders were restored in full. It is this background which helps to explain both the low bimetallic ratio of the years 1419-31 and the fact that, shortly after the 1429 crisis, the Burgos merchants were in a position to offer a substantial and regular flow of silver.

What was the position with respect to gold? If the bimetallic ratio calculations are at all accurate, then the supply of gold must have been relatively more abundant than that of silver. There were two sources of gold. In the first place there were the sums paid by the Muslim rulers of Granada as tribute money to the Castilian rulers. These payments, known as *parias,* still await a detailed study, but some aspects regarding them are clear. Although the age of huge booty and *parias* lay well in the past, the sums collected by the fifteenth-century Castilian kings were far from negligible.[91] Indeed at one stage John II almost pulled off a brilliant success, when, in 1431, his client-king, Yusuf IV, promised the equivalent of 408 marks of 19 carat gold in annual tribute payments in return for Castilian help in securing his position in Granada. In the event Yusuf IV died and the agreement remained unfulfilled.[92] Yet the sums which are known to have been paid were still substantial. For example in the published documentation on the 1439 truce negotiations between Castile and Granada, the Castilian quest for large gold payments, the final compromise, and even some of the receipts for instalments of the *parias* can be studied in detail. In this particular instance John II once again pressed hard for *parias* equivalent to 408 marks per year, but in the event he had to content himself with 490 marks spread over the three years of the truce.[93] Of course, not all the tribute payments were always as large as this: a *paria* of only 265 marks, for example, was obtained for the three years of truce negotiated in 1421.[94] Yet, considering that the late medieval frontier was more often at peace

[90]Suárez Fernández, *Navegación y comercio,* p. 98.

[91]For a useful survey of the classic age of *parias* in the eleventh century see J.M. Lacarra, 'Aspectos económicos de la sumisión de los reinos de taifas (1010-1102)', in *Homenaje a Jaime Vicens Vives,* I (Barcelona, 1965), 255-77.

[92]On this incident see L. Suárez Fernández, *Juan II y la frontera de Granada,* pp. 21-2. It should be noted that *parias* were always paid in gold *doblas.* My conversion of these into marks is based on the *dobla* being of 19 carats and 1/49 to the mark.

[93]J. Amador de los Rios, *Memoria histórico-crítica sobre las treguas celebradas en 1439, passim.*

[94]*Crónica de Juan II* (BAE., LXX, Madrid, 1878), p. 405.

than at war,[95] these fluctuating and no doubt irregular payments must have added up to a considerable amount during the century preceding the fall of Granada.

The other source for Castilian gold was North Africa. Usually historians attach considerable significance to the various stages marking the reappearance of gold coins in the European economy — for example, the Florentine florin (1252), the Aragonese florin (1346), and the Portuguese *cruzado* (1457). As far as Castile is concerned, however, it must be remembered that al-Andalus had for long been a part of North Africa and that the Castilian monetary system was in many ways an extension of an Islamic world in which gold coins had been common. Thus, whereas areas like Aragon and Catalonia formed part of the 'Carolingian sterling area', the histories of coins such as the *maravedí* and the *dobla* illustrate the extent to which the Castilian-Leonese monetary system had developed within a Muslim orbit. When Alfonso VIII, for example, began to mint gold *maravedíes* in 1172, they were not only patterned on the Almoravid *morabitín* but they actually displayed Arabic lettering. Similarly the Almohadic gold *dobla* was subsequently adopted by Castile in the thirteenth century. In this way, therefore, the rise and fall of the North African Berber empires was reflected in a Castile where, unlike the rest of Europe, gold coins had circulated from a very early date. Even as late as the fifteenth century, John II deliberately patterned some of his gold *doblas* on those issued by Muslim mints.[96]

It is against such a background that the evidence for the supplies of North African gold must be placed. Although the Castilian sources are disappointingly silent on this problem, there can be no doubt as to the existence of regular trading contacts in which gold was one of the prized commodities. The organization of customs duties in Andalusia catered for two distinct areas of trade with Muslims — the *diezmo y medio diezmo de lo morisco* was levied on trade with Granada, and the *renta de Berbería* formed part of the complex *almojarifazgo* duties. The *renta de Berbería* was levied on trade between the Maghreb and towns such as Seville, Cádiz, Jerez, Puerto de Santa María and Sanlucar de Barrameda.[97] Unfortunately the fiscal documents of the Crown reveal little, if anything, about the nature of this trade, although it is clear from other sources that it was by no means limited in scope. In 1469, for example, Seville alone imported

[95]Elsewhere I have calculated that there were approximately 85 years of peace and only 25 years of war during the period 1350-1460: A. MacKay, 'The Ballad and the Frontier', 20.

[96]See below, p. 50.

[97]On the customs duties in general see above, pp. 7-10.

6,720 tons of grain from the Barbary coast.[98] Moreover, a petition of the *cortes* of 1465 makes it obvious that African gold was regularly brought to Seville:

> Furthermore . . . we entreat Your Highness that when you require coins to be minted . . . you should order them to be minted generally in all the established mints in the same way as they are minted at Segovia, and that for the present Your Highness should issue licences to the said mints of your realms for the issuing of gold, silver, and especially billon coins, for because of the scarcity of these, most trading activities in Burgos, Toledo, Seville, and the other cities and towns of your kingdoms have come to a halt. More particularly, it is well known that in the said city of Seville the gold which was regularly brought from Barbary when the said mint was functioning, has come and is coming to a halt because it is found extremely inconvenient to bring the gold to the mint at Segovia, especially during times such as these, and as a result Your Highness is losing large sums of *mrs* each year from the [minting] rights which could be obtained.[99]

The petition, therefore, makes it clear that the Seville mint was regularly supplied with African gold but that in and around 1465 this supply was beset by problems. This evidence, of course, fits in perfectly with that of the bimetallic ratios: which indicates that the years 1464-1469 were precisely those during which gold was at a premium. What reasons can be adduced to explain the problems which beset this regular supply of gold during these few years?

One possible explanation for this relative scarcity of gold is suggested by the 'bullion famine' thesis.[100] The network of exchanges which characterised the trans-Saharan trade was disrupted during the late fourteenth century, the empire of Mali disintegrated, the Berber kings of Tlemcen could not protect the Saharan caravans against the bedouins, and Jewish participation in the trade collapsed. But it should be emphasised that the chronology of this argument is very vague — and certainly of no help in establishing an explanatory link with the precise years, 1464-9, which interest us here. Indeed, the trans-Saharan gold trade is said to have 'picked up again' during the second half of the fifteenth century, and a subsequent collapse is equally vaguely dated.

[98] AM, Seville, box 1468-70, accounts headed 'Del pan de berueria'. These accounts only concern imports arranged by the town council during a grain crisis and do not relate to the 'private' activities of merchants.

[99] This passage from *Cortes*, III, 755-6 is cited in Ladero, 'Mondeda y tasa', 104.

[100] For what follows see Day, 37-9.

But perhaps another possible explanation lies in the chronology of Portuguese expansion — for example, the establishment of Arguin as an outpost in the gold trade from Timbuktu, the appearance of the gold *cruzado* in 1457, and the arrival at the coast of Guinea in the late 1460s? Was Portuguese gold already drying up the overland flow from the Sudan to North Africa ? It seems unlikely: any such displacement would come at a later date, and as Spooner argues, 'even after the palmy days of Portuguese trade, gold continued to flow toward the Maghreb and Egypt'.[101] In any case, although the evidence cannot be reviewed here in detail, it is still far from clear that the Castilians were slow off the mark in making for the gold of Guinea or that relations with the Portuguese were necessarily always hostile.

For their part, the *procuradores* laid the blame for inadequate gold supplies on the centralisation of mint operations at Segovia and on the troubled times which made the transportation of gold to the centre of the kingdom a dubious proposition. These arguments were to some extent justified. In September 1464 Henry IV had halted all minting operations with the sole exception of the Segovia house, and the anarchic political conditions certainly led to some spectacular 'losses' of bullion.[102] But, as will be seen, the suspension of minting operations was a temporary phenomenon, and it was preceded and followed by a proliferation of mints.[103] Moreover, the way in which the *procuradores* phrased their petition was ambiguous. Were they in fact alleging that the Barbary gold trade *in general* had come to a halt, or were they merely stating that the supply of this gold *to the mints* (at Seville and Segovia) had collapsed? The fact that Genoese and Florentine merchants were active in the Seville gold markets during these years certainly suggests that African gold was still available and that it is this latter interpretation which must be accepted. In any case another factor must be introduced into the picture at this stage. Ladero has convincingly argued that the root cause of much of the trouble at this time was a crisis in business confidence in Seville and other large towns.[104] Many merchants and money-changers had suffered from some of the provisions of an ordinance of 1462 and not a few seem to have departed from Seville. Moreover, since the ordinance had attempted to reduce the value of gold coins in terms of

[101] Spooner, p. 14.

[102] The minting directive is in AGS, EMR., Leg. 519, doc. 27. For an act of banditry which cost the *alcaide* of Carmona his life and 50,000 gold doblas, see Garci Sánchez, *Los Anales de Garci Sánchez, jurado de Sevilla,* ed. Juan de Mata Carriazo (Seville, 1953), p. 56.

[103] See below, pp. 71-4.

[104] Ladero, 'Moneda y tasa', 103-4.

silver, it may well be that a low mint price for gold (as well as the official prices for coins) starved the mints and encouraged foreign purchasers. Only some explanation along these lines can explain the odd fact that, while the *procuradores* complained of a shortage of gold at the mints, the Florentine galleys, according to Heers, were being loaded with gold for Italy, Flanders and England: 'Les chargements des galères florentines au retour d'Occident comportent, parmi les marchandises prises à Séville, des cuirs, de la grana, mais aussi de l'or: pour 40,000 ducats en 1466 et pour 10,000 doubles "tiberi" en 1468. Les Florentines en prennent aussi pour la Mer du Nord; à la même époque [1467] leurs galères amenent de l'or en Flandre ou Angletèrre.'[105]

The preceding discussion has attempted to suggest that, apart from periods of a few years (for example, c 1429 for silver and c 1464-9 for gold), Castilian supplies of precious metals were abundant. It cannot be assumed, however, that the supplies of gold and silver were solely destined for the royal mints, and the demand factor must also be taken into account. The discussion began with a comparison between Castilian and Genoese bimetallic ratios, and it is to the Genoese example that we must now again turn. Heers convincingly demonstrates that by the later middle ages Andalusia was already western Europe's most important market in precious metals. Much of the gold and silver which flowed into Castile, therefore, was re-exported and this factor must be take into account. In a general way the point is well illustrated by Heer's analysis of a Genoese customs register of 1377. The register lists gold imports into Genoa over a period of ten months, and it underlines the overwhelming importance of the Iberian bullion markets to the Genoese:

Sources	Totals (in Genoese lire)
From Palermo	1,000
From Valencia	6,000
From Malaga	6,000
From Seville	9,500
From Spain in general	45,000
Indeterminate sources	1,100
	68,600

[105]Heers, *Gènes,* p. 68.

This was African gold and the great clearing markets for it were in Spain: 'Le trafic se fait par l'intérmediaire des ports chrétiens, et presque exclusivement, par ceux de la péninsule ibérique. Le royaume d'Aragon et celui de Grenade restent fort loin derrière la Castille. Dès la fin du XIVe siècle, le grand marché de l'or pour les Génois et, sans doute, pour tous les marchands d'Occident, c'est l'Andalousie avec Séville et Cadix.'[106] But what of the evidence which the royal officials provided with respect to the output of silver coins from Castilian mints? Does this not provide the necessary proof of an adequate supply of silver for the specific purpose of minting? It does — but unfortunately it tells us nothing about the fate of the coins after they issued from the mints, and such coins were often valuable commodities in international trade. Disparities in bimetallic ratios, for example, could stimulate complex flows of coins across frontiers. Indeed, the Castilian royal ordinances repeatedly alleged that *blancas* and other coins were being illegally exported, and these allegations appear to have had some foundation in fact. The crisis of 1429/30, for example, was preceded by a flight of silver towards Portugal,[107] and during the reign of Henry IV the Genoese exported *blancas* by the million and even admitted that this illegal trade was a well-established and regular feature of their activities in Seville.[108]

What, then, can we conclude about the supply of precious metals in Castile? Like the other states of western Europe, Castile suffered from a bullion famine during the course of the fifteenth century. But within this context it is still possible to speak of 'a *relative* abundance' and, as we have seen, it does seem to be the case that late medieval Castile, and in particular Seville, was already one of Europe's most important distribution centres for precious metals. Of course, this does not mean that the Castilian mints necessarily enjoyed constant and plentiful supplies of gold and silver. For if, on the one hand, merchants from Burgos could confidently offer to supply substantial quantities of silver at fixed prices over a period of ten years, royal officials were sceptical about such promises and clearly believed that constant mint prices would collapse in the face of market shortages. Still, even the calculations of the sceptics seem to indicate that Castile enjoyed a relative advantage of supply. Against this background the bimetallic ratios show that while gold appreciated

[106]*Ibid.*, pp. 69-70. The term 'Spain' obviously meant Castile. See Day, 37 and Hamilton, *Money Prices and Wages,* p. 34, where it is also suggested that Castile was the supplier of gold to the Crown of Aragon.

[107]*Crónica de Juan II,* p. 467.

[108]Heers, *Gênes,* pp. 70-1.

during the 1430s and 1460s, the demand for silver increased during the 1420s, 1440s and 1470s. More important, the 'liquidity crises' that can be detected do not quite match the general European pattern. Day locates the major European 'famine' in the period 1395-1415. In Castile, however, the acute crisis in silver came in 1429/30 when the Crown was forced to contemplate the confiscation of Church plate. Day assigns another important European shortage to the period 1440-60, and he refers to Spufford's findings in words which are apposite for Castile as well: 'In the Low Countries too it was primarily debased seigneurial issues that were responsible for what Peter Spufford calls "the small change inflation" of 1440-66'.[109] Later we will see that in Castile also there was a 'small change inflation', that 'not enough copper could be imported from Flanders and other kingdoms'[110] for the minting of 'black money', and that seigneurial and other counterfeiters were largely responsible for the phenomenon. But once again there was a time-lag, because this particular crisis hit Castile during the period 1462-74. How then are these variations from the general European pattern to be explained? The answer is to be found by connecting the relative abundance (or scarcity) of Castilian supplies of precious metals to the political history of the period. If, other things being equal, Castile had managed to ride out these crises, she would not have been alone. Referring to the shortage of 1440-66, Day observes that, for unknown reasons, only England 'seems to have learned to live with a chronic scarcity of cash in the famine years without recourse to surrogate "black money" whether foreign or domestic'.[111] But Castile also managed tolerably well for most of this period and only failed to cope later. The differences are surely to be explained by the fact that, despite their relatively advantageous supplies, the Castilian kings encouraged — or found themselves falling victim to — wars or political situations which imposed an unbearable strain on fiscal resources. In other words, the coins to be minted from the metals became the agents of royal plans which, in Pierre Vilar's phrase, constituted 'a means of policy'.[112] The Castilian situation was finely balanced — without the bullion famine political factors (particularly, foreign wars) need not have entailed debasements and devaluations, but without these factors Castile, like England, might have learned to live with the scarcity.

---

[109]Day, 46.
[110]See below, pp. 79-85.
[111]Day, 46.
[112]See below, pp. 60, 96-7.

2

PRICES, ROYAL DEBASEMENTS AND COUNTERFEITING

The Evidence and its Problems

Most of the quantitative data in this study are derived from the *Libros Redondos* of the cathedral of Burgos. These were the yearly account books kept by the canons. Each book contains approximately 250 paper folios and includes several specialised accounts as well as a general account in which all figures on income and expenditure are brought together to cast the yearly balance.[1] Bound in parchment and arranged in chronological order,[2] the account books only begin to display a reasonable degree of continuity from 1390 onwards.[3] From 1427 onwards the series is complete. Since the *Libros* do not usually specify the day or the month corresponding to the quantitative data, it is important to note the time limits of the accounts. The financial year of the *Libros Redondos* began in May of the title year and ended in April of the following year: hence, for example, a price ascribed to 1393 corresponds to the period running from 1 May 1393 to 30 April 1394.[4]

Evidence for some prices is taken from accounts in the municipal archive of Seville. Although these prices have not been published before, I have described the sources in another study in which the nominal movement revealed by these figures is also discussed.[5] Here it need only be noted that while the Seville prices provide a useful counterpoint to those of Burgos, the Seville accounting year ran from July to June rather than from May to April.

[1] The specialised accounts usually include general expenses (*despendimos*), repairs (*rehazimientos*), income from land (*heras, heredamientos*), the distribution of income in kind and cash among the chapter officials (*matriculas*), and the rents of houses, mills and orchards (*rentas*). The archive, of course, contains other account books and *cuadernos de contabilidad*.

[2] Two of the Libros are incorrctly dated: the one marked '1389' is for 1390, and the one marked '1414' should be ascribed to a year in the fourteenth century (probably 1376).

[3] There are *Libros Redondos* for 1352, 1365, 1368, 1371, 1376 (? marked '1414'), 1384, and 1385. There are no *Libros* for the following years between 1390 and 1427: 1392, 1399-1401, 1403, 1405-6, 1408-11, 1413-5, 1417, 1420, 1426.

[4] The actual 'taking' of the account could be effected at a slightly later date. In the case of the 1393 *Libro*, for example, it took place in June 1394.

[5] A. MacKay, 'Popular Movements and Pogroms in fifteenth-century Castile', *Past and Present*, no. 55 (1972), 33-67.

Burgos quotations for many commodities, such as fish, grain, olive oil, coal, vinegar and firewood, have had to be discounted for varying reasons — for example, insufficient regularity to warrant their tabulation, changes in the quality of the items, and the use of imprecise terminology. Thus the data which have been tabulated may seem to relate to a somewhat restricted and odd collection of commodities and coins. Yet this by no means detracts from the usefulness of the evidence for a later medieval Castile for which no figures at all are available, and the data serve as a fairly reliable indicator of the trend of prices.

The inclusion of wax prices (*cera*) in cathedral accounts is only to be expected, although quotations for sacramental wine are strangely lacking. The wax for candles was distinguished in the accounts from the smaller purchases of *cera bermeja* and *cera colorada* which, as the accounts frequently specified, was used *para sellar las cartas*. It should be noted that wax prices for the years 1448, 1452 and 1466 are explicitly referred to in the accounts as being prices paid for bulk purchases at the fairs of Medina del Campo.

The nature of the wine prices has to be defined for the obvious reason that wine qualities varied greatly. The red and white wines tabulated here were quality wines used for 'superior' occasions. This point emerges clearly when the occasional quotations for low-quality wine, used for Lenten meals provided for the poor, are compared with quotations for the high-quality wines used for special canonical celebrations, such as that which took place in April. This difference in quality was occasionally referred to in the accounts in fairly precise terms. For example, the *Libro* of 1385 makes it clear that the superior *vino de Toro* was almost double the price of the *vino de la tierra*. Precise descriptions, however, are generally confined to the more detailed entries of the accounts of the earlier years. The quality white wine is variously described as *añejo, añejo de Madrigal,* and *de Madrigal,* and the red wine, although it is twice described as *tinto de allende los puertos,* is usually referred to as *de Toro* or *colorado de Toro.*[6] In short these were not local wines but were of a type equivalent to 'Toro Red' and 'Madrigal de las Altas Torres White', both of these being wines from areas close to Medina del Campo and the so-called *tierra del vino.*[7]

[6]These descriptions are to be found in the *Libros* for 1384, 1390-1, 1393-7, 1402, 1407, and 1438-9.

[7]The famous wines of the period, including those of Madrigal, are listed in Jorge Manrique's *Coplas a una beuda que tenia empeñado un brial en la taberna.* The white wines of the Medina region were among the few which were allowed to mature — hence the term *añejo* which is applied to 'Madrigal white'. Cf. also, Juan Ruiz, *Libro de Buen Amor,* ed. R.S. Willis (Princeton, 1972), p. 363: 'do an vino de Toro non beven de valadi'.

Parchment quotations present problems of a different kind since it is difficult to determine uniformity of size and the state of preparation. However, the accounts frequently facilitate matters by distinguishing between ordinary *pieles* and *pieles mayores,* and by giving information about preparation in terms of scraping and cleaning (*el raer e esponçar*). These factors help to create some confidence in the figures. In the first place the quotations in the accounts usually make it clear that prices include the cost of preparation. Secondly, since it seems obvious that the quantities purchased were for the use of the cathedral officials, the documents of the archive itself provide a reliable indicator as to size. In effect the large parchment sheets — the quotations for which are tabulated in this study — must have been used for the huge *Cuadernos de contabilidad,* and these parchments, bound in massive wooden covers, measure approximately 65 x 45 centimetres.

Similar considerations apply to the quotations of paper prices. Quite apart from the *Libros Redondos* themselves — and they used up some 25,000 folios during the period under review — paper was also needed for the other account books and for the *actas capitulares.* The size and quality of the paper remained fairly constant, although given the idiosyncratic movement of paper prices slight changes in size may have been of some importance. Down to 1456 the size used in the *Libros Redondos* remained at a constant 34 x 24 centimetres. Thereafter sizes varied somewhat before settling down to 30 x 22 centimetres from 1465 onwards.[8]

The two remaining commodities for which Burgos quotations are given require little comment. Plaster prices (*yeso*) have been taken from the 'repairs' accounts. Rabbits were an essential element in one of the Christmas festivities, and for this reason their continuous quotation, along with that for the cathedral dog-ejector's salary, constitutes one of the more bizarre features of the *Libros Redondos.*

Salaries of officials in Seville were often calculated on a basis of cash, cloth and grain, and it is for this reason that quotations for Bruges and Courtrai cloths are given with a fair degree of regularity. The respective importance and quality of these cloths within an Iberian context can now be gauged by reference to Iradiel's recent work on the Castilian cloth industry.[9]

[8] The precise variations in centimetres between 1456 and 1465 are as follows: 1457-8 = 30 x 22; 1459-60 = 34 x 24; 1461-3 = 30.5. x. 22; 1464 = 34 x 24. I owe these precise measurements to the kindness of Don Matías Vicario, who checked out my much more approximate calculations.

[9] P. Iradiel Murugarren, *Evolución de la industria textil castellana en los siglos XIII-XVI* (Salamanca, 1974).

The rather unsettling absence of Burgos wage quotations during the 1450s and 1460s is to be explained by the cathedral clergy's progressive disinclination to involve themselves in the direct management of property. This tendency, already obvious in the demesne accounts of the later fourteenth century, did not effect the accounts of repairs to urban property until the fifteenth century. But then, with leases increasingly shifting the burden of repairs on to tenants, residual repair work was contracted out and wage quotations petered out in the account-books.[9] The phenomenon was most marked in the case of the work-force of female labourers (*obreras*). But even with the carpenters there was a subtle change of emphasis. During the first half of the fifteenth century the account-books listed day-rates for numerous carpenters engaged on relatively extensive repairs. The *Libros* from the 1450s onwards, on the other hand, list only one carpenter per year and give his remuneration as a yearly salary.[11] Not until the 1470s are there signs that this tendency was at last being reversed.

Since there are adequate English translations for the terms *obreros, retejadores* and *carpinteros,* the work of those whose wages are quoted requires little comment. Inadequate data has prevented efforts to avoid the distortions of day-wage averages by seasonal variations. But although the percentages of seasonal fluctuations cannot be reliably calculated, the evidence suggests that any margin of error is not wide. For example, the dating of the wage-rates quoted in the *Libro Redondo* of 1424 is specific enough to show that while the day-wages of carpenters dropped by two *mrs* from November through to April, those of tilers and workmen were entirely unaffected by seasonal fluctuations. The account-books give no information about any payments in kind, and the quotations are for money wages.[12]

The problems posed by the series of salaries are so varied and technical that they are best dealt with in an Appendix. The most obvious general point concerning them is that, since they all refer to specialised employment within the cathedral, their restricted nature makes it virtually impossible to make viable deductions of general significance.

[10]Obviously this movement away from direct exploitation and management is a feature of great importance for the study of the economy of the period. Its very complexity, however, means that it deserves a separate study rather than the totally inadequate substantiation of a footnote.

[11]For example, 100*mrs* to *Hamete de perros moro desu salario deste anno por carpintero del cabildo* (Libro Redondo, 1453).

[12]This conculsion supports the lengthier comments of Hamilton who was obviously preoccupied on this point: Earl J. Hamilton, *Money, Prices and Wages,* pp. 66-7, 111,

The series of coin quotations include three of the more valuable monetary units in circulation in fifteenth-century Castile — gold *doblas*, gold Aragonese florins, and silver *reales*. Discontinuous quotations are given for French gold crowns, gold francs, gold ducats, the gold *enriques* minted by Henry IV of Castile (1454-74), and the *alfonsíes* minted by his half-brother, the pretender-king, Alfonso XII (1465-8).[13]

The evidence relating to the face values of these coins presents various problems. Quite apart from the difficulties arising from variations in weight, fineness, clipping and wear and tear, the very terminology used by the accounts often reveals that similar names could refer to intrinsically different coins. The term *dobla* is a good example, for the documents not only refer to *doblas* but also to *doblas valadíes, doblas de la banda, doblas castellanas, doblas blanquillas* and *doblas de oro moriscas*.[14] In addition to carefully distinguishing between such variations, however, the historian has to differentiate between different types of coin 'prices' given in the accounts. In the case of the Burgos *Libros Redondos*, from which the present quotations are taken, there seem to have been three basic types of coin 'prices'. In the first place there was what may be termed the 'market' price — that is to say, the value of a coin, such as an Aragonese florin, was given in *mrs* at the rate at which it circulated in practice. At times of rapid monetary change, of course, these 'market' prices themselves displayed considerable variation. Secondly, the *Libros Redondos* were sensitive to royal attempts to establish fixed prices for coins. 'Official' coin prices, therefore, appear as transitory phenomena in the accounts. The only clue to their appearance is an uncharacteristic and transient change in coin values, and when the 'official' values laid down in the royal ordinances are unearthed it becomes apparent that the corresponding Burgos quotations are exactly the same or represent a compromise between the 'official' and 'market' prices. Thirdly, the Burgos accounts use totally fictional coin values which may be termed 'management' prices. The nature of these is best explained by giving a specific example. On 12 March 1464 the cathedral chapter discussed the leases and income

[13] The *alfonsí* was simply another version of the *enrique*. As might be expected, large numbers and varieties of coins are mentioned in the Burgos accounts. Although most of these were 'exotic travellers', some areas of the kingdom were obviously more open to their influence. See, for example, the *so pena* clause of *mill doblas coronas de oro de la moneda del Rey de Francia* in an early fifteenth-century Guipúzcoan document in *Colección de documentos inéditos para la historia de Guipúzcoa* (San Sebastian, 1958), I, 17-22.

[14] Similarly, it should be remembered that divisions and multiples of some of these coins were in circulation.

relating to some of their houses in the Moorish quarter of Burgos. These houses had been given in *censo* in 1427 to Maestre Hali and Mahomad de Lerma in return for a payment of ten Aragonese gold florins per year. The houses, however, were now in a bad state of repair, the original tenants had died, the value of the florin had risen sharply until it now stood at 150 *mrs,* and the present tenants were threatening to leave unless the canons 'should wish to fix and moderate the florins to a reasonable price'. The canons, in fact, agreed to this proposal, and the 'price' of the florins was henceforth fixed at 107 *mrs* each.[15] Fortunately, although the *Libros Redondos* are full of such 'management' prices, they are usually easy to detect either because they are listed separately or because with the passage of time the differences between 'management' and 'market' prices became glaringly obvious. In this study the 'management' prices have been entirely ignored, 'market' prices have been averaged out where necessary, and the occasional interferences of 'official' prices have been taken into account as representing the transient but real effects which royal ordinances had on the money market.

Despite the effort involved in differentiating the various prices and coins, the construction of price series for the coins selected presents positive advantages. For, if we attempt to classify the Castilian monetary system in the light of Braudel and Spooner's illuminating framework, it must be concluded that the *maravedí*-based system was a 'light' currency group — that is, the billon coinage played a leading role in determining the devaluation of the money of account while at the same time there was a 'crying-up' of the full-bodied gold and silver coins.[16] The increase in the face-value of the coins selected, therefore, is one way of obtaining an approximate measure of the devaluation of the *maravedí* in terms of bullion.

But is it possible to analyse the fortunes of the *maravedí* more precisely? Since it was 'fictional' and did not exist as a coin, it is difficult to approach the problem in terms of weight and fineness.[17] A relatively precise analysis, however, is possible by using the price series for both Aragonese gold florins and silver. As will be seen later,

[15]This example is taken from the *censo* discussions and arrangements recorded in A.C. Burgos, Libro 2, *Censos de Pedro Rodriguez Velforado,* 1457-75, fos. 145-6 *v.*

[16]F. Braudel and F. Spooner, 'Prices in Europe from 1450 to 1750', in E.E. Rich and C.H. Wilson, eds., *Cambridge Economic History of Europe,* IV, *The Economy of Expanding Europe in the sixteenth and seventeenth centuries* (Cambridge, 1967), 378-82.

[17]It is certain that for most of the period under review the *maravedí* did not exist as a coin. In the ordinance of 1462, however, Henry IV ordered the minting of *maravedies* of 24 grains and 1/96 to the mark. Whether these were ever minted remains uncertain. For a discussion of the measures of 1462 see below, pp. 66-72.

there is general agreement as to the stability of the weight and fineness of the Aragonese florin, and this makes it possible to measure the devaluation of the *maravedí* in terms of gold. Of course, 'silver, more than gold, reveals the larger and more real perspectives of economic activity',[18] and for Castile there are unfortunately no data for the mint prices of silver. But since a greater number of indicators lead to firmer conclusions, Burgos quotations for the price of silver deserve consideration as being suitable for 'measurement' purposes.

During the period 1404-74, one and a half ounces of silver were registered among the various items of income listed by the *Libros Redondos*. As with all such items, the silver was priced in *maravedí*es in order to enable the accounting procedures to be put into operation. Provided, therefore, that some confidence as to the nature of this silver can be established, the fortunes of the *maravedí* can be measured in terms of silver during these seventy years. Indeed it is on the nature and relationships of the coins and the silver that attention must now be focussed.

Aragonese florins, modelled on those of Florence, were first minted by Peter IV of Aragon in 1346 and were probably 24 carats fine and 1/68 of a mark. This purity was shortlived: in 1352 the fineness was reduced to 22 ¾ carats, in 1362 to 22 carats and in 1365 to 18 carats, with the weight remaining stable at 1/68 of a mark. The important point, however, is that from 1365 onwards the fineness and weight remained constant and, as Hamilton put it, 'the gold content of the florin established at this time never changed.[19] Thus, apart from exceptional quotations for the 'old' florin in the *Libros Redondos* of 1390 and 1391, all Burgos figures for florins refer to the Aragonese florin of 18 carats and 1/68 of a mark.

Although there are less data on the fineness and weight of the silver *real* of Castile, such evidence as there is suggests that this coin, like the florin, remained relatively stable throughout this period. Thus, in a remarkable ordinance of 1442 in which he admitted having debased *blancas*, John II insisted on the maintenance of the silver *real* at its traditional standard:

> Furthermore, I ordered and order my said treasurers (of the mints) to mint . . . *reales* and half *reales* and quarter *reales* of

[18]F. Braudel and F. Spooner, 'Prices in Europe', 381.

[19]The presence of large numbers of these florins in Castile is partly to be explained in terms of this stability which led to an under-valuation of gold in the Crown of Aragon. Round about 1420, for example, the Aragonese monarch was presented with a mint memorandum which argued in favour of an alteration of the content of the florin in order to eliminate the profits to be made from its exportation. Hamilton, *Money, Prices and Wages,* pp. 12-14, 22-3.

silver at a fineness of eleven *dineros* and four grains and at a weight of sixty six *reales* to the mark, which is more or less the same fineness and weight that King Henry my father, and King John my grandfather, and King Henry my great grandfather ordered in their times for the minting of silver *reales* . . .[20]

According to John II, therefore, the silver *real* of 11 *dineros* and 4 grains and 1/66 of a mark had 'more or less' maintained its stability — and a tolerance margin of two grains was normal — ever since the reign of Henry II (1369-79). Moreover it was probably to remain stable for, although in the 1460s Henry IV was to reduce its weight to 1/67 of a mark, its fineness appears to have remained fairly constant.[21] It is true that allegations about debasement of the *real,* voiced by Henry IV's enemies, cannot be lightly set aside,[22] yet nowhere in the *Libros Redondos* do we find those distinctions between 'old' and 'new' *reales* which were made with respect to other debased coins, and the increase in the face value of the *real* more or less matched that of the Aragonese florin.

The Castilian gold *dobla*, minted intermittently from the reign of Ferdinand III (1217-1252) onwards, presents greater difficulties than the florin or *real*. For the period under review its notional fineness was 23¾ carats and its weight 1/50 of a mark.[23] However, the different adjectives used to describe the *doblas* clearly indicate different types of coin. In the cortes of Madrid of 1435, for example, the *procuradores* referred to *doblas blanquillas* and *doblas valadíes*:

> there are many frauds (perpetrated) in the *doblas baladis* which now circulate in your kingdom, not only because many of them are not good, but also because the money changers who change them claim that (all the *doblas*) are *blanquillas*, despite the fact that many of them are good, and they only give eighty five *mrs* for them in exchange; in this way the money changers take in the good ones, and often these (same) *doblas* are bought from the exchangers at ninety six *mrs*. . . .[24]

[20]Ordinance of 29 January 1442, BN, MS., 13259, fo. 313 (Appendix A-3).

[21]Minting directive of 20 November 1468 in AGS EMR., Leg. 519; ordinance of 10 April 1471 in *Memorias de Don Enrique IV de Castilla* (Real Academia de la Historia, Madrid, 1835-1913), II, 641.

[22]In fact there was only one specific allegation with reference to the *real* — that made by the Pretender, Alfonso, in a letter of 25 Nov. 1465. See O. Gil Farres, *Historia de la moneda española* (Madrid, 1959), p. 220, and L. Sáez, *Demostración histórica del verdadero valor de todas las monedas que corrían en Castilla durante el regnado del Señor Don Enrique IV* (Madrid, 1805), pp. 20-1.

[23]Gil Farres, p. 216.

[24]*Cortes,* III, 232-3.

What exactly were these *doblas valadíes*? There can be little doubt that these were Muslim *doblas* or the so-called Castilian *doblas de la banda* which John II consciously modelled on the Muslim *dobla* when he began minting them in 1430. This relationship between the Muslim *doblas* (*doblas valadíes, doblas moriscas, doblas granadinas*) and the *doblas de la banda* was described by the king himself in 1442:

> I ordered and order the treasurers of the mint . . . that in each mint they should work a furnace for *doblas* of gold, and that each one of these should bear my royal arms and, on the other side, the *banda*. These *doblas* are to be smaller in circumference than those which exist . . . And, inasmuch as I had sure information that, at the time when the good *doblas baladis* were being used and circulated in my kingdoms and lordships, they had been and were being minted in the mint of Málaga and elsewhere, and were of a fineness of nineteen carats of fine gold and of a weight of forty nine *doblas* to the mark, and were worth in my kingdoms at that time eighty or eighty two *mrs* in terms of *blancas viejas,* therefore these *doblas de la banda* which I ordered to be minted are to be of the same fineness and cut and weight.[25].

There were, therefore, two main types of *doblas* in circulation — the *dobla* of 22¾ carats and 1/50 of a mark, and the *dobla de la banda* of 19 carats and 1/49 of a mark. The reference to *blanquillas*, of course, makes it clear that, during the 1430s at least, debased versions of either or both of these *doblas* were in circulation.

The infrequent quotations presented here for *enriques, alfonsíes,* or other gold coins hardly help to throw much light on the little that is known about them. Henry IV's *enrique* and his rival's *alfonsí* were notionally of a fineness of 23, 23¼ or 23¾ carats and a weight of 1/50 of a mark.[26] However, the existence of 'new' and 'old' *enriques* indicates that these coins were subjected to changes which it is impossible to quantify with any precision. Indeed, if we accept one contemporary assessment, it would seem that *enriques* of only 7 carats were being minted by 1470.[27]

However, in contrast to most of the 'heavy' coins just examined, there can be little doubt that the 'light' or billon coins in circulation were characterized by a chronic instability which seriously affected

[25] Ordinance of 29 January 1442, BN, MS., 13259, fo. 312 *v* (Appendix A-3).

[26] For these variations see AGS, EMR., Leg. 11, fo. 98, 11 February 1468; *ibid.,* Leg. 519, docs. dated 15 February 1468, 20 November 1468, 25 August 1469, 9 August 1469; *Memorias de Enrique IV,* pp. 640-1, 10 April 1471.

[27] See L. Sáez, p. 4; Gil Farrés, p. 220.

the fortunes of the money of account to which they were intimately linked. In almost any set of fifteenth-century accounts, the historian is brought face to face with the fact that, when the need to define the *maravedí* arose, contemporaries invariably defined it in terms of the billon coinage, and in particular by referring to the coins known as *blancas*. Thus, if we take random samples from the documentation of Sahagún monastery, we find the monks describing the nature of the money of their rents and prices as follows: in 1410 they referred to 4,000 *mrs* 'of this usual money in which two *blancas* make one *maravedí*'; in 1438, 200 *mrs* 'of this usual money in which two *blancas* make one *maravedí*'; in 1451, 200 *mrs* 'of this usual money in which two old *blancas* make one *maravedí*'; in 1459, 3,500 *mrs* 'of this usual money in which two old *blancas* or three new ones make one *maravedí*'; in 1464, 2,000 *mrs* 'of this money in which two old *blancas* and three new ones make one *maravedí*'.[28] It will have been noticed, of course, that both old and new *blancas* have insinuated themselves into the descriptions. And it certainly does not help to clarify matters if we note that, prior to the old and new *blancas*, 'old' and 'new' *maravedí*es had also existed and, as fictional moneys of account, are to be found jostling each other in the accounts of the late fourteenth and early fifteenth centuries. Thus, to take another Sahagún example, in a dispute in 1407 over seigneurial dues, the 'old' *maravedí* was defined as being the equivalent of ten *dineros novenes* or two 'new' *maravedí*es.[29] Despite the apparent confusion, however, it is clear that the *maravedí* was invariably defined in terms of billon coins. A typical set of equivalencies between old and new coins, for example, would be couched in terms of billon and might be expressed as follows:

1 'old' *maravedí* = 2 'new' *maravedí*es = 4 *blancas* = 6 'old' *cornados* = 12 'new' *cornados* = 10 'old' *dineros (novenes)* = 20 'new' *dineros* = 60 'old' *meajas* = 120 'new' *meajas*.[30]

But two points remain to be elucidated. How is the existence of two types of *maravedí* to be explained, and where do the 'old' and 'new' *blancas* fit into the picture?

The existence of the schizophrenic *maravedí* presents problems as far as the early years covered by this study are concerned. Prior to

[28]AHN, Clero, Pergs., Carp. 941, doc. 23, 3 November 1410; Carp. 943, doc. 4, 3 March 1438, and doc. 11, 15 March 1451; Carp. 944, doc. 1, 27 March 1459, and doc. 3, 27 January 1464.

[29]AHN, Clero, Pergs., Carp. 941, doc. 6, 7 March 1407.

[30]These early fifteenth-century equivalencies, of course, were hardly ever expressed in their totality in one and the same document. For a convenient tabulation, in which the columns for the *real* and the *maravedí* of Charles IV should be ignored, see L. Sáez, p. 183.

1390, in effect, a disastrous civil war, the intervention of French and English armies in Castilian politics, and a bullion famine had led the monarchy to indulge in massive debasements in order to meet war expenditure and repay foreign debts. By 1387, therefore, a series of complicated measures began to be introduced to restore some order in the monetary chaos that prevailed. The general upshot of all these measures, however, was fairly clear: the intrinsic value of the debased coins of low denomination was declared to be half the value of the 'old' coins bearing the same name. For example, in the *cortes* of 1391 one 'new' debased *dinero* was declared to be worth only half an 'old' *dinero*. But, since the *maravedí* was related to such coins, 'old' and 'new' *maravedíes* also came into existence. Thus the new *maravedí* (= 6 new *cornados* = 10 new *dineros* = 60 new *meajas*) was worth half the old *maravedí* (= 6 old *cornados* = 10 old *dineros* = 60 old *meajas*).[31]

For some years after 1390, therefore, accounting procedures used both old and new *maravedíes* with final reckoning being calculated on a simple 'two to one' basis. The new *maravedí*, however, emerged victoriously as the standard money of account, and for the purposes of this study the few quotations in old *maravedíes* have been retained as such in the tables but have been converted into new *maravedíes* as far as the graphs are concerned. In effecting such conversions, in fact, I have merely done what the Castilians of the period themselves did.

It has already been seen from the Sahagún examples that the new *maravedí* was usually defined in terms of *blancas*. Fortunately, although little is known about the fineness and weight of many of the billon coins in circulation, there are sufficient data to outline the fate of the *blanca* itself. As its fineness and weight deteriorated during the course of the fifteenth century, so too was the *maravedí* affected by devaluation and the ubiquitous adjectives 'old' and 'new' reappeared and were attached to the *blancas*. Henry III's *blancas*, first minted in 1390, had a fineness of 24 grains and a weight of 1/112 of a mark. But John II reduced the *blanca* to 20 grains and 1/118 of a mark, by 1469 it had dropped to 11 grains and 1/160 of a mark, and by 1470 it was as low as 8 grains and 1/170 of a mark.[32] Distinctions between 'old' and 'new'

---

[31] For the pre-1390 background see Gil Farres, pp. 212-5; J. Valdeón Baruque, 829-45; *Cortes,* II, 359-62, 399-407, 420-3, 517-23.

[32] Gil Farres, p. 218, gives the fineness of Henry III's *blancas* as 21 grains, but the precise data both for these and for the *blancas* of John II are given in the ordinance of 29 Jan. 1442, BN, MS., 13259, fo. 312 (Appendix A-3). The data for 1469 and 1470 are in AGS, EMR., Leg. 519, docs. of 9 August 1469 (Appendix A-8) and 28 January 1470. It should be stressed that only selected data are given in the text since, at this stage, the purpose is merely to sketch the fate of the *blanca*.

blancas arose as a result of royal attempts to halt the slide in the value of the *maravedí* which followed on from these changes in the billon coinage. In 1442, for example, John II tried to cope with the problem by establishing parities which would leave the *maravedí* unscathed: 3 'new' *blancas* (that is, John II's debased *blancas*) = 6 *cornados* = 2 'old' *blancas* (of Henry III) = 1 *maravedí.*[33] Similarly, in 1473, Henry IV decreed that 'my coins of *blancas* which have been minted in my six mints, and two of which used to be worth one *maravedí*, are to be henceforth valued at three *blancas* for one *maravedí. . .* '[34] The success or failure of such measures will be examined later. The main purpose here has been to review briefly the main characteristics of the florins, *doblas* and *reales*, and to explain why *maravedíes* and *blancas* were divided into 'new' and 'old' categories for considerable periods of time.

There remains the problem of the nature and quality of the silver for which prices are given in the *Libros Redondos*. This silver was paid in the form of *censo* rents for houses in the *Cal de las Armas* and in the area in front of the church of San Esteban.[35] Unfortunately a search through the surviving registers of *censos* has failed to uncover the documents corresponding to the *censos* of these particular houses. However, all is not lost and we can be certain of two things. In the first place we can be sure that the 'quality' of the silver remained constant over the years. Although rather more complicated in theory, for our present purposes the *censo* may simply be described as a perpetual lease.[36] In setting up such *censos* the canons carefully defined the nature, method and quality of the payments in order to protect the long-term interests and income of the cathedral. Thus, although we do not know what these definitions were in this case, there can be little doubt that a fixed standard was laid down. Secondly, it is certain that none of the prices quoted for silver in the *Libros Redondos* were 'management' prices. At no point, therefore, were these rents subjected to an artificial price adjustment such as has already been described in the example of the houses in the Moorish district.

[33] The parities were established in more than one ordinance. See, for example, BN, MS., 13107, fos. 181-92, and 13259, fos. 316 *v*-8 (Appendix A-4).

[34] Ordinance of 12 May 1473, *Memorias de Enrique IV*, p. 691.

[35] This information is derived from the separate accounts for houses. See, for example, A.C. Burgos, *Cuaderno de contabilidad,* 9, años 1445-9, fo. 6 for the year 1449.

[36] I define it in this way simply to emphasise its long-term nature and to avoid a lengthy digression. For a discussion of some of the complexities and for further bibliographical data, see Charles Jago, 'The Influence of Debt on the Relations between Crown and Aristocracy in seventeenth-century Castile', *Economic History Review,* 2nd ser. XXVI (1973), 218-36.

The 'quality' and amounts of silver, therefore, were constant factors. Is it possible to determine the fineness and weight of this silver precisely? Fortunately, the evidence for the silver prices is from *Burgos* cathedral, and this fact alone seems to point in only one direction.

According to Gil Farres, the mark of silver in use in late medieval Castile was the Cologne mark of 230 grams which was divisible into 8 ounces, 64 *ochavas,* 384 *tomines* aand 4,608 grains. The ounce of silver, therefore, was 28.75 grams.[37] Of course, to posit the existence of one standard system of weights and measures for any medieval kingdom, let alone Castile, immediately presents difficulties. But in the case of the Castilian mark of silver the sources are particularly explicit. Thus, although there were indeed frequent complaints in the *cortes* about conflicting systems of weights and measures, as far as silver was concerned it was the *Burgos* mark which was stipulated as the norm for the whole kingdom. The acts of the *cortes* of 1435 and 1436, for example, make it abundantly clear that the Burgos mark was the same as that of Cologne, that its fineness was 270/288 grains, and that it had been established as the standard mark over a century earlier.[38] Similarly, it was for this mark of silver that the monarchy attempted to fix prices, and even the conditions for farming the royal mints stipulated 'that all the said [minting] houses must work according to one mark and standard and that this mark should be that of Burgos . . .'[39] Now, even if it is assumed that in practice the Burgos or Cologne mark of silver was not in universal use throughout the kingdom, it would obviously be the standard mark for Burgos itself. Thus the one and a half ounces of silver listed in the *Libros Redondos* referred to silver which was weighted in terms of the Burgos mark. But this does not necessarily prove that its fineness was 270/288 grains because, although this might have been the standard fineness, it is obvious that silvers of different finenesses must have been in circulation. Fortunately, the terminology of the period comes to our aid. In 1442 John II stipulated that the price of the mark of silver of 270/288 grains should be no more that 560 *mrs.* But another version of the very same ordinance, instead of giving the fineness of the silver, stipulates exactly the same price for '*el marco de plata quebrada en pasta*'.[40] This latter terminology, therefore, must have been an

[37]Gil Farres, p. 19.

[38]*Cortes,* III, 226-7, 251-8.

[39]The passage quoted is from AGS, EMR., Leg. 11, fo. 99, 11 February 1468.

[40]For this ordinance of 6 April 1442, see BN, MS., 13259, fos. 318-9 (Appendix A-5). For the variation in terminology see the eighteenth-century copy in BN, MS., 13107, fo. 182 *v.*

alternative way of referring to silver of 270/288 grains, and it is precisely this terminology which is employed in the more specific references of the *Libros Redondos*. The conclusion, therefore, is that the silver prices of the Burgos accounts refer to silver of 270/288 grains and 230 grams to the mark.

Prices, Wages and Salaries

Before attempting to interpret the statistical data it is necessary to justify the manner of their presentation and to emphasize the caution which must obviously govern any generalizations derived from such limited information.

All the statistics given in the tables are presented on semi-logarithmic graphs in the form of index numbers in order to facilitate the perception of percentage changes and the comparison of the various series. The base year of 1435 has been chosen because it is at the centre of most series.[41]

Isolating cyclical fluctuations by means of moving averages has been rejected for the purposes of the present study. What is of interest here is both the long-term trend and the irregular fluctuations, and since there is no obvious case for arguing that regular cyclical factors affect the data, the determining of such cycles and their periodicity can be left until more quantitative information becomes available. Similarly another expedient has been rejected: given the extent of irregular fluctuations in most of the series, no attempt has been made — for example, by using the least-squares method — to calculate appropriate interpolations for missing values in the various series. There is one exception to this rule. Down to the second decade of the fifteenth century there are one or two years for which we have prices and wages expressed in *maravedíes* but no values for these *maravedíes* in either silver or Aragonese florins. Since these missing *maravedí* values are part of a fairly predictable pattern, interpolations have been effected in these few instances in order to calculate real prices and wages, but they have not been used for any other purpose. These interpolations are clearly marked in the relevant tables.

Do the inadequacies of the present indices have to be emphasized? Prices for vital commodities are lacking, the price and wage series show alarming gaps, data on salaries are obviously open to serious

---

[41] Although not impossible, the selection of a more extended base — such as the 1421-30 base used by Hamilton — would necessitate the use of interpolations.

objections, nothing of any significance emerges about regional price variations, nominal prices in Seville are converted into real prices by using evidence from Burgos, and most of the evidence is gathered from precisely those cathedral and municipal institutions so suspect to price-historians of later periods. Yet in the context of later medieval Castile the present quantitative data marks an advance in a forest of ignorance. All the generalizations and conclusions are open to question, but they also invite other historians to collect more material in order to substantiate or alter the arguments propounded here.

With few exceptions, the first impression given by the nominal price indices is that of a considerable similarity of agreement in both the long-term trends and the short-term fluctuations (Graph 2). With the exception of paper, nominal prices from 1390/1400 to 1470/80 are characterised, in very general terms, by an upwards inflationary movement. Within this very general movement, however, it is possible to detect shorter periods of similar patterns. If we disregard the few rather conflicting and fluctuating movements prior to 1400, there is in the first place a rather indeterminate period of stability between c1400 and c1430: wax and wine prices fluctuate round the base line to a greater degree than those of paper; the prices of rabbits and plaster reveal a moderate upward bias; cloth prices in Seville fluctuate upwards in the years around 1410, and then, after a pause at the end of the second decade, settle down to more or less their initial level; parchment prices may be said to behave in a similar manner to those of cloth, but with a time-lag and with a downward bias in the settling-down level round about 1430. Pronounced inflation, therefore, was chiefly a feature of the period from the 1430s onwards. But even here we can detect accelerations and pauses in the upwards movement: from c1430 to c1441 acceleration; an indeterminate and fluctuating pause in the 1440s which in some cases is prolonged into the 1450s; accelerated inflation during the 1460s (with the exception of wine); finally, in those cases where there are data for the 1470s, a suggestion that a new high plateau has been reached.

These patterns in the nominal price indices are to a large extent mirrored by the indices of the face-values of coins and silver (Graph 4). The crying-up of these values only becomes serious after a period of relative stability prior to 1430. From c1430 to c1441 coin face-values and silver prices accelerate sharply upwards, there follows a dip and a pause for part of the 1440s (less marked in the case of *reales*), a higher plateau is reached in the 1450s, and then accelerated inflation characterises the late 1450s and early 1460s onwards, although both florins and *reales* dip sharply c1462 and there is the hint of a new high plateau being reached in the 1470s.

The remarkable concordance of these movements is well illustrated by plotting the devaluation of the money of account in terms of silver and Aragonese florins (Graph 1). There are, it is true, significant disparities between the silver and florin components in the early years of the 1440s, 1460s and 1470s, and attention will be focused on these episodes later. But apart from these exceptions, these movements remain almost inextricably entwined over the century and, as might be expected, the devaluation perspective reveals the same periodisations. Down to 1430 the *maravedi* retained its value fairly well in what may be termed a gently inclined downward phase of stability. Thereafter, however, its fortunes declined sharply in plunges punctuated by brief pauses or rests: sharp devaluation characterises the periods c1430-41, 1445-51 and 1462/64 onwards; pauses and even partial reversals of the downward trend are evident during the years c1442-5, c1451-6/9, and c1460-4.

It is clear from the foregoing analysis that the rhythms of the nominal price movements were to a considerable extent determined by the devaluation of the money of account. To clinch the point we need only look at the flattening-out effect which is produced when nominal prices and wages are expressed in terms of silver (Graphs 3, 5). Indeed some real prices actually show a downward trend, although it is much harder to generalise about these indices because, having eliminated the effects of the common factor of devaluation, each commodity movement tends to acquire its own particular characteristics. Nevertheless the falling trend of paper prices is also discernible to a lesser extent in the cases of parchment, cloth and perhaps plaster. Moreover, while the indices of wax, rabbits and wine tend to maintain a more or less fluctuating movement along the base line, there is no case where a long-term trend of rising prices can be detected. Further than this it is difficult to generalise with any certainty. During the first two decades of the fifteenth century real prices tend to be high, from c1420 to c1435 there is a downward movement (with two exceptions), during the following decade there is a partial recovery marked by fairly violent fluctuations, and at differing points during the 1460s there is perhaps a tendency for prices to pick up again. Is it also possible to detect a long-term rhythm over twenty-year periods — c1412-32, 1432-52, 1452-72?

Although there are only three wage indices (and they are far from complete!), these tend to confirm some of the general points made about the price movements (Graph 5). In each case the movements A-A and B-B intersect in a manner which reveals that, while there was a long-term rise in nominal wages, the benefits of this increase were eroded to such an extent that real wages appear to have declined considerably by the 1470s. Once again, too, it would seem that, despite fluctuations, the years up to the 1430s were ones of relative stability. But the buoyancy of the series for workmen and carpenters is prolonged for some time after the devaluation of the *maravedí* had set in (Graph 5), and in the absence of further quotations it is impossible to determine at what point, prior to the late 1460s, the collapse in real wages occurred. The relative wage-earning capacities of the various occupations are self-evident (Appendix B-4), but in the absence of any data on the regularity of employment and of any gauge of the cost of living (however approximate), it is impossible to make any quantitative assessment of changes in the value of real incomes.

In Appendix B-5 a detailed description is given of the jobs to which the salary data refer, and the more technical problems which these figures pose are analysed. In general terms the most striking phenomenon revealed by the data is that of stability over long periods. During the whole of the period, for example, the salaries of the *raedor* and the *portero* remained constant — a fact which makes it irrelevant to construct a graph since the result would merely be to superimpose a straight base-line (nominal salary) on the devaluation of the *maravedí* (real salary). Stability of this kind, of course, implied a long-term erosion of salaries in real terms, as can be most easily seen in the cases of the *mayordomos del libro redondo* and the *escribano del cabildo* during the period c1450-80. In both these cases, however, abrupt compensating advances in the indices, in 1418 and in 1450 respectively, reveal that real salaries were much the same at the end of this period as they had been at the beginning. Only in the case of the *mayordomo* was there a substantial rise over the period as a whole, possibly because this official was in the most commanding position with respect to the financial affairs of the cathedral. Whatever the explanation, however, this one case stands in contrast to the drastic fall in the real salaries of most of the officials (for example, the *contadores, troxeros, escribanos del consistorio,* and *raedores).* But it is absolutely essential to emphasize that these comments on the salary data cannot be used to make any general deductions. Indeed, given the existence of *pluriempleo* and the fact that most of these officials were also canons (see Appendix B-5), it is clear that the data on salaries refer to specific tasks of work rather than to the income of specific individuals. For example, the statement that there was a drastic fall in the real salaries of the *contadores* cannot be taken to refer to the economic fortunes of those individuals who counted this particular salary among their many other sources of income.

The preceding descriptions of the various series and indices have helped to establish two points of a methodological nature. Firstly, it is clear that at present no further advances of significance can be made along the front of real prices and wages. The evidence from Burgos and the few examples from Seville can hardly be used to generalize about the Castilian realms as a whole. Moreover, even if we restrict discussion to the Burgos region alone it is still difficult to make confident pronouncements about the movements of real prices and wages in general. All that can be said is that the limited evidence suggests that real prices and wages in Castile may have tended to stagnate or decline over the period as a whole — and this suggestion at least has the merit of agreeing with the western European experience in general. Secondly, the extent of the devaluation of the *maravedí* was on such a scale as to convert stagnating and even declining real price trends into sharp nominal inflation. This fact in itself was of importance to contemporaries since the perceived reality of rampant inflation affected the behavioural system of their society. For example, we only need to posit the existence of a powerful nobility with fixed incomes (in terms of money of account) to realize the importance of exploring the problems of debasement and nominal inflation further. But is is not enough merely to catalogue contemporary complaints relating to these phenomena, although these accord well enough with the various pauses and bursts of inflation which have already been deduced from the quantitative data.[42] Cannot the contemporary reactions to these phenomena also help to explain the hidden mechanisms which prompted many forms of political action and social unrest? In effect, more often than not the devaluation of the *maravedí* depended on the monetary policies of the monarchy, and this fact by itself meant that the issue of inflation was perceived in political terms. Let us first see, therefore, to what extent the fortunes of the *maravedí* were linked to the monetary policies of the Crown.

The Chronology of Devaluation and Royal Debasements

The following discussion on debasements and devaluations is full of an apparently bewildering variety of coins, finenesses and weights. Two points about these need to be emphasised at the outset. In the first place both the distinction and the confusion between the contents and the names of coins must be constantly kept in mind. Pierre Vilar has neatly summarized the point:-

[42]In general terms if we exclude protests about price rises due to bad harvests, the volume of complaints begins *c*1435 and reaches a crescendo in the 1460s when, for example, the *sentencia* of 1465 presented demands for reform because of price increases of over 50 and 60 per cent.

The money-changer of the fifteenth century *weighed* his *écus*; for him they were a commodity. The royal official might see in money something *created by the State*, a means of policy. Only the 'stupid and crude populace' (to use the phrase of President de Lusson in an unpublished memoir), incapable of finding its way among the 80-odd forms of coin which circulated in seventeenth-century France, had to put its trust in *denomination* alone, only to be robbed when one sort of coin was changed for its equivalent denomination in another.[43]

This tripartite distinction is important. Obviously, in terms of content, the *blanca* of 1400 (24 grains and 1/112 of a mark) was not the same coin as the *blanca* of 1470 (8 grains and 1/170 of a mark). The difference was appreciated by those who always sought the reality behind the denomination — for example, the money-changer who weighed his *écus*. But the denomination did not change. On one occasion, it is true, a change in contents did result in a confusion of denominations and a transvestite *dinero* was accepted into circulation as a *blanca*.[44] This case, however, was exceptional, and the result was that the changing contents of coins of fixed denomination affected the value of the *maravedí* and of other coins to which they were related. In the Castilian case, as we will see, the changes became so frequent that the populace in the end refused to put its trust in denomination and even resorted to barter. It is obvious, too, that changes in the contents of the coins were created by the State, but the hypothesis that these changes constituted a means of policy must be set aside for discussion in a separate section.[45] Secondly, if we are to analyse subtle changes in the scale of monetary disturbances, a method of calculation must occasionally be applied which allows us to weigh and compare the various coins. It was for this purpose that I constructed the equation $P = xy/z$.[46]

Although the evidence is not as plentiful as one would like, it is possible to describe and date most of the royal manipulations of the monetary system which relate to the nominal movements already analysed.

The first three decades of the fifteenth century, as we have seen, were characterised by relative stability. In effect the only notable features of this early period are the fairly simple processes of readjustment between 'old' and 'new' *maravedíes* which were the

[43] Pierre Vilar, 'Problems of the Formation of Capitalism', 29.

[44] See below, pp. 68-71.

[45] See below pp. 96-101.

[46] For a detailed explanation of the equation see the Preface.

legacy of the Crown's solution to the last major monetary upheaval of the previous century. A late and typical example of such a process is contained in a letter of 1416 from Queen Beatriz to the town council of Toro, and concerns the levying of the seigneurial tax known as the *martiniega*:

> You well know that some problems have arisen over my *martiniegas* from the said town of Toro and its lands between your council and those who have to collect and levy these *martiniegas*. These problems relate to whether the *martiniega* payments should be in *moneda vieja* ['old' *mrs*] or in *moneda blanca* ['new' *mrs*], whether half asessments should be listed so that those who are not fully assessed should also pay, and whether those who . . . claim to be exempt should not pay the said *martiniega*. . . . It is my wish and I order and declare that from now on the said *martiniegas* should be collected in the following manner. He who is assessed at 120 *mrs of moneda vieja* or at 240 *mrs* of *moneda blanca* is to pay the full amount of 12 *mrs* of *moneda vieja* or 24 *mrs* of *moneda blanca*. And he who is not assessed at the said amount but at 60 *mrs* of *moneda vieja* or 120 *mrs* of *moneda blanca* is to pay the half contribution of 6 *mrs* of *moneda vieja* or 12 *mrs* of *moneda blanca*. . . .[47]

Clearly the 2:1 relationship between 'new' and 'old' *mrs* posed few problems, but some of the other implications of these readjustments need to be briefly mentioned. The creation of the 'new' *mr* did not cause an immediate and massive devaluation of the money of account. Certainly the use of *mrs* apparently doubled the nominal figure of any sum expressed in 'old' *mrs*, but as the example just cited shows, any price, wage, or tax-contribution could be expressed in either type of *maravedi*. However, the 'old' *mr* was in the long run affected by devaluation in exactly the same way as the 'new' *mr*. For example, if in the 1440s a noble insisted that royal *mercedes* or seigneurial dues, which had been established in terms of 'old' *mrs* at the beginning of the century, should be paid to him at double the rate in 'new' *mrs*, he avoided any loss involved in the change to the new money of account; but since the conversion was established on a 2:1 basis, he could not avoid the fact that the devaluation of the 'new' *mr* since 1430 also dragged the 'old' *mr* in its wake.[48]

[47]ADM, Villalonso, Leg. 3, doc. 36, 6 November 1416.

[48]The salaries of the *contadores* of Burgos cathedral also illustrate the point (Appendix B-5). Down to the *Libro Redondo* of 1453 these salaries were entered as 500 'old' *mrs*, but from 1454 onwards the entry was changed to 1,000 'new' *mrs*. Thus, while the process of doubling the figure presented no problem, the salaries, whether expressed in 'old' or 'new' *mrs*, were still affected by the devaluation that had set in a quarter of a century earlier.

The evidence suggests that 1430 was in fact the first year in which John II debased the coinage.[49] To establish this we must begin with documents dating from 1442. In that year the king, without referring to a specific date, explained the reasons which had led him to mint *doblas*, *blancas* and *cornados* at the four mints of Burgos, Toledo, Seville and La Coruña, and in particular he referred to his issue of *blancas* of reduced fineness and weight (20 grains and 1/59 to the mark as against Henry III's *blancas* of 24 grains and 1/56 to the mark).[50] When did this debasement take place? In discussing the ordinances of 1442, the chronicle of John II states that these *blancas* had been minted a long time before (*mucho tiempo antes*).[51] In fact, although he had blamed counterfeiters, the king had already admitted in 1439 that debased coins were in circulation,[52] and the *cortes* of 1435 and 1436 had complained about dubious *doblas* and *moneda non buena* in general.[53] Now, prior to these admissions and complaints, only 1429/30 and 1435 can be considered as possible dates for the debasement. In 1429, as the chronicle of John II relates, a political crisis was accompanied by prolonged monetary deliberations which resulted in a decision to mint considerable amounts of coin.[54] But Gil Farres, while emphasizing the minting decisions of 1429, also states that there was another issue of *blancas* and *cornados* in 1435.[55] In choosing between these two dates, however, the evidence points overwhelmingly to 1429/30. For, not only does the devaluation graph clearly point to a date prior to 1435 (Graph 1), but as will be seen later, the very nature of the political crisis of 1429 was such as to induce the king to resort to his first manipulation of the coinage.[56] That this first debasement was repeated in 1435 is, of course, by no means improbable.

The first attempts to deal with the inflation arising from this debasement were John II's ordinances of 1438 and 1439. But these

[49] After working out the arguments contained in this paragraph, I was delighted to discover that a late fifteenth-century version of parts of the chronicle of John II, which is located in the British Museum (Egerton 1875), contains a passage which fully supports my deductions. I am extremely grateful to Dr. Dorothy Severin for drawing my attention to the version in question.

[50] See, in particular, the ordinance of 29 January 1442 in BN, MS., 13259, fos. 312-4 (Appendix A-3).

[51] *Crónica de Juan II,* p. 608.

[52] Ordinance of 20 December 1439, BN, MS., 13259, fos. 189v — 90v (Appendix A-2).

[53] *Cortes,* III 230-3, 265-7.

[54] *Crónica de Juan II,* pp. 467-8.

[55] Gil Farres, p. 218.

[56] See below pp. 95-6.

were makeshift measures, and despite provisions for the immediate withdrawal of patently inferior coins and the piercing and eventual withdrawal of dubious coins, little had changed by 1442 when a determined effort at reform was launched.[57] This began in January when the king laid down standards for the fineness and weight of *doblas*, *reales* and *blancas*, and ordered all his debased *blancas nuevas* to be withdrawn from circulation.[58] Debasement, the king argued, had resulted in the *maravedí* losing one-sixth of its value.[59] He was not far wrong. In fact, to be more precise, if the *maravedí* had actually existed as a coin, its weight and fineness would have been approaching 20 grains and 1/29.5 to the mark; by withdrawing debased *blancas* the *maravedí* would notionally climb to 24 grains and 1/28 to the mark.[60]

By March, however, John II had been persuaded that the withdrawal of the debased *blancas* was not a satisfactory solution.[61] In the first place, the *procuradores* of the *cortes* pointed out, the withdrawal of these *blancas* would necessitate an expensive new issue of billon coins. Secondly, however good these new coins might be, the experience of the past few years would make people undervalue them, and this in turn would be detrimental to price levels. Finally, past experience suggested that a new issue would lead to a wave of counterfeiting both in neighbouring kingdoms and in Castile itself. Rather than withdraw the *blancas nuevas*, therefore, the *procuradores* urged that they be allowed to circulate at their proper value. Accepting these arguments, John II now decreed a series of equivalencies that linked both kinds of *blancas* to the *maravedí* at different levels of value: 1 *mr* = 2 'old' *blancas* = 3 'new' *blancas*. With this solution, it was now confidently expected, most problems had been resolved — new billon coins would not have to be minted, and the prices of coins and commodities would stabilize.

This confidence was unfounded, and within a month a new ordinance was issued imposing fixed price levels on gold coins and silver: the value of the *dobla de la banda* was fixed at 100 *mrs*, the

[57]Ordinance of 11 July 1438 in L. Sáez, pp. 473-80; ordinance of 20 December 1439, BN, MS., 13259, fos. 189*v*-90*v* (Appendix A-2). The debased *blancas* continued to circulate, and it was precisely because of this that new measures had to be taken in 1442.

[58]Ordinance of 29 January 1442, BN, MS., 13259, fos. 312-4 (Appendix A-3).

[59]*Ibid.* fo. 312*v*.

[60]These calculations, in line with those of the ordinance, assume that the fortunes of the *maravedí* were determined by the *blancas nuevas*.

[61]For what follows see the Ordinance of 10 March 1442 in BN, MS., 13259, fos. 314-8 (Appendix A-4).

florin at 65 *mrs*, and the mark of standard silver at 560 *mrs*.[62] The intention was clearly deflationary: in 1441 the Burgos cathedral accounts had quoted the *dobla de la banda* at 136 *mrs*, the florin at 75-80 *mrs*, and the mark of silver at 720 *mrs*. In fact, judging from the Burgos data, the ordinance of March was attempting a return to the price levels of the mid-1430s.

Once again, however, the relative failure of these deceptively simple measures led to a more complicated ordinance being promulgated in the same year at Madrigal.[63] The king admitted that the measures taken in April had failed to produce an effect on prices. He then cited a *cortes* petition which reviewed the continuing inflationary spiral in prices and wages and urged that price controls should be imposed on commodities other than gold coins and silver.[64] The next section of the ordinance states that John II had reacted to this petition by ordering the establishment of official prices and wages. Unfortunately, the ordinance gives no further details about these, although it does make it clear that they provoked both foreign and native merchants to complain that the official levels which had been established were too low and needed to be modified. Consequently John II set up a commission, including native and foreign merchants and 'experts' from appropriate wage sectors, to study foreign price levels, particularly those of Flanders, past and present price levels in Castile itself, and the effects on prices of taxes imposed on goods in transit. Armed with the information of the commission, and bearing in mind the reforms already carried out with regard to the *blancas* and gold coins, a modified set of price measures was introduced and explained in the ordinance. The reasoning behind these new measures was that, despite regional variations, most Castilian prices were ultimately 'orchestrated' by the dealings at the international fairs at Medina del Campo. Prices, therefore, were to take their cue from the next October fair at Medina. Most regional prices would consequently represent the Medina levels plus the costs of transport and transit taxes. On the other hand, areas such as Seville, the coastal towns of the north, and the centres of the textile industry — that is, areas which sold rather than bought at Medina — were to deduct transport and tax costs from the price levels of the ordinance in order to arrive at the

[62]Ordinance of 6 April 1442, *Ibid* fos. 318-9 (Appendix A-5). A small degree of tolerance in coin prices was allowed to money-changers.

[63]The following details are taken from an eighteenth-century copy of the ordinance in BN, MS., 13107, fos. 181-92. This copy does not give the exact date of the ordinance, but it is obvious from internal evidence that it was issued after the previous measures in April and before the October fair at Medina del Campo.

[64]The petition was preoccupied, above all, with prices and wages in the textile sector of the economy.

prices for goods sold in their place of origin. The scheme envisaged was certainly complicated, but curiously enough when the price levels were established, these were related exclusively to a wide range of cloths, and in the majority of cases they applied to imports from abroad.[65]

The range of decisions taken during the course of 1442 raises interesting problems. Clearly, if we restrict the discussion to the price-fixing for which we have specific quotations, the measures were only directed at cloth and, in particular, imported cloth. Is there a suggestion here that devaluation had stimulated exports and priced imports beyond tolerable levels? It is possible, but it should also be remembered that the fixing of cloth prices represented the modification of a previous ordinance on prices for which we do not have the details. It may well be that this previous ordinance covered a much wider range of commodities, and in any case an attempt had been made to dampen down all price levels by deflating the prices of gold coins and silver.

How effective were the measures? The rather indeterminate and fluctuating stability in the nominal price levels of the 1440s suggest that they were not entirely without effect. Indeed, to judge from the Burgos evidence on coins and silver, the measures were relatively successful. The average quotation of the florin dropped from 77.5 *mrs* in 1441 to 68.67 *mrs* in 1442 and to 68.17 *mrs* in 1443; in fact, for the first time in eight years some quotations of the florin in 1442 dropped as low as the 65 *mrs* which had been laid down by the royal ordinances. However, silver prices, reacting with less emphasis, dropped from 720 *mrs* per mark in 1441 to a plateau of 640 *mrs* per mark from 1442 to 1445 (Appendices B-2, 3). It is this variation in the reactions to the official prices of florins and silver that explains the deviation in the gold and silver calculations of devaluation around 1442, and it was not until 1445 that both trends began once again to move in some sort of unison (Graph 1). Both this disparity and the pause in devaluation from 1442 to 1445 illustrate that the royal measures were moderately successful, and we will see that a similar situation was to arise precisely twenty years later.

Although the records are silent on the point, the devaluation graph raises suspicions of further royal debasements around 1445 and 1449. Moreover, a lengthy digression into the circumstantial evidence

[65] An astonishingly wide range of cloths was covered, including several varieties each from Florence, Malines, London, Ypres, Courtrai, Bruges, Flanders, Valencia and Saragossa. The only Castilian textile centres mentioned were Segovia, Valladolid and Palencia.

of the political history of these years would indicate that such suspicions would be more than justified.[66] For the next *direct* evidence on debasement, however, we must skip these two years and the stability of the 1450s, and begin with the rather vague allegations of a debasement in 1461 and the more precise data of the royal ordinance of 1462. First of all there is the statement in the *Anales* of Garci Sánchez: 'And in this said year [1461] there began the minting of *blancas* . . . And the minting of this money was ordered by the magnificent King Henry [IV], and 130 *mrs* of the new money were given for 100 *mrs* of the old *blancas*.'[67] Secondly, according to Diego de Valera, Henry IV 'ordered the minting of money which was much baser than that which King John [II], his father, had minted, or that which King Henry [III], his grandfather, had minted, which was much better. And he ordered this minting in order to make a profit, to the great damage of his subjects.'[68] Vague as these statements are, they are of crucial importance to an interpretation of both the debasement of 1461 and the royal ordinance of 1462. Both Valera and Garci Sánchez, it will be noted, make unambiguous references to a debasement, but whereas Valera makes a rather vague reference to money, Garci Sánchez not only states that *blancas* were minted but actually tells us that people exchanged them at a rate of 130 *mrs* of 'new' *blancas* for 100 *mrs* of 'old' ones.

At first sight the royal ordinance of 1462 confuses our picture of this debasement by contradicting the precise details given by Garci Sánchez. However, if we add a fifteenth-century version of this ordinance to the seventeenth-century copy which Ladero used in his study of the 1462 measures, it is possible to resolve the contradictions within a quantitative framework.[69]

[66]In 1445 Alvaro de Luna and John II won the decisive battle of Olmedo, and in 1449 Luna's imposition of an extraordinary tax sparked off the Toledan rebellion. The likelihood of debasements during these two years fits in perfectly with the analysis of the connection between monetary and political history which is outlined below, pp. 87-101.

[67]Garci Sánchez, p. 44.

[68]Mosén Diego de Valera, *Memorial de diversas hazañas,* ed. Juan de Mata Carriazo (Madrid, 1941), p. 64.

[69]The fifteenth-century copy of the ordinance is in AM, Burgos, Leg. 1290-1317, doc. 1315. This is a *traslado,* dated 3 September 1462, of a confirmation, dated 5 June 1462, of the original ordinance which was issued in Madrid on 22 May 1462. In M.A. Ladero Quesada, 'Moneda y tasa', 91-115, the author bases his study on a seventeenth-century copy in the Real Academia de la Historia. Although Ladero does not publish this version of the ordinance, it is possible to combine his summary of it with the fifteenth-century copy in order to resolve problematical points. It will be seen from the comments which follow that I do not agree with one or two of the interpretations suggested by Ladero.

The fifteenth-century Burgos version of the ordinance begins with a general review of the monetary problems of the immediately preceding years. The key passage states:

> Know . . . that I, understanding it to be in my service . . . and also because of the shortage of moneys resulting from the melting down and exportation out of my kingdoms of old and new *blancas*, with the agreement of the members of my council and of the other persons knowledgeable in this matter, ordered the minting of *quartos* and half *quartos* of sixty grains per mark and of sixty two coins to the mark, and *dineros* and half *dineros* of twelve grains and of one hundred and sixty coins to the mark . . .

But after this, the document goes on to point out, the king was informed that if these coins continued to be minted, the face value of gold coins and prices in general would continue to rise sharply. It was because of these inflationary fears that the measures contained in the rest of the ordinance were being introduced.[70]

The preamble, therefore, agrees with the statements of Valera and Garci Sánchez in so far as it clearly implies that a debasement had taken place. Why else would prices and the face value of coins continue to rise sharply? Similarly, when we come to consider the problems in the supply and demand of precious metals, it will be seen that Henry IV's reasoning about the disappearance of *blancas* was essentially accurate.[71] But what are we to make of the 'debased' *quartos* of 60 grains and 1/62 to the mark, and the 'debased' *dineros* of 12 grains and 1/160 to the mark?

The data on coins present two problems. In the first place, whereas Garci Sánchez states that the new coins were *blancas,* the ordinance states definitely that they were *quartos* and *dineros*. Was Garci Sánchez so badly informed that he not only got the coins wrong but that he actually went on to invent fictitious values for them? Such an explanation is hardly credible, given his interest in and knowledge of such matters.[72] Secondly, despite the fact that Valera, Garci Sánchez and Henry IV all agree that a debasement had taken place, the data on coins given by the ordinance suggest at first sight that the opposite was the case and that the silver content of the coins was increased. To be more precise, it is the *dinero* coin which presents the puzzle. The traditional scheme of equivalencies was: 10

---

[70]AM, Burgos, Leg. 1290-1317, doc. 1315, fos. 1-2.

[71]See below, p. 78.

[72]Of course, Garci Sánchez did make errors. Ladero, 'Moneda y tasa', p. 101, for example, notes the chronicler's mistakes relating to the 1462 *tasa* of coins. But in general terms Garci Sánchez was remarkably accurate, and if he did confuse *dineros* with *blancas*, then he was certainly not the only one to do so.

dineros = 2 *blancas* = 1 *mr*. Now, although we do not know the fineness and weight of previous *dineros*, the silver content of the new ones clearly represented a considerable increase. Indeed, later in the ordinance, Henry IV decreed that only three *dineros* (not ten) were to be worth one *maravedí*.[73] This point obviously puzzled Ladero and encouraged him to wonder whether the seventeenth-century copyist had blundered in his transcription.[74] But since the Burgos document makes exactly the same point, there can be no doubt as to the intended 3:1 relationship. However, this was to be the relationship *in future* (i.e. from 1462 onwards) and the coins had been minted in 1461. Calculating from the Burgos quotations for 1461 and 1462, the price of a mark of fine silver was between 1,067 and 1,075 *mrs*. But if, when minted, the new *dineros* had entered into circulation on the basis of 10 *dineros* = 1 *maravedí* the silver content of these coins would price the mark of silver at about 385 *mrs* only. Far from being devalued, therefore, the *maravedí* would have appreciated enormously. How, then, can all the talk about debasement be squared with this evidence?

The answer must surely lie with Garci Sánchez's statement about the minting of *blancas*, the fact that former *blancas* were disappearing from circulation, and Henry IV's acceptance of both the existence of debased coins and the fears of further inflation. In short, as the evidence of Garci Sánchez shows, the so-called new *dineros* were accepted into circulation not as *dineros* but as *blancas*, and as such they represented a real threat in terms of debasement and devaluation. As has been seen, the Burgos data give a price of between 1,067 and 1,075 *mrs* for the mark of fine silver. If the new coins had entered into circulation as *blancas* and on the basis of 2 *blancas* = 1 *maravedí*, the mark of fine silver would have jumped to 1,920 *mrs* and the *maravedí* would have fallen in value at a truly alarming rate. Garci Sánchez, however, reveals that the new coins circulated at a less damaging ratio: '130 *mrs* of the new money were given for 100 *mrs* of the old *blancas*'. At this ratio the mark of fine silver would have climbed to between 1,400 and 1,500 *mrs* — a devaluation which, if less marked, was still considerable. It was precisely for these reasons that Henry IV established the less damaging ratio of three of the new coins to one *maravedí* in the 1462 ordinance.

If this interpretation is correct, there remains the problem of Henry IV's probity and intentions. Of course, the possibility of mis-

---

[73] AM, Burgos, Leg. 1290-1317, doc. 1315, fo. 8v.

[74] Ladero, 'Moneda y tasa', p. 98.

calculation cannot be discounted.[75] Valera, however, asserted that the king's actions were deliberately calculated and that they were motivated by both political considerations and a desire for profit.[76] Moreover, this is by no means the only occasion on which we will encounter Henry IV resorting to monetary subterfuge and deception,[77] and it is difficult to believe that a king with such a record of debasements was actually intending to *improve* the quality of *quartos* and *dineros*. It may be objected that a confusion in the denomination of the coins seems an unlikely hypothesis, but we will see later that the similarities between the new coins and *blancas* were indeed striking.

After reviewing the problems arising from the debasement of 1461, the remainder of the ordinance of 1462 was taken up with explaining new monetary measures in detail. Broadly speaking these were designed to deal with the two most important issues, the elaboration of a coherent minting strategy, and the manipulation of prices and wages in order to secure a degree of stability.

The new monetary strategy envisaged a considerable degree of recoinage.[78] Henry III's 'old' *blancas* and John II's 'new' *blancas* were to be completely withdrawn from circulation within six months. The minting of gold coins, silver coins, *quartos* and *dineros* was, with few exceptions, to be brought to an immediate halt. Coins of these denominations which had already been minted, however, were not to be withdrawn and were to continue to circulate freely. A key role in the reformed monetary structure was assigned to new coins (perhaps one should say 'yet newer coins'!) that were to be minted — that is, *maravedies* of 24 grains and 1/96 to the mark, *blancas* of 19 grains and 1/152 to the mark, and half-*blancas* of 19 grains and 1/304 to the mark. The coherence between these new coins and the former silver and billon coins which were still to circulate was achieved by establishing the following relationships:

1 *maravedi* = 2 *blancas* = 4 half-*blancas* = 1/16 *real* = 1/4 *quarto* = 1/3 *dinero*.

The weight of the new *blancas* by itself illustrates the degree to which devaluation had taken its toll on the *maravedí*: whereas Henry

[75] The argument in favour of an 'honest' miscalculation in monetary policy would rest on (*a*) the circulation of *dineros* of a type not too far removed from *blancas* at a time when the latter were scarce; (*b*) a variant of Gresham's Law; and (*c*) the alacrity with which the king, after introducing the new coins in 1461, moved to stabilize the situation in 1462.

[76] Valera, p. 64. For a discussion of the political factors see below, pp. 87-101.

[77] See below, pp. 75-6.

[78] All the data in this paragraph are from AM, Burgos, Leg. 1290-1317, doc. 1315, fos. 1*v*-8*v*.

III had minted 56 *blancas* from each mark of silver, Henry IV proposed minting 152. However, it would be wrong to assume that the 1462 measures constituted yet another sudden and dramatic debasement. The last previous quotations available for *blancas* relate to those minted by John II in 1429 (20 grains; 1/59 to the mark), and we cannot discount further debasements, particularly around the years 1435, 1440, 1445 and 1449. In fact, the evidence suggests that the 1462 ordinance was a remarkable attempt to stabilise the *maravedí*. The point is well illustrated by the devaluation graph (Graph 1). In it, the appreciation of the florin component has its own particular explanation and must be discounted for the moment.[79] The silver component, however, far from revealing a sudden drop in the value of the *maravedí*, indicates a short period of stability. If we analyse the data of the ordinance, it can be seen that this levelling-out phenomenon is no mere quirk of the Burgos documentation. As has been seen, the Burgos quotation for 1462 gives the mark of fine silver an approximate value of 1,075 *mrs.*[80] Calculating on the basis of the 1462 ordinance's data on the coins forming part of the new monetary system, the approximate values of the mark of fine silver would be as follows:

Coins	*Value of mark of fine silver*
Maravedí: 24 grains, 1/96	1152 *mrs*
Blanca: 19 grains, 1/152 (= ½ mr)	1152 *mrs*
Half *Blanca*: 19 grains, 1/304 (= ¼ *mr*)	1152 *mrs*
Dinero: 12 grains, 1/160 (= 1/3 *mr*)	1280 *mrs*
Quarto: 60 grains, 1/62 (= 4 *mrs*)	1190 *mrs*

It will be seen that while the new half-*blancas*, *blancas* and *mrs* were 'absolutely' related, the ordinance was also fairly successful in creating a 'family' relationship with the awkward *dineros* and *quartos* as well. But even more important was the successful integration of the new *mrs* and *blancas* at a level close to the value of the money of

[79]See below, p. 72.

[80]The Burgos quotations for silver remain stable from 1460 to 1464. If the 1461 or 1463 quotations were used instead of that for 1462, the results would not be significantly different.

account as determined by the previous *blancas* — an integration which is revealed by comparing the figure of 1,152 *mrs* (calculated from the new *mrs*) with the figure of 1,075 *mrs* (calculated from the Burgos data). Indeed, given the in-built margin of error in both the figures of the *Libros Redondos* and the equation used for these calculations, a difference of only 77 *mrs* is remarkable.

It must be concluded that the 1462 measures did not constitute any significant debasement or devaluation of the *maravedí*. But if this latter interpretation is correct, then why was it necessary to introduce the measures at all? The answer must surely be that the 'transvestite' *dineros* minted in 1461 had in fact gone into circulation as *blancas*, and the resulting threat of a devaluation of the *maravedí* prompted the promulgation of the ordinance which, in this light, must be seen as a measure of revaluation and reform.

But surely, it might be objected, this confusion between *dineros* and *blancas* would have been impossible? In fact the coins must in many respects have been similar. The ordinance of 1462 assumed that *blancas* at 1/152 to the mark would be accepted into circulation without demur. Why, therefore, after a history of successive debasements, should the 1461 *dineros* at 1/160 to the mark not have been initially confused or accepted as *blancas*? Only a clear differentiation in design would have prevented this happening, and Garci Sánchez's description of the coin suggests that this was not the casè.[81] Thus, with *blancas* becoming scarce, the 'transvestite' *dinero* of only 12 grains clearly posed a serious problem. To clinch the argument, moreover, we need only note that the 1462 measures were only temporarily successful and that, within a few years, *blancas* of only 8 grains and 1/170 to the mark (cf the 1461 *dinero* of 12 grains and 1/160 to the mark) would be introduced into circulation.[82]

As well as dealing with minting problems, the measures of 1462 also attempted both to fix the value of gold coins and silver, and to impose price and wage levels. The details are ably analysed by Ladero,[83] and it is clear that the measures constituted a policy of deflation very similar to that attempted by John II in 1442. Moreover, as in 1442, the effects were momentary in nature and characterized by relative confusion.[84] A comparison between the

---

[81]Garci Sánchez, p. 44: '. . . *se comenzó a labrar moneda de blancas, y tenie una cara y un castillo, y debaxo del castillo granadas.*'

[82]See below, p. 74.

[83]Ladero, 'Moneda y tasa', *passim.*

[84]*Ibid.* pp. 97, 101-7.

coin prices of the ordinance and the Burgos quotations, for example, not only illustrates the deflationary intentions of Henry IV's *tasas*, but also repeats the 1442 experience of a partial and short-term reaction to the official prices, which was particularly pronounced in the case of the florin and hardly apparent in the case of silver.[85] It is this phenomenon which once again accounts for the disparity in fluctuations between the florin and silver components of the devaluation graph.

The short period of stability initiated by the reforms of 1462 only lasted until 1464. Between this latter year and 1465 the devaluation graph registers another sickening lurch downwards which is followed by a short pause until 1467. The evidence supporting the suspicion of a debasement in 1463 or 1464 is abundant, but unfortunately the documentation gives few specific details about the nature of the operation. The first hint of trouble comes in a royal writ of 1464.[86] In this, although Henry IV referred to a previous order halting all minting operations in his realms, the officials of the Segovia mint were ordered to continue with issues of gold *enriques* and silver *reales* on the pretext that the coinage in circulation was in short supply. This exception was to apply to the Segovia mint only, and its officials were to issue coins at the finenesses and weights prevailing prior to the ban until such time as the king, the royal council and the *cortes* could formulate new monetary measures. The implications of this writ, then, are that the ban on minting and the projected reforms had been provoked by a debasement.

The writ to Segovia was issued on 13 September. Two weeks later Henry IV's opponents issued a long manifesto of grievances which confirms the debasement:

> And the extent of the damage and evils inflicted on your kingdoms and on all the three estates by the corruption of the moneys . . . is manifest to everybody . . . And all the poor and middling estates are lost since they cannot maintain themselves because of the alteration of coins which Your Highness ordered without that advice and agreement of your realms which Your Highness was legally obliged to receive. And because of some profits, a reduction in the fineness of the money, which Your Highness ordered to be minted, was approved, and those who debased it were not punished. And this was the cause of the rise

---

[85] The official prices which the ordinance of 1462 stipulated for florins, *reales,* and silver were 103 *mrs,* 16 *mrs,* and 930 *mrs,* respectively. A comparison with the Burgos quotations for these items (Appendices 2, 3) reveals the partial and uneven reaction already described.

[86] AGS, EMR., Leg. 519, writ of 13 September 1464.

[in the face value] of money and the increase in the prices of goods and everything else, and your subjects suffered and daily suffer the extremely damaging consequences. And because of certain gains Your Highness has not imposed the appropriate penalties on those who debased the *reales* and *enriques*.[87]

Three months later, in January 1465, the complex *sentencia* of Medina del Campo, described by one historian as a Magna Carta which was never put into effect,[88] proposed that a special commission be set up to reform the coinage. The need for this reform, of course, arose because of debasement and price inflation, and the *sentencia* meanwhile attempted to cater for the most pressing problems by restricting the issue of all coins to the Segovia mint and imposing price levels on the 'heavy' coins.[89] Instead of bringing reform, however, the *sentencia* heralded the beginnings of political and monetary anarchy.[90] For, if the documentation of 1465 provides no clear evidence of further debasement, it reveals that a unified control and administration of the coinage no longer existed, and that the monetary problem was now a matter for political propaganda. In fact, Henry IV's *enriques* and *reales* now had to compete with the *alfonsies* and *reales* minted by his rival, the pretender-King Alfonso.[91] But it was not simply a matter of two kings and two minting administrations. By September, the Alfonsine chancery was virtually referring to an epidemic of counterfeiting[92] and alleging that Henry IV, desperately short of money, was engaged in minting *reales* of a greatly reduced fineness.[93] Clearly, whatever the exact nature of the debasement in 1463 or 1464, the monetary situation was threatening to get out of all control. In the event, after a short pause, this is exactly what happened.

[87] *Memorias de Enrique IV,* p. 330, 28 September 1464.

[88] See L. Suárez Fernández, 'Los Trastámaras de Castilla y Aragón en el siglo XV', in R. Menéndez Pidal, ed., *Historia de España,* XV (Madrid, 1964), 261.

[89] *Memorias de Enrique IV,* pp. 394-6.

[90] For the political troubles see Suárez Fernández, *Los Trastámaras,* pp. 262 ff.

[91] The statement of Garci Sánchez, p. 54 to the effect that these *alfonsies* and *reales* circulated at the same value as their Henrician equivalents suggests that, in the initial stages at least, the Alfonsine coins were of the same fineness and weight as their competitors. If so, this would help to explain the slight pause in devaluation after 1465.

[92] A document appointing an *alcalde mayor* to the Valladolid mint empowers him 'que do quier que quales quier falsadores de moneda pudieren ser avidos e alcançados en la dha villa de valladolid e en su tierra e termino e jurediccion que vos el dho ferrand sanches mi alcalde . . . podades faser justicia dellos . . . .' See AGS, EMR., Leg. 1, fos. 190-1, dated 18 September 1465.

[93] This oft-quoted allegation is contained in a propaganda letter sent to the count of Arcos on 25 September 1465: *Memorias de Enrique IV,* p. 516.

The years from 1465 to 1470 constituted a fiscal nightmare for the Castilian realms. Two letters sent by Henry IV to the municipality of Seville at the end of this period summarise some of its basic features.[94] The letters concerned the subsidies voted by the *cortes* of Ocaña in 1469, but in explaining the background to these grants, the king briefly surveyed events since 1465. At the *cortes* of Ocaña the members of the royal council urged the *procuradores* to vote substantial subsidies because, after five years of civil war, money was desperately needed to strengthen the monarchy and pacify the kingdom. These arguments, according to Henry IV, were supported by the *procuradores* but, in arriving at an appropriate figure for the subsidies, the taxes voted in the *cortes* of Salamanca in 1465 were used as a yardstick. At that *cortes* 87 million *mrs* had been granted in the form of *pedidos* and *monedas* — one half to be collected in 1465 and the remaining half in 1466. Because of the civil war, however, these subsidies had never been collected and it was now proposed that the same 87 million *mrs* be granted afresh at Ocaña. Yet everyone agreed that there were strong reasons for granting an additional sum and, among these, changes in the coinage during the intervening years, the drop in the real value of the *maravedí*, and the cost of projected minting reforms figured prominently. Accordingly the total grant was raised to 93 million *mrs*. The civil-war years after 1465, in short, had witnessed a paralysis in royal income and further waves of debasement. Inevitably the picture of these years of anarchy is rather confused, but certain features are clear.

As to debasement there can be no possible doubt. It is not simply a matter of phantom coins, such as the debased Alfonsine *quartos* which were minted in 1466 and withdrawn after being in circulation for only two days.[95] The royal minting orders themselves reveal the process of debasement, especially with regard to billon coins. As against the 1462 *blanca* of 19 grains and 1/152 to the mark, for example, a mint directive of August 1469 stipulated *blancas* of 11 grains and 1/160 to the mark,[96] and within five months this was followed by an order for the issue of *blancas* of only eight grains and 1/170 to the mark.[97] The data in this latter order also reveal the plunge of the *maravedí*: in 1462 it stood at 24 grains and 1/96 to the mark, but by January 1470 it was as low as eight grains and 1/85 to the mark.

[94] For what follows see AM, Seville, box 1468-70, letters dated Ocaña, 3 May 1469 and Madrid, 18 October 1470.

[95] See Garci Sánchez, pp. 58-9.

[96] AGS, EMR., Leg. 519, docs. of 9 August 1469 and 25 August 1469 (Appendix A-9).

[97] AGS, EMR., Leg. 519, 28 January 1470.

The fall was sharp and dramatic, and even after the apparently hopeful discussions at the *cortes* of Ocaña, Henry IV was busily engaged in debasement. The provisions of this one writ of January 1470, for example, meant that the Cuenca mint by itself would add almost one million *maravedíes* of debased billon coins to the specie in circulation.[98]

Worse still, we cannot even be sure that the data contained in minting directives always reveal the full extent of the debasements, because Henry IV was obviously at his most devious during these years. In a politically motivated appointment to the Coruña mint in 1468, for example, the King ordered that, despite all his 'public' bans on minting, this house was to continue issuing gold, silver, and billon coins.[99] The suspicion that an 'open' or 'public' monetary policy was being continually undermined by secret directives is transformed into a certainty by the terms used in a minting order sent to Seville on 25 August 1469. In this, although the king referred to a previous 'public' and 'open' order relating to the issue of gold *enriques* (23 grains; 1/50), *quartos* (54 grains; 1/70) and *blancas* (11 grains; 1/160), the remainder of the directive contained secret instructions. The mint officials of Seville were to make the terms of the 'open' order public, but in practice they were to carry out a two-monthly check on the finenesses and weights of the coins minted at Segovia and Jaén, and they were then to bring the Seville issues into line with those of the two 'directing' mints.[100] The choice of Segovia (Henry IV's 'capital') and Jaén (staunchly Henrician under Miguel Lucas de Iranzo) as the 'directing' mints is easily explained in terms of politics. But what other reasons, apart from debasement, can be adduced to explain this deliberate undermining of 'public' policy by secret orders?[101]

The years from 1470 to 1474 were characterised by various painful attempts to return to some form of stability. Diego Enríquez del Castillo, although rather naively suggesting that debasements

[98]*Ibid*. The Cuenca officials were ordered to mint 10,000 marks of billon in *maravedíes, blancas* and *medias blancas*.

[99]AGS, EMR., Leg. 519, 18 January 1468.

[100]AGS, EMR., Leg. 519, 25 August 1469 (Appendix A-9). Henry IV was almost certainly referring to decisions contained in an order of 9 August 1469 (Appendix A-8). This document, issued in Alcalá de Guadaira, reported on what were obviously 'public' discussions in Seville and during which the *'mayor'* and *'mas sana parte'* came up with the finenesses and weights which are specified both in this document and in the secret directive.

[101]The secret orders sent to Seville were not exceptional. A similare directive was sent the following year to Burgos: AGS, EMR., Leg. 519, 25 November 1470. The Burgos officials were empowered to recoin a wide range of moneys and had to follow the lead of the Segovia and Madrid mints.

only came to light in 1470, gave a succinct description of the first steps taken to stem inflation:

> This year [1470] a great deception in the coinage was discovered. The great quantity of bad coins was minted to such an extent by so many and different minting houses, that it was necessary to reduce them — not only with respect to the billon coinage, but the gold and silver coins as well. This resulted in a great loss to many people in different places, and gave rise to grave scandals and riots in the towns. But this reduction which was carried out was very necessary and needful for the common weal of the kingdom; because all the coins, and especially the gold coins, were so false that none of them were at their rightful price. On the contrary, the coins had risen by more than half of their real value.[102]

In effect, in late 1470 and early 1471 concerted efforts were made to end all minting and impose deflationary measures until such time as the monarchy, the *procuradores* and monetary experts should decide on the appropriate reforms.[103] The temporary measures were directed principally at controlling operations in *enriques* and *quartos*. The 'new' or debased *enriques* were reduced sharply to 310 *mrs*, and *quartos*, officially valued in 1462 at four *mrs*, were reduced to two *mrs*. Repeated declarations of the ban on all minting, however, openly referred to the failure to comply with the royal orders.

In theory at least, the period of temporary and confusing measures was of short duration because in April the promised reforming ordinance was promulgated.[104] The result of deliberations involving *procuradores* and minting experts, the reform envisaged a considerable amount of recoinage but contained few surprises. In contrast with what appears to have been a royal preference for a monetary system based on *blancas* of pure copper, the ordinance aimed at a stabilization of the *maravedi*, an improvement in the quality of the 'heavier' coins, and an end to those defects in the minting administration which had led to a proliferation of debasements. No provision was made for the minting of *maravedi*es but, with the traditional 2:1 ratio being continued, the *blanca* was fixed at ten grains and 1/205 to the mark. *Enriques* were restored to 23¾ carats and 1/50 to the mark, *reales* were confirmed at 268 grains and 1/67, and the following face-values were

---

[102]Diego Enríquez del Castillo, *Crónica del rey Don Enrique el Cuarto* (BAE, LXX, Madrid, 1878), p. 204.

[103]The details that follow are taken from the relevant documents, dated 24 December 1470 and 22 January 1471, in *Memorias de Enrique IV*, pp. 623-4, 628-9.

[104]*Ibid.* pp. 639-56 gives the full text of this ordinance of 10 April 1471.

established: *enrique* = 420 *mrs; dobla de la banda* = 300 *mrs*; Aragonese florin = 210 *mrs; real* = 31 *mrs*. A whole series of measures were drawn up in order to eliminate minting abuses and restrict operations to six official houses.

How successful was the reform of 1471? To judge by the devaluation graph, the last few years of Henry IV's reign were apparently ones of relative stability. The Burgos quotations, moreover, confirm that the ordinance picked up the tendency of the trend in order to achieve stability. Thus the florin, quoted at 190 *mrs* in 1469 and 200 *mrs* in 1470, settled at the 'official' price of 210 *mrs* in 1471 and virtually retained that level till the end of the reign. Similarly the *real*, already quoted at 25-31 *mrs* in 1470, was to remain at or below the 'official' price for the rest of the decade (Appendix B-2).

Despite these successes, however, serious problems still remained unsolved after the 1471 ordinance, and the king discussed them at length in a widely circulated letter issued in July.[105] The existence of *quartos* of varying intrinsic values obviously continued to cause a great deal of trouble. Accordingly, Henry IV reduced the value of the *quarto* to three *blancas* and introduced measures to remove unsatisfactory *quartos* from circulation. This reduction, however, could only be effective if all was well with the *blancas*, and the king had already been warned that the intrinsic value of these coins 'with which the larger coins are measured' was not well adjusted to the structure of the reformed monetary system.[106] In fact, applying the equation $P = xy/z$, the data on these *blancas* give the mark of fine silver an approximate value of 2,952 *mrs*, whereas the data on *reales* only give 2,232 *mrs* and the Burgos silver data for the years 1470-2 give 1,963-2,133 *mrs*. An undervaluation of the *blanca*, therefore, threatened to undo the projected reforms.

It was against this background that Henry IV introduced the last of his reforms in March 1473. The *enrique* was reduced to 400 *mrs*, the Aragonese florin to 200 *mrs*, and the *real* to 30 *mrs*. More important, the undervalued *blanca* was reduced to a new ratio of three *blancas* to the *maravedí*.[107] This latter measure, giving an approximate value of 1,948 *mrs* to the mark of fine silver, brought the *blanca* and the *maravedí* into a closer relationship both with the new rate for the

[105]For what follows see the letter of 30 July 1471 in L. Sáez, pp. 498-500.

[106]*Ibid.* The warnings were to the effect that the fineness was too low. However, it is clear from both my calculations and the royal measures of 1473 that the *blanca* was undervalued at this stage.

[107]For these reforms, which were recapitulated in a royal letter of 12 May 1473, see *Memorias de Enrique IV*, p. 691.

real (= 2,160 *mrs* per mark of fine silver) and the Burgos quotations (1473 = 1,962 *mrs* per mark of fine silver). But the details of this measure are known from a royal letter, issued in May, in which Henry IV described the obstacles to their successful implementation. According to the king, the main problem was the fact that debased coins, issued by mints other than the six established houses, were still causing monetary chaos. Indeed, in condemning the following illegal and evil transactions, Henry IV gave a fair description of the operation of Gresham's law:

(i) 'Good' and 'official' coins and *blancas* issued by the six established mints were being hidden, and men were using 'corrupt' or debased coins.

(ii) Coins issued by the official mints were being bought and sold at prices well above those officially established.

(iii) The lower classes (*gente menuda*) and the people in general were being persuaded to part with sound coins by deliberately fomented rumours that the king was about to order further reductions in the values of *blancas* and other coins.

Consequently, according to the king, not only was bad money driving out good, but prices were rising, and shopkeepers and tradesmen had ceased to buy or sell goods because of the confusion. Fulminating against these practices, Henry IV reiterated the measures he had taken and solemnly promised that no more reductions or alterations in the coinage would be put into operaton.[108] Quite obviously, therefore, the reform of 1471 had only been moderately successful, and at this precise moment of time in 1473 something akin to a *grand peur* was affecting mens' attitudes to the coins in circulation. Even at the end of this stormy reign the monetary situation was affected by convulsions and confusions.

Counterfeiting

The foregoing discussion has concentrated on the details of the monarchy's debasements and reforms during the fifteenth century. But before the main features of these are briefly summarised, we must also take into account the repeated allegations that, quite apart from the royal houses, many illegal and semi-legal mints were at work issuing debased coins. Although the very nature of their work makes it hard to find detailed evidence of the activities of these counterfeiters, the following famous description of the state of affairs during the last

[108]*Ibid*. pp. 690-3.

few years of Henry IV's reign illustrates the importance of attempting some analysis of the problem:

King Henry lived for another four years after Prince Ferdinand, husband of Queen Isabella, entered Castile, and during this period the number of robberies and mischiefs in the kingdom increased to such an extent that it pains me to write about them . . . As I have already said, being like a man without a son and heir, he [Henry IV] had little interest in his kingdom: and having already alienated everything, there being no revenue, place or fortress which he had not given away and there being left no *juros* or other revenues for further grants, he began to hand out minting houses in signed letters. And whereas it was the custom for there to be no more than five royal mints in the kingdom for the issue of all the coinage, within the space of three years he issued letters, orders and licences until there were 150 houses in the kingdom. Besides these there were many more illegal [houses], where people minted as much as they could or wished without any fear — and this not only in the fortresses but also in any houses of the cities and towns. So much was this the case that silversmiths and men of other trades could labour at this at the doors and in the houses where they worked with royal permission, and the coins which they produced this month, they melted down in the following month and reissued at a lower fineness. As a consequence there was such a great deal of business in the mints that [it seemed] there was no other occupation in the kingdom. There were mints which brought in 200,000 *mrs* to their lords in one day without taking into account the profits of the moneyers and dealers. Because of all this the kingdom was plunged into such great confusion that the *vara* of cloth, which used to be worth 200 *mrs*, rose to 600 *mrs*, the mark of silver, which was worth 1,500 *mrs*, rose to 6,000 *mrs*, and the *quintal* of copper, which was worth 2,000 *mrs*, rose to 12,000 *mrs* — so much was this the case that not enough copper could be imported from Flanders and other kingdoms, and there was not a cauldron or pot to be bought in the kingdom for less than six times what it was worth.

The confusion was so great that, of the billon coins, a *cuarto* which was worth five *maravedi*es when issued by a mint licensed by the king, was not even worth one *blanca* and did not even have the same fineness. When *enriques* were first minted they were of 23½ carats, but of those minted during this period the royal houses ended up issuing some of only seven carats, and the illegal mints issued them at as low a fineness as they wished. Livestock and all other goods in the kingdom were sold for such high prices that the poor *hidalgos*, men dealing in such goods, and all other people were ruined. And when matters had reached such a state of utter confusion, a reduction was decreed with the result that the *quarto* which was worth five *maravedies* was to be lowered to three *blancas* No possible price could be put on gold [coins] save by determining the number of carats in each coin. The reduction was so great — what was worth ten *blancas* was to be worth only three — that all the merchants who had made profits were lost and impoverished. And when the reduction was made, some paid up the debts they owed [at low prices] in contrast to those who had paid up prevously at high prices, and those who were to receive the payments did not wish to accept them and there arose many disputes, clashes, deaths and such a great deal of confusion that men did not know what to do or how to live.... Travellers on the roads could find nothing to eat because the peasants refused to accept money at any price — high or low. So many were defrauded by the [monetary] swindles that the people of Castile lived like the Guineans, and without coins or law they exchanged bread for wine and bartered one thing for another. . . .[109]

It is hard to envisage a more devastating description of monetary anarchy, and examples have often been cited from this famous passage. Again and again, for example, historians have accepted the figure of 150 mints and the existence of *enriques* of only seven carats. But is the description accurate or is it wildly exaggerated? And if there is some measure of truth in it, does all the blame attach only to the last three or four years of Henry IV's reign? Fortunately, the anonymous writer gives enough specific information to enable us to test his general accuracy. In the first place, the writer seems to exaggerate the workings and effects of the reduction of *quartos*: in fact it would appear that his statement that prices were reduced by a ratio of 10 *blancas* = 3 *blancas* can only be accepted if we take into account the reductions of the *quarto* decreed in 1470 and 1471, accept the writer's version of this reduction, and ignore the revaluation of the *blanca* in May 1473. Nevertheless, on this point his description is not by any means wide of the mark. More serious distortions, however, seem to have been introduced into the description of the price behaviour of silver and cloth. The writer has the mark of silver — presumably the standard mark — rising from 1,500 *mrs* to 6,000 *mrs:* the Burgos quotations show the mark rising from 1,520 *mrs* in 1469 to 1,840 *mrs* in 1474 (Appendix B-3). The writer has a *vara* of unspecified cloth rising from 200 *mrs* to 600 *mrs:* the Seville quotations show the *vara* of Courtrai rising from 190 *mrs* in 1461 to 280 *mrs* in 1474, and the *vara* of Bruges rising from 210 *mrs* in 1454 to 400 *mrs* in 1474 (Appendix B-1). In short, unless the writer has

[109]L. Sáez, pp. 2-4.

picked on extreme cases (for example, cloth prices which were affected by supply and demand factors as well as debasement), or has extended the range of his quotations to include periods before and after the latter years of Henry IV's reign, it is difficult to avoid accusing him of wilful exaggeration.

Despite the special pleading, however, there is a good deal of substance in the passage, and this consideration probably applies to the description of counterfeiting. The basic features of this description are as follows:

(i) The wave of counterfeiting occurred during the period c1470-4.

(iii) The writer distinguishes between 'legal' debasement, 'semi-legal' counterfeiting in licensed mints, and 'illegal' counterfeiting.

(iii) The number of mints shot up from five to 150 licensed houses. There were many more unlicensed houses.

(iv) Men found it a relatively easy matter to counterfeit coins, and this stimulated the enormous increase in this activity.

Long ago Hamilton pointed out that medieval counterfeiting was facilitated by the nature of the handicraft mint processes and the fact that heterogeneity in 'official' production made it difficult to detect false coins.[110] The picture of an uncontrolled epidemic of counterfeiting, therefore, is by no means implausible. In fact as early as 1439 John II alleged that counterfeiters were responsible for circulating debased coins, and in 1442 he quoted the argument of the *procuradores* to the effect that the minting of false money both within Castile and in the neighbouring kingdoms was a relatively easy occupation to indulge in.[111] But in 1439 the king was attempting to cover up his own debasements, and the argument cited in 1442 merely posited the consequences of a monetary policy which was never put into effect. Thus, if we are to judge by the volume of protests and allegations, there can be no doubt that wide-spread counterfeiting was a phenomenon which was effectively limited to the reign of Henry IV. This argument is confirmed by an analysis of the proliferation of 'legal' and 'semi-legal' mints.

The survey of monetary problems, almost certainly dating from the mid-1430s, makes it clear that the existing Castilian mints were

[110]Hamilton, p. 120, note 3.

[111]Ordinances of 20 December 1439 and 10 March 1442 in BN, MS., 13259, fos. 189v-90v, 314-8 (Appendix A-2 and 4).

Seville, Toledo, Burgos and La Coruña.[112] To these must be added the house at Cuenca which was probably operating as early as 1435.[113] These were the 'core' mints and there is no serious evidence that new houses were created during the remainder of John II's reign.[114] In Henry IV's reign a house was in operation in Segovia from at least 1455, but when minting accounts were settled after the reform of 1462 no more new houses had appeared.[115] Thus the six houses listed in the accounts of 1462 were the traditional 'five' mints to which the anonymous writer referred: Seville, Toledo, Burgos, Segovia, Cuenca and La Coruña.

From 1462 onwards, and particularly after Henry IV's enemies proclaimed his half-brother, Alfonso, as king, new mints were set up with increasing rapidity. In the years after 1462 Genoese associates were (illegally?) turning out large numbers of *blancas* and Portuguese *reales* at a mint in Coca,[116] an Alfonsine appointment to the Valladolid mint survives from 1465,[117] a house was established in Jaén in 1466,[118] and in 1467 a mint was established in Medina del Campo.[119] After this stage of early growth the proliferation of mints achieved a 'take-off' in 1468. Calculations on royal income from the beginning of 1468 list 'the six authentic houses' (*seys casas autenticas*) and a mere three houses 'newly created' (*fechas de nuevo*): Valladolid, Madrid and Ciudad Real.[120] But in the tenders for the farms of the royal minting rights, houses in Palencia, Avila and Murcia are mentioned,[121] Medina del Campo and Jaén continued to

---

[112]AGS, D. de C., Leg. 4, doc. 56 (Appendix A-1). This important document is discussed at length above, pp. 30-5. The same mints are listed in the acts of the *cortes* of Madrid of 1433: *Cortes,* III, 168-9.

[113]A taxation *cuaderno* for 1435 lists 43 *escusados* who were *monederos* of the Cuenca mint: Escorial, Z.1.8, fo. 235.

[114]Without citing sources, Gil Farres, p. 218 states that some minting was carried out in Avila and Valladolid in 1451.

[115]The accounts covered the period from 1 January 1455 to 24 January 1462 and included the Segovian mint: AGS, EMR, Leg. 655, two docs. both dated 28 March 1462.

[116]J. Heers, *Gênes,* p. 71.

[117]Dated 18 September 1465, in AGS, EMR., Leg. 1, fos. 190-1.

[118]Juan de Mata Carriazo, ed. *Hechos del Condestable Don Miguel Lucas de Iranzo* (Madrid, 1940), p. 310.

[119]AGS, EMR., Leg. 519, 12 October 1467.

[120]*Ibid*. Leg. 11, fos. 6-9v. On the Ciudad Real mint see also *ibid.* Leg. 519, 20 October 1468.

[121]*Ibid*. Leg. 11, fos. 104, 138, and 519, doc. 17. For further details on the setting up of the mint in Palencia see *ibid.* Leg. 519, two docs. both dated 4 November 1468.

operate,[122] and in 1469 new mints were established in Toro, Salamanca and Ciudad Rodrigo.[123] In short, although we are far from our total of 150 houses, it is clear that in the seven years after 1462 the royal mints had at least tripled. How does this proliferation fit in with the allegations that 'licensed' or 'semi-legal' houses were granted out as gifts (*mercedes*) by Henry IV?

Without going into a detailed description of the minting administration, it is clear that in addition to the traditional system of royally appointed officials and financial accountability, other alternative systems were operative. The coinage rights of the Crown and even the mints themselves, for example, could be farmed out, and licences extended the facilities of the mints to individuals. Thus, we not only have the Alfonsine conditions for farming out the mints in 1468 but we also have the records of some of the tenders, such as those offered for the Murcian mint by the treasurer of the Avila house, a Genoese residing in Toledo, and a Jewish financier from Segovia.[124] As far as licences granting individuals the right to mint in established houses are concerned, these must have been common enough. In 1469, for example, Henry IV granted Diego de Palencia of Burgos the right to mint 7,000 marks of *quartos* in the Burgos house.[125] Within a Castilian context, none of these administrative techniques could be termed irregular, although the system of farming mints could obviously pose problems despite the accountability of the farmers to the royal financial administration. But the documentation confirms the allegation that, from 1468, Henry IV in effect *alienated* some of the royal mints and this obviously marked a radical and dangerous departure from administrative norms. In April 1468, for example, Henry IV not only granted all the royal rights from the Coruña mint for life to one of his chaplains, Juan de Salsedo, but he also surrendered all control by making the mint officials accountable to Salsedo and not to the royal administration.[126] In November of the same year the king alienated the mint at Avila to no less a person than the future Queen Isabella: she received the royal rights for life, was given control over all appointments, and had her house exempted from any future royal ban on minting activities, even if such a ban

[122]For example, *ibid*. Leg. 519, docs. dated 5 February 1468 and 25 August 1469 (Appendix A-9).

[123]*Ibid*. doc. 20(Salamanca), doc. 25 (Toro), and doc. 12 (Ciudad Rodrigo).

[124]For the farming conditions and the bids for the Murcian mint, *ibid*. Leg. 11, fos. 98-100, 11 February 1468, and Leg. 519, doc. 17 (Appendix A-6).

[125]*Ibid*. Leg. 519, 25 September 1469.

[126]*Ibid*. 25 April 1468.

should be issued at the request of the *cortes*.[127] Given the total lack of Crown control, how effective was the proviso in this grant that the Avila house should issue its coins in accordance with the finenesses and weights of the royal mints?

There was worse to come. The alienations just mentioned affected houses which had been in operation prior to the issue of the gifts.[128] In 1469, however, we find Henry IV creating and alienating mints at one and the same time. Thus, in the space of one royal letter, the king created a mint in Toro, appointed Rodrigo de Ulloa as its treasurer for life, empowered him to control and appoint all the mint officials up to a limit the number of which was left as a blank, alienated all the royal rights to Ulloa for life, and freed him from any accountability to the royal administration.[129] The mint at Salamanca was established and alienated to Pedro de Fuentiveros in a document which was couched in precisely the same terms, even to the extent of leaving a blank for the number of officials to be appointed.[130] In the following year further alienations of a rather more restricted nature were made with respect to the mints at Valladolid and Seville.[131]

The allegations relating to licences and alienations, therefore, must be considered as proven. It was all very well for the papal legate to fulminate against the 'illegal' mints, and there can be little doubt that they were many.[132] But Henry IV himself admitted in the ordinance of 1471 that he had alienated minting rights and issued licences for the establishment of new houses.[133] Moreover, even if the figure of 150 mints seems exaggerated, it must be remembered that not all the royal licences and alienations may have survived. Alonso de Palencia, for example, alleged that the count of Benavente had the king's blessing for minting debased coins at Villalón, and despite

[127]*Ibid.*, 15 November 1468.

[128]Despite the 'establishment' of the Avila mint on the same day as the grant to Isabella — for which, see *ibid.* doc. of 15 November 1468 — there are earlier references to the existence of this house.

[129]AGS, EMR., Leg. 519, 20 March 1469 (Appendix A-7). The point about granting the right to appoint mint officials is that such appointments bestowed tax-immunity on the recipients. Thus, by leaving the number of such appointments blank, the king was virtually letting Ulloa determine the extent of his new source of patronage. *Ibid.*, doc. dated 8 December 1462, is an example, relating to the Coruña mint, of the appointment and registering of such *escusados*.

[130]*Ibid.*, doc. 20, undated.

[131]Life grants of the Valladolid *derechos,* and the alienation of the Seville *derechos* for 28 years: *ibid.* docs of 27 February 1470, and 20 July 1470.

[132]The legate's letter of 15 February 1473 is in L. Sáez, pp. 502-4.

[133]*Memorias de Enrique IV*, pp. 653-5.

this chronicler's obvious bias against Henry IV, there is no reason to doubt his word in this particular instance.[134]

This lengthy discussion of royal debasements, reforming ordinances, and the proliferation of mints has necessarily involved the presentation of intricate detail. In summing up the results, however, the main features can be conveniently linked to the devaluation graph of the *maravedí* and presented as in the graph on the facing page. With this clear pattern of debasement and reforms in front of us, it is now time to try and link it to political factors.

[134]See L. Sáez, p. 7.

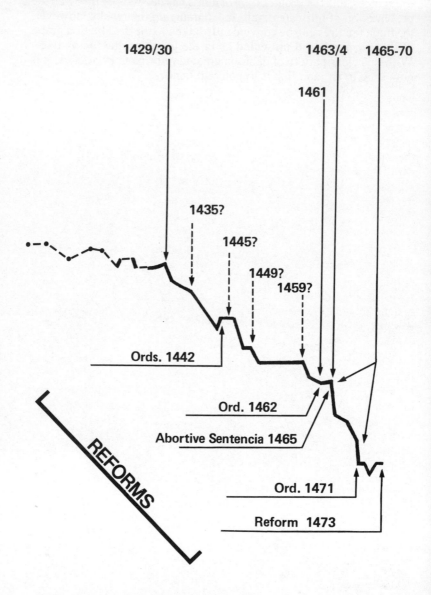

DEBASEMENTS

1429/30   1463/4   1465-70

1461

1435?

1445?

1449?

1459?

Ords. 1442

Ord. 1462

Abortive Sentencia 1465

REFORMS

Ord. 1471

Reform 1473

3

POLITICS, DEBASEMENTS AND DEVALUATION

The monetary phenomena examined in this study must be seen against a general background of two great cycles of wars which, when taken together, may roughly be equated in relative magnitude to the Hundred Years War in France. The first of these cycles covered the years c1350-c1390 and was constituted by several related wars — the civil war between *emperogilados* and Trastamarans, the intervention of the French and English in support of the opposing sides, the resistance of the successful Trastamarans to English attempts to press the claims of the duke of Lancaster to the Castilian throne, and a war with Portugal which involved a disastrous Castilian defeat at Aljubarrota. This cycle ended towards the close of the 1380s when the Trastamaran monarchy signed treaties with Lancaster and the Portuguese and terminated what may be called the Iberian or Castilian phase of the Hundred Years War.[1]

The years c1390-c1420 marked a pause between the two cycles of wars. Of course, these years were certainly not entirely free from political unrest. Moreover, many of the seeds of future civil wars were sown during the latter part of this period.[2] But in terms of the magnitude of international and internal warfare there can be no doubt, the reign of Henry III (1390-1406) and the minority of John II's reign (1406-1454) were years of relative peace and stability.

The second cycle of wars covered the years c1420-c1476, and like the previous cycle it was made up of several related episodes — the long drawn-out struggle between John II and Alvaro de Luna on the one hand and the *Infantes* of Aragon and their Castilian supporters on the other, the civil wars and anarchy of Henry IV's reign, and the wars to determine the succession to the Castilian throne after Henry IV's death.[3]

---

[1] The best narrative political histories on this first cycle are P.E. Russell, *The English Intervention in Spain and Portugal in the time of Edward III and Richard II* (Oxford, 1955), and L. Suárez Fernández's section in R. Menéndez Pidal, *Historia de España*, vol. XIV: *España cristiana: crisis de la reconquista, luchas civiles* (Madrid, 1964).

[2] It was during John II's minority that Ferdinand of Antequera laid the foundations of his family's political and economic power, thus paving the way for the later struggles between the Crown and the so-called 'Aragonese party'.

[3] A standard account of these political events is that by L. Suárez Fernández, *Los Trastámaras*.

The present data on prices and money, therefore, cover a period which, in political terms, was constituted by the 'pause' of relative stability ($c1390-c1420$) and by the second great cycle of wars ($c1420-c1476$). In these rather general and simplified terms there can be little doubt that the monetary phenomena reflect the long-term vagaries of political history. But if, having sketched the background in a very general way, we now proceed to a more detailed analysis some remarkably interesting patterns emerge.

In the first place it is clear that, in terms of political history, the second cycle of wars itself contained periods of greater or lesser instability. Two periods of lesser instability were the years 1420-29 and the years 1454-1461/3. In effect, although John II and Alvaro de Luna began to move against the 'Aragonese party' as early as 1418, historians are virtually unanimous in agreeing that the skirmishes and war-like episodes of these early years only reached their crisis point towards the end of the 1420s. In 1428 John II of Castile felt himself strong enough to order the king of Navarre to leave the kingdom and to envisage full-scale war with Aragon and Navarre. Success meant that, as Ladero put it, '1429 was consequently a year of monarchical apotheosis. With the *Infantes* of Aragon beaten, don Alvaro de Luna rapidly reached the height of his power. The team of royal financial officials changes, the administration becomes efficient again. . . .'[4] As far as the years 1454-1461/3 are concerned, it is enough to note that almost all historians contrast Henry IV's early and relatively successful years with the anarchy of the second half of his reign. Suárez Fernández, for example, concluded that until 1463, with varying fortunes, Henry IV appeared to be a great king. His power inspired fear in Castile and confidence in Catalonia.[5] Ladero shortens this initial period by two years, but makes the same point: 'The reign began in an optimistic atmosphere, which would be prolonged until 1461 . . .'.[6]

The monetary evidence supports these judgements on political history to a remarkable degree. The devaluation graph, for example, suggests that stability was prolonged into the early years of the second cycle of wars and that the crisis of the *maravedí* coincided with the politically decisive year of 1429/30. Similarly, the evidence of the devaluation graph and the relatively effective royal control over the mints down to 1462 reflect the political stability or 'optimism' which characterized the early years of Henry IV's reign. Despite the 'drop'

[4]M.A. Ladero Quesada, *La Hacienda Real de Castilla en el siglo XV* (La Laguna, 1973), p. 241.

[5]Suárez Fernández, *Los Trastámaras*, p. 221.

[6]Ladero, *La Hacienda Real,* p. 242.

in 1459, for example, the devaluation graph reveals a very sharp contrast between the stability of the years 1454-62 and the disastrous fall in the value of the *maravedí* during the anarchy from 1463 onwards. It is important to note, however, that the coincidence is not absolute: the political 'optimism' of Henry IV's reign begins with his accession in 1454, but the stability or 'optimism' of the *maravedí* stretches back into the last years of John II's reign. Obviously, therefore, the accession of the new king cannot by itself explain the stability of the money of account. This point will be taken up again in due course,[7] but for the moment another obvious feature must be commented upon.

Given the traditional picture of an irresponsible and greedy nobility, it is interesting to note that debasements must be ascribed to the monarchy and reforming ordinances to the king's enemies. In almost all the cases of debasements, the monarchy was acting freely and in accordance with its chosen advisers. The debasement of 1429, for example, was carried out at a time when decisions at court were being freely taken by John II and Alvaro de Luna. Similarly, however incompetent Henry IV was, and however anarchical the conditions were during the second half of his reign, the king it was who chose his favourites and issued his secret mint orders in the teeth of what had been advised by *procuradores* and councillors. The same applies to the debasements which the evidence suggests might have taken place in 1435, 1445, 1449 and 1459. For, if debasements did take place during these years, they were effected at times when the monarchy was free to follow the monetary policy of its choice. The demands for monetary reform and a halt to price inflation, on the other hand, were made both by the *procuradores* of the *cortes* and the nobility in opposition. When one reads the relevant sections of the *sentencia* of Medina del Campo of 1465, for example, it is clear that the nobility demanded an end to the monetary irresponsibility of the king and a return to a sound coinage and stable prices.[8] Of course, such demands may have been demagogic in character, but the specific example of the reforming ordinance of 1442 demonstrates that much more was involved than mere propaganda.

In 1429 John II and Alvaro de Luna triumphed over their adversaries: by 1440, however, Luna had been beaten by a coalition of Castilian nobles and the *Infantes* of Aragon, and John II was no longer free to act in accordance with what he himself referred to as his

[7]Below, pp. 90-3.

[8]References supporting all these points about the political history would entail inordinately long footnotes: some specific examples are discussed below in greater detail

'absolute royal power'. Government, in fact, was to be controlled by the royal council, and in 1441 Luna was sentenced to six years of exile from the court. Thus the nobility and the Aragonese party, led by the king of Navarre, were in effective control of the court and the council, and it was within this political context that the various reforming ordinances of 1442 were promulgated.[9] Indeed the ordinances specifically refer to decisions taken at meetings of the royal council which were attended by the king of Navarre, the *Infante* Enrique, and other members of the Aragonese party, such as the admiral, don Fadrique.[10] The devaluation graph registers these political events perfectly — the triumph of the royalists in 1429 is accompanied by debasement and devaluation, and the triumph of the king's enemies in the early 1440s is accompanied by a recovery in the fortunes of the *maravedí* as a result of the reforming ordinance. Is this recovery of too short a duration to be convincing? On the contrary, although it only lasted until 1445, it was precisely in that year that John II and Alvaro de Luna gained a decisive victory over their enemies at the battle of Olmedo. And as the graph shows, the triumph of the monarchy was once more accompanied by a decline in the fortunes of the *maravedí*.

There was, then, a contrast in monetary attitudes between monarchical 'irresponsibility' and the demands of the opposition nobility for reforms. But before discussing the reasons for the Crown's 'irresponsibility', some curious links between monetary history and that of the political figures of the period must be emphasized. After all, even during those periods when the king was 'free' to rule, his choice of a particular policy often depended on the advice of his favourites or trusted councillors. In the case of kings like John II and Henry IV, moreover, it is obvious that any theory of royal 'irresponsibility' must be related to the activities of those men to whom these kings so often entrusted the formulation of royal policies. Looked at in this way, the data on devaluation produce the following links with political history.[11]

(a) *c*1429-*c*1451. Apart from the brief recovery in the fortunes of the *maravedí* during those years in the early 1440s when the Aragonese party was in power, this period witnessed the first long-

[9]For the content of these reforms see above, pp. 62-5.

[10]On the political background see Suárez Fernández, *Los Trastámaras*, pp. 106-83. For an example of a specific reference to royal councils attended (and controlled) by members of the Aragonese party see the ordinance (*sobre lo de la moneda vieja e nueva*) of 10 March 1442, BN, MS., 13259, fos. 314-8 (Appendix A-4).

[11]See, in general, Suárez Fernández, *Los Trastámaras, passim.*

term fall in the value of the money of account. But these years also constituted the age of Alvaro de Luna's almost complete domination of the royal court of Castile. By 1451 he was struggling to maintain his position and in 1453 he was executed.

(b) c1451-c1461/3.　Apart from a drop in value in 1459, the *maravedí* remained remarkably stable during this period. After the execution of Luna and until his own death in 1454, John II was helped in the task of government by a group of men who may be labelled *politiques*. The rest of this period constituted the 'optimistic' years of Henry IV's reign during which the court was dominated by the royal favourite, Juan Pacheco, marquis of Villena.

(c) c1462-c1468.　These were the catastrophic years during which the *maravedí* fell vertically and the kingdom was plunged into civil war. In terms of court politics, Pacheco was replaced by the worthless *hombres nuevos,* and men like Beltrán de la Cueva dominated the mind (and perhaps the body) of the king.

(d) c1468-c1474.　After the agreement of Toros de Guisando (1468), Juan Pacheco once more returned to power at court. His return heralded the reforming ordinances which attempted to restore order and put an end to monetary chaos.

Is it possible to speak of 'the Alvaro de Luna and Beltrán de la Cueva periods of debasement' and of 'the Pacheco years of monetary stability', or are the links too hypothetical to be of any use? The latter may be the case, but the coincidences are too striking to be rejected out of hand, and they do help to explain some rather puzzling features of the political history of the period.

The most convincing link is that between the first long period of devaluation and Alvaro de Luna's years of personal rule. It would be no exaggeration to state that many of the nobility detested the constable not simply on personal grounds but because he was complete master of the royal administration and because many of his policies ran counter to their fundamental interests. One of these was the desire for a stable monetary system, and there can be no doubt at all that the Crown's opponents held Luna personally responsible for the debasements of the period. Here, for example, is the section on monetary affairs from the manifesto of political grievances which the nobility sent to John II in 1440:

> And among the other things which he [Alvaro de Luna] did in order to become all-powerful in your kingdoms and dispose of them according to his own will, was to ensure that all the *maravedí*es of the revenues of your realms should be in his power and at his will and command, and he personally appointed

the treasurers and tax collectors. He also took over control of your mints and had coins made which were much inferior to the assay which Your Highness ordered with the agreement of those of your council. And this was done by false pretences and was carried out because the officials of these mints were all the constable's men and appointed by him. And with this same tyrannical aim he appointed *contadores mayores* . . . so that he could the more easily cover up what he wished to take.[12]

The allegation, therefore, was very specific, and it supports the theory of a Luna phase of debasements. He had gained unrestricted power at court in 1429, his domination was to last until the early 1450s, and he certainly practised a policy of appointing his own supporters into key positions in the financial and minting administration. The value of the *maravedí*, in short, continued to fall until Luna himself fell from power.

In political terms the period of monetary stability from 1451 to *c*1461 presents more of a problem. It is understandable that, after Luna's fall from power, those who controlled royal government should have opted for stability — they had, after all, to maintain a difficult equilibrium between the interests of an aging king, the resurgent nobility, and the increasingly important figure of the heir to the throne.[13] The real puzzle is provided by the years of Juan Pacheco's control of the royal court. The judgements of historians on the marquis of Villena have invariably been unfavourable. Undoubtedly he possessed rare diplomatic talents, but his domination of Henry IV was not accompanied by that devotion to the task of strengthening royal power which Luna is held to have displayed. Both Luna and Pacheco, of course, feathered their own nests as did all royal favourites, but the devious marquis had dealings with the nobility behind the king's back and he 'betrayed' Henry IV in negotiations with Louis XI.[14] Why, then, should this master of duplicity have rejected the financial benefits to be reaped from a policy of debasements? The answer surely lies in the fact that Pacheco *did* try to side with the nobility as well as the Crown, and his aristocratic outlook was coupled with a profound knowledge of the interests of a nobility who viewed monetary manipulations with hostility. This hypothesis is

[12] This particular section is contained in the complete version of the manifesto given in *Crónica de Juan II,* pp. 560-2.

[13] Suárez Fernández, *Los Trastámaras,* p. 212.

[14] *Ibid.,* pp. 219-53. A good analysis of the tensions between men like Pacheco and Carrillo, on the one hand, and the emerging group of *hombres nuevos,* on the other, is given in the editor's introduction to Fernando del Pulgar, *Claros varones de Castilla,* ed. R.B. Tate (Oxford, 1971), p. xv.

supported by some other puzzling features of Pacheco's conduct. As will be seen below, one of the main causes of debasements was war. But the option between peaceful negotiation or war, after all, was often a matter of choice, and whereas Alvaro de Luna sought confrontation and decisive battles, Juan Pacheco preferred compromise and negotiation. Indeed, it was this very factor which led to his loss of power at court in 1462. For, when the rebellious Catalans invited Henry IV to be their king, it was Pacheco and his supporters who resisted the grandiose and costly schemes which would involve war in Aragon, Catalonia and Valencia. In fact it was after the debasement of 1461 and the reform of 1462 that Juan Pacheco and Alfonso Carrillo, archbishop of Toledo, made one last and determined stand against the Catalan ambassadors who came to seduce Henry IV into making costly military commitments. The Catalans, they argued, should send the necessary cash *before* the Castilian military intervention.[15] They were overruled, and it is against this background that the 'betrayal' in the negotiations with Louis XI must be viewed. Pacheco, in short, emerges as a cautious politician with a dislike of debasement and rash military expenditure. When he fell from power in 1462 it is clear that many of the nobility shared his views, and he was one of the two representatives of the nobility who negotiated that *sentencia* of Medina del Campo (1465) which, as has been noted, contained demands for monetary reform.[16] By this time, however, Henry IV and his new favourites — of whom Beltrán de la Cueva was the most prominent — had already plunged into a frenzied succession of debasements and minting concessions, and it was only after Pacheco's return to power in 1468 that the work of reform would once again be taken up.

In stressing these links between monetary history and the important political figures of the age, however, other and more important factors have to be taken into account. Chief of these was war itself. During the second half of the fourteenth century both Henry II and John I had frantically debased the coinage in an attempt to meet the financial strains imposed by war. Valdeón Baruque, in studying the monetary policies of Henry II, quite rightly points out that 'devaluation

---

[15]In addition to the standard account by Suárez Fernández, already cited, see also the detailed descriptions of Pacheco and Carrillo's stand against the Catalan venture in *Estudio sobre la "Crónica de Enrique IV" del Dr. Galíndez de Carvajal,* ed. J. Torres Fontes (Murcia, 1946), pp. 181-9; Enríquez del Castillo, *Crónica del rey Don Enrique el Cuarto* pp. 122-7.

[16]The reform commission was made up of two supporters of Henry IV (Pedro de Velasco and Gonzalo de Saavedra), two members representing the interests of the disgruntled nobility (Juan Pacheco and the count of Plasencia), and an 'independent' or neutral member. The full text of the *sentencia* is in *Memorias de Enrique IV,* pp. 355-479

was nothing more than a disguised and partial bankruptcy which was used to lighten the weight of the public debt.'[17] Pero López de Ayala, in fact, gave an almost perfect description of such a disguised and partial bankruptcy in his chronicle:

> King Henry [II], being in Burgos, took counsel because, since he had to make large payments to Mosen Beltran [Beltrand Du Guesclin] and to the other foreigners who had come with him as well as to his own men, he could not fulfill [these obligations] however great the taxes which might be repartitioned throughout the kingdom. Moreover, he wished to preserve rather than anger the many regions of the kingdom which supported him. For all these reasons he decided to mint money; and so he minted coins known as *cruzados,* each one of which was worth one *maravedí,* and other coins known as *reales* which were worth three *maravedí*es. These coins were of a low fineness. . . . And then he took advantage [of these operations] and paid Mosen Beltrán and the foreigners who had come to serve him, to whom he owed great amounts, and also much of what he owed to many of his own men. But these coins caused a great deal of harm for a considerable time because things became so expensive that a *dobla* was worth three hundred *maravedí*es, a horse cost sixty thousand *maravedí*es, and so it was with the prices of other things.[18]

Obviously the costs of this cycle of wars had been enormous. Quite apart from the expenses of civil war, for example, Henry II had to pay and reward his French allies, and in the end John I had to buy off Lancastrian claims to the throne with a capital payment and an annual pension which far exceeded any *parias* paid by the rulers of Granada.[19]

The same close links can be established between the fifteenth-century cycle of wars and the chronology of debasements. What, for example, are the crucial dates which mark the turning points between periods of relative monetary stability and the subsequent years of prolonged devaluation of the *maravedí*? They are 1429/30 and 1461, and these are precisely the years when it is beyond doubt that the demands of war had outstripped the financial resources of the Crown. They are also, interestingly enough, the two occasions when the monarchy decided to wage war *abroad*. In the case of the crisis of

[17] J. Valdeón, 832.

[18] Pedro López de Ayala, *Crónica de Enrique II de Castilla* (BAE, LXVIII, 1953), p. 3.

[19] On the Lancastrian payments and pensions see Russell, ch. XIX and doc. XI of the appendix. The extent of the war-debts to the French remains unknown, but documents relating to some payments survive: for example, AM Burgos, Leg. 963-1070, doc. 1009, and Leg. 1125-1214, docs. 1138-1141.

1461 it has already been noted how Pacheco and Carrillo resisted grandiose schemes for Castilian intervention in the political affairs of the Crown of Aragon, and of course Diego de Valera explained the debasements of these years in terms of Henry IV's expeditions '*con gran gente*' to '*fazer guerra en Navarra*'.[20] The mechanisms of the monetary crisis, in fact, were much the same as they had been in 1429, and for this latter year there is enough documentary evidence to analyse the problems in greater detail.

The outbreak of hostilities between John II and his enemies in 1429 was precipitated by the expulsion of the king of Navarre from Castile in 1428. Hamilton has already examined the way in which this crisis led the king of Navarre to borrow plate and debase the Navarrese coinage in order to secure a victorious return to the Castilian court.[21] But in the latter kingdom John II found himself equally short of funds:

> While the king was in Burgos he took counsel about those things which were necessary for waging war in the kingdoms of Aragon and Navarre in the following year. . . . And when the *contadores* had done their calculations, it was found that 100,000,000 *mrs* were necessary to pay the wages of the said men for six months and to pay for all the other items listed. After many discussions on this matter it was agreed that the king should mint money in three or four of the houses where this was customary, because little remained of the money which King Henry, his father, had minted, and much had been taken out of these realms, especially to the kingdom of Portugal, to the great detriment of this kingdom. In this way the king would have more money available for the great expenditure which he needed to incur. To this end, he could borrow plate from many areas of his realms where [not enough] money was to be had, and his Majesty was advised to send and ask for the loan of plate from the principal churches and monasteries of these realms as well as from some prelates and some individuals who, it was thought, could provide it. The king accepted this as good advice, and he ordered coins to be minted in Burgos and Seville, and he ordered that the *blancas* should be of the same fineness, weight and price as the *blancas* already in circulation, which King Henry, his father, had minted. . . .[22]

If the chronicler was at all accurate, then the king was indeed desperately short of money. He needed 100,000,000 *mrs* for war expenditure, but the oldest surviving Castilian budget, significantly

---

[20]See Valera, *Memorial de diversas hazañas,* p. 64, where the debasement is placed concisely within the context of the Catalan venture.

[21]Hamilton, *Money, Prices and Wages,* pp. 129-32.

[22]*Crónica de Juan II,* pp. 467-8.

enough also dating from 1429, estimated a total regular income of only 60,812,290 *mrs* and an already assigned recurrent expenditure of 55,245,008 *mrs!*[23] Of course, the possibility of *cortes* subsidies could make a great difference, but it is clear from all the evidence that the decision for a confrontation with the Aragonese party entailed a fiscal commitment of enormous magnitude.

The chronicle relates that in the end it was also decided to approach the towns for loans, and the process can be followed through more than one set of documents. On 24 November 1429, for example, the town council of Burgos was presented with a royal demand for a loan of 15,000 gold florins,[24] but since 250 of the more substantial citizens of Burgos were also approached for a forced loan of 2,000 marks of silver, and since the king had mounted an operation to commandeer the plate from all churches in the diocese, the town council attempted to reduce the amount it had to pay.[25] John II did in fact reduce his demand to 10,000 florins, but the unwillingness of the council to pay up reached such a point that on 30 November the king sent a stiff letter to the oligarchs in which he also attempted to appeal to inter-urban rivalry by pointing out that Seville had already advanced him two million *mrs*. It was hardly an accident that, at the same council meeting at which this letter was discussed, the treasurer of the Burgos mint appeared and demanded that matters be speeded up so that the essential supplies for the mint should not be held up.[26]

Although similar documentation exists for the demands which John II made in Córdoba and Seville, the main points of the war-debasement relationship have already been established. At a time when John II and Alvaro de Luna were in full political control at court, they anticipated heavy military expenditure by resorting to forced loans and a debasement of the coinage.

Was there more to the series of late medieval debasements than the pressing demands of military expenditure? Or, to use Vilar's

[23] The most recently printed version of the 1429 budget is to be found in Ladero, *La Hacienda Real,* pp. 268-70.

[24] AM, Burgos, *Actas capitulares,* 1429-30, fos. 84v-85, meeting of 24 November 1429. The demand was contained in a royal letter of 20 November and presented by one of the King's secretaries. The initial willingness of the Burgos officials to provide the money was recorded at a meeting on the following day: *ibid.* fo. 85v.

[25] *Ibid.,* fos. 86-88v, meeting of 26 November 1429. The copy of the royal letter detailing the measures for the requisitioning of church plate breaks off without giving the date. The grounds for the town's claim that the total should be reduced were that both the 250 *monederos* in Burgos and the 250 contributors to the 2,000 marks of silver would be exempted from paying towards the 15,000 florins.

[26] *Ibid.,* fo. 90v, meeting of 6 December.

phrase, did the monarchy use money in other ways as 'a means of policy'? Alvaro de Luna, as has been seen, was accused by his enemies of a 'tyrannical' manipulation of the coinage, and a total lack of monetary responsibility was one of many serious charges levelled at Henry IV. Although the reasons for this unease and concern on the part of the nobility are fairly obvious, another detailed study would be needed to substantiate them in detail. But even if we disregard the important implications for the nobility's income of the lack of demesne exploitation, the prevalence of long-term land leases, and the fixed nature of seigneurial income, it is clear that the famous royal privileges or *mercedes* were of vital importance to many of the Castilian nobility. Yet almost without exception, all such financial rewards, pensions and payments which the Crown granted to nobles were calculated in terms of fixed amounts of *maravedí*es.[27] Thus a noble with an annual pension of 75,000 *mrs* in 1429 would find that its real value would fall along with that of the money of account, indeed the graph of its devaluation would be exactly the same. Crown income, on the other hand, was not inelastic because, since the royal revenues were farmed out to the highest bidders and since many of the taxes were *ad valorem* impositions, total income could rise in nominal terms.[28] Quite apart from other considerations, therefore, while any debasement of the coinage entailed a corresponding devaluation of all privileges held from the Crown, royal income was not necessarily affected to the same extent and the king reaped a profit from the debasement itself. The detrimental effects of debasements on important sources of noble income, therefore, raise the possibility of a deliberate royal policy and remind one of Thomas Wilson's comment on Henry VIII's debasement: 'Notwithstanding, some report that this [debasement] was not done without the pollicy of the King, who by this meanes weakened the ability of his nobility and thereby clipped the wings of their insolencys.'[29]

Although there is plenty of evidence to show that the Crown rewarded its own supporters and that the effects of devaluation weakened 'the ability' of noble opponents, it is difficult to determine whether Castilian kings deliberately pursued such a policy. However, there are several considerations which help towards the formulation

[27]The literature on *mercedes* is enormous, but for an important study of the various types of privileges, which also illustrates the fact that payments were in *mrs,* see L. Suárez Fernández, 'Un libro de asientos de Juan II', *Hispania,* XVII (1957), 323-68.

[28]Much, of course, depended on the degree of political stability. For figures on royal income see below, p. 100.

[29]Sir Thomas Wilson, 'The State of England (1600)', ed. F.J. Fisher, in *Camden Miscellany,* vol XVI (Camden Society, 3rd ser. LII, 1936), 39.

of a judgement. In the first place the Alvaro de Luna and Beltrán de la Cueva phases of debasements were, in political terms, very different in nature. During the 1460s the monarchy was desperately on the defensive and Henry IV was subjected to the humiliation of having his effigy deposed, his half-brother raised up against him as 'King' Alfonso, and his daughter's legitimacy called into question. In these circumstances it must surely be concluded that debasements were due to the king's extreme penury and debility, and that there was no subtle scheme to weaken the opposition nobility. The impression given by the years of Alvaro de Luna's domination, on the other hand, is quite different. These were the years when the king and his favourite actively promoted a policy of absolutism. John II justified many of his arbitrary policies and actions by stressing that he acted 'as king and lord, not recognising a superior in temporal matters, and by virtue of my own will, certain knowledge and absolute royal power'. Moreover, laws were promulgated by the king alone and his absolute royal power was used to declare them to be as valid 'as if they had been made in *cortes*'. Together the king and favourite sought military confrontations with opponents who, for their part, preferred to negotiate rather than fight.[30] Indeed, although the nobility carefully avoided making accusations against the king himself, they bitterly attacked Alvaro de Luna for his 'usurpation' of royal power and for his 'tyrannical' policies. Had they, one wonders, been reading Nicholas Oresme's *De Moneta*?

> I submit, as a point already proved and often repeated, that to take or augment profit by alteration of the coinage is fraudulent, tyrannical and unjust, and moreover it cannot be persisted in without the kingdom being, in many other respects also, changed to a tyranny. Wherefore, it not only brings disadvantages of its own, but involves many other evils as either its conditions or its consequences. For this course can only be the advice of evil-minded men, ready to counsel any fraud or tyranny, if they see a prince inclined to it or willing to listen to it.
>
> To sum up my argument, I say that a thing which tends to bring a realm to ruin is disgraceful and harmful to the king and his heirs, my first premiss; that it extends and changes to a tyranny, my second; and that it does so by alteration of the coinage, my third.[31]

Bearing in mind the 'absolutist' or 'tyrannical' context of these years, a calculated policy of debasements, which not only helped to

---

[30] See MacKay, *Spain in the Middle Ages*, pp. 131-42.

[31] Nicholas Oresme, *De Moneta*, ed. and trans. Charles Johnson (London, 1956), p. 48.

meet the financial demands of war but also served to weaken the nobility, cannot be ruled out as improbable. While those who supported John II and Alvaro de Luna received extra *mercedes*, a noble who was out of favour at court would find that the real value of his financial income from all sources was falling at an alarming rate — indeed, in real terms the value of all his fixed income in 1429 would have been halved by 1451 (and halved yet again by 1471). Moreover, even if there was no deliberate attempt to clip the wings of the nobility's 'insolence', it is clear that both the Crown and its opponents were fully aware that debasement entailed such a consequence. In effect, in 1442, after Luna had been exiled from the court and the king was trapped by his opponents, John II was forced to declare that one of the reasons for introducing monetary reforms was precisely the fact that debasements had entailed a fall in the value of privileges held from the Crown:

> Furthermore seeing that it was a burden on my conscience that the places, towns, frontier castles, and all the other people of my realms . . . who . . . hold from me great sums of *mrs* in *mercedes* for life or in perpetuity, money-fiefs (*tierras*), maintenances, salaries, and in many other ways . . . and considering that, because of the fineness of the money which I ordered to be minted, the value of what each person holds from me . . . is reduced by one sixth, it was and is my wish . . . to return to the situation which prevailed before I ordered the said money to be minted. . . .[32]

The nobility, of course, were hardly likely to accept the consequences of debasement with equanimity. Time and again, therefore, the various groups of nobles jockeyed for positions of political importance at court in an attempt to secure those extra *mercedes* or 'increments' which would restore their financial fortunes to that 'situation which prevailed before I ordered the said money to be minted . . .'. In addition, however, there were the inevitable demands for monetary reform and stability, and in the last resort a recourse to sustained military action could seriously disrupt the income of the monarchy at the local or regional level and reduce a king like Henry IV to desperate straits.[33]. Here again a political contrast emerges between the Alvaro de Luna and Beltrán de la Cueva phases of debasements. In the following table Ladero's figures for

---

[32]Ordinance of 29 January 1442, BN, MS., 13259, fo. 312v (Appendix A-3).

[33]For an excellent example of the complete disruption of royal income at a regional level during the reign of Henry IV see J. Torres Fontes, *Don Pedro Fajardo,* pp. 17-19, 99, 103, 116-9, 245-62. *All* the royal revenues in Murcia during the period 1465-74 fell into the hands of Pedro Fajardo.

royal income have been indexed in terms of silver to allow for a comparison with a rate of devaluation of the money of account.[34]

	Royal income — mrs	Royal income — silver 1406 = 100	maravedí — silver 1406 = 100
1406	60,000,000	100	100
1429	60,812,290	89	88
1430	57,555,709	86	89
1444	73,578,561	76	62
1453	c80,000,000	60	45
1458	85,814,000	64	45
1465	67,370,325	35	31
1474	c73,250,000	26	22

The first impression derived from these figures is that debasements in the end devalued royal income and the *maravedí* to approximately the same extent. However, the rate of devaluation over the years was not the same in both cases, and to account for this difference other factors, such as the authority of the monarch and the general efficiency of the royal administration, must be taken into account. In fact throughout both Alvaro de Luna's rule and the period of Pacheco's domination, royal income increased in nominal terms and devalued at a much slower rate than the *maravedí* itself. Even as late as 1458, despite the civil wars and the various debasements which had taken place, the monarchy was still well ahead in the fight to defend itself against the full effects of devaluation. The same was not

[34]The figures for royal income are taken from Ladero, *La Hacienda Real,* p. 43. Ladero himself attempted to index the real value of royal income by converting *mrs* into *doblas.* However, given the unsatisfactory nature of his *dobla* values, his calculations are very approximate and they underestimate the real fall in royal income. Even if we stick to calculating real values in terms of gold by using the present data on Aragonese florins, the discrepancies are substantial:

	Index: Aragonese florins	Index: Ladero's *dobla*
1429	100	100
1430	92	95
1444	83.5	122
1453	66	90
1458	60	95
1465	38	55
1474	30	60

true of the turbulent years which came after the 'optimistic' period of Henry IV's reign and during which the value of royal income fell alarmingly. Does the contrast emphasise the statesman-like qualities of Alvaro de Luna or does it rather confirm the incompetence of Henry IV and men like Beltrán de la Cueva? In any case the two phases are different — under Alvaro de Luna the Crown appeared to hold the initiative, but during the 1460s there was an almost complete collapse.

It is time now to turn to other aspects of political and social unrest. In another study I have attempted to demonstrate that the popular movements and pogroms of the period were related to a general deterioration in economic conditions.[35] Among these, crises of subsistence and rising prices were particularly important in causing urban unrest from about 1435 onwards. In either real or nominal terms, of course, it could be argued from the data presented here that prices and wages tended to move in sympathy over the whole period. For the purposes of the history of social unrest, however, the evidence must be analysed in terms of the perceived reality of contemporaries, and from this point of view the expressed grievances of the period can leave little room for doubt: prices were seen to be rising sharply, the increasing burdens of taxation were felt to be unjustified or even 'tyrannical', and men like Alvaro de Luna and his Jewish or *converso* 'allies' were accused of plotting to ruin the king, the nobility, the towns and the Old Christians. But in the context of the data presented in this study, the striking feature is the relationship which can be detected between monetary reductions and the more important, savage, and widespread pogroms.

The period under review opened with the great pogrom of 1391 and closed with the savage massacres of *conversos* in numerous towns in 1473 and 1474. Although a detailed analysis of these crises cannot be given here, it must be emphasised that they were among the worst pogroms of the whole of the medieval period and were clearly much more serious than the other more isolated outbreaks of anti-semitism or hunger riots.[36] But the period also opened and closed with attempts at monetary reform which were similar in nature and yet different from other types of reforms which had been attempted. Were there any connexions between these reforms and the violent uprisings?

In both cases the monetary reforms dated from the last years of each of the two long-term war cycles, which have already been

[35] A. MacKay, 'Popular Movements', 33-67.

[36] See P. Wolff, 'The 1391 Pogrom in Spain. Social Crisis or not?', *Past and Present*, no. 50 (1971), 4-18; A. MacKay, 'Popular Movements', *passim*.

discussed, and the evident aim was to deal with the urgent problems arising from the chronic nominal inflation and instability of previous decades. In neither case were the reforms introduced in one comprehensive package and at one specific point of time. On the contrary, the measures consisted of more than one attempt to deal with the monetary problems of the two periods in question:

(a) Towards the end of the first cycle of wars John I promulgated reforms in the *cortes* of Bribiesca of 1387, and these were followed by further ordinances issued by Henry III in 1391.[37]

(b) During the last years of the second war cycle Henry IV introduced his reforms of 1471 and subsequently promulgated further deflationary measures in 1473.[38]

It is important to note that all these measures, in their various ways, aimed at securing a *reduction* of billon coins which were held to be responsible for provoking inflation. In 1387 John I reduced the coins known as *blancos*, and in 1391 Henry III ordered further reductions in these same coins and issued an 'Ordinance on the reduction of *blancos* and on the value of the old money'. In 1470-1 Henry IV reduced the *quartos*, and in 1473 he reduced the *blancas*.

Now, successful though these measures may have been in the long run, the immediate result was to create a total confusion in financial transactions which was duly recorded in urban records. Here, for example, is the entry for 1391 in the *Libros de Acuerdos* of Burgos: 'There came to this meeting Diego Fernandez, *bachiller* and *alcalde* of the kings court and *alguacil* of the court, and they told him that there existed great confusion with this money because [men] did not wish to take it, and they were rejecting the good money in favour of the bad, and they asked that they should remedy the situation. And the *alcaldes* and officials said that no remedy could be effected at present until a meeting of the *cortes* is held.'[39] Similarly, the confusion arising from the reduction of 1471 was immediately recorded on the very first page of the *actas* of Burgos for that year: 'Inasmuch as there is great confusion in this town over the exchange rate of *quartos* because some people allege that the king . . . has reduced them to two *mrs* each while others say that they are worth four *mrs* or that they are at their accustomed value. . . .'[40] Moreover, since the reduction applied to *billon* coins, both the *maravedí* itself and the populace at large were more directly affected. After all, coins such as *quartos* and

[37]*Cortes*, II, 359-62, 420-4, 517-24.

[38]For details of the measures see above, pp. 76-8.

[39]AM, Burgos, *Actas capitulares, 1391-92, fo. 17v,* meeting of 28 September 1391

[40]*Ibid. Actas capitulares,* 1471, fo. 1.

blancas were literally the meat and drink of the vast majority of the Castilians, and the fortunes of the *maravedí* were determined by the billon coinage in general. It is hardly surprising, therefore, that the discussions and violent tensions relating to these reductions should have spilled out from the closed meetings of the urban oligarchs and ended up in the public squares and streets. This at least is what happened in Carmona in 1471. Caught between Henry IV's order to reduce *quartos* and the possible violent consequences of such a reduction, the oligarchs decided to protect themselves by announcing a full public discussion of the issue in the town square. In the event, despite the heated arguments and 'murmuring', this shrewd move produced a temporary solution to the problem.[41] Not all towns, however, managed to avoid the scandal and murmuring among the people and the risk of disobedience.[42]

The reasons for the scandals and confusion arising from these reductions in the billon coins are obvious enough. Any substantial reduction immediately created problems about payments, particularly of debts, and in any transaction one party was inevitably left with a grievance. How, for example, was a man to repay a debt of 300 *mrs* after the reduction of 1473? Originally borrowed at the old rate (2 *blancas* = 1 *maravedí*), a repayment at this same rate would be rejected by the lender; but equally the borrower would refuse to repay at the new post-reduction rate (3 *blancas* = 1 *maravedí*). It was precisely because of this kind of confusion that Henry III introduced the incredibly complicated ordinance of 1391 in which, along with the *procuradores* of the *cortes,* he distinguished between all the various ways in which loans, debts, rents, leases and taxes were to be paid.[43] In practice, of course, such labyrinthine measures only led to further confusion and the accumulation of more grievances.[44]

In the short term, therefore, the curbing of price inflation by reductions in key billon coins led to convulsions in those very

[41] AM, Carmona, *Actas capitulares, 1471,* meetings of 26 and 27 January 1471. I am greatly indebted to Prof. Manuel González Jiménez who kindly sent me photocopies of the relevent documents in Carmona. The result of the public deliberations in Carmona was a decision to adopt the policy practised in Córdoba — that is, to allow *quartos* from the seven 'established' mints to circulate at four *mrs* and reduce the *quartos* from other mints to two *mrs*. This, of course, was envisaged as a temporary expedient until such time as the Crown should provide a definite solution to the problem.

[42] The phrase is taken from Nicholas Oresme, p. 13.

[43] *Cortes,* II, 517-24.

[44] See the comments, already cited, by Diego Enríquez del Castillo and the anonymous writer when describing the social effects of 'reductions': above, pp. 75 6, 79-80.

activities and social sectors in which the Jews and *conversos* were most active. Indeed, the precise chronology of the respective reductions and pogroms confirms this diagnosis of precipitating causes and effects. On the 22 January 1391 Henry III ordered a further reduction in the value of *blancos;* on the 24 April he issued his complicated ordinance on the various methods by which appropriate adjustments were to be made in financial transactions; on the 6 June the pogrom started in Seville and quickly spread to other major towns. Similarly, we know from a royal letter of 12 May 1473 that Henry IV had promulgated his reduction of *blancas 'de dos meses a esta parte'*.[45] The reduction, therefore, must have taken place in March, and it was during March and April that the pogroms of 1473 took place with the most serious massacre occurring in Córdoba on the 10 March.[46] And when, in May 1473, Henry IV described the monetary confusion, the rumours of further reductions, the refusal of tradesmen and shopkeepers to carry on business, and the general anarchy affecting financial transactions, was he not in fact describing the very atmosphere and context within which these popular movements of unrest had taken place?[47]

[45]*Memorias de Enrique IV*, p. 691.
[46] Suárez Fernández, *Los Trastámaras,* p. 308.
[47] See above, pp. 77-8.

APPENDICES

APPENDIX A: DOCUMENTS

1

Undated (first half of the 1430s)

Minting policies and silver supplies: proposals and discussions between Burgos merchants and royal officials.

AGS, D. de C., Leg. 4, doc. 56.

[1r]Petiçion que dieron los mercaderes de Burgos al Rey don Iohan sobre la moneda que mandaua labrar e la respuesta que sobre ello se les dio.

P.   Que el Rey nuestro señor de el ofiçio de la thesoreria de la casa con las condiçiones e salario que oy la tiene el thesorero.

P.   Iten que el dicho señor Rey de las costas que oy da e por el preçio que oy estan e con las mesmas condiçiones e ofiçiales.

P.   Fasiendo el dicho señor Rey lo sobre dicho daran dies mill marcos de plata e mas la que menester fuere para labrar la casa continua mente syn estar vaca dies años primeros siguientes, e labraran de la ley e manera que oy se labra syn que ponga el dicho señor Rey plata nin dinero alguno, e que la dicha plata sea tasada por el tiempo que bien visto fuere por preçio de quinientos e çinco mrs cada marco, e que non sea quitada la dicha thesoreria e casa e costas enlos dichos dies años. De lo qual piden que aya respuesta fasta el jueues primero siguiente por que los nauios de que se han de proueer han de partir en breue, que en otra manera non podran faser cosa alguna fasta el año que viene.

Respuesta

P.   Disen los thesoreros que en lo que toca al ofiçio de las thesorerias, que pues el Rey nuestro señor syn lo ellos procurar nin demandar su merçet gela diera, en lo qual siguieron a su altesa con mucha lealtança, disponiendose a muchos trabajos e dexando la administraçion de sus fasiendas, e non auiendo

106

fecho por que con justiçia les deua ser tirada, que tienen muy grand fiusa en su merçet que non gelo quitara, por que seyendo les tirado a su senoria non recresceria en ello seruiçio, e a ellos seria grand infamia por que muchos entenderian que por algund fallesçimiento que fisieran en el dicho ofiçio les fuera quitado.

P.   A lo que toca a lo de las costas, disen que pues las dichas costas se arrendaron e remataron, e los que las arrendaron fisieron [1v] recabdos de tener e conplir todo lo contenido en las condiçiones con que se arrendaron e remataron, e tienen fecho sobre ello muchas costas e espensas asi en los petrechos que conpraron para forneçimiento de la dicha casa como cobre e rasuras e otras cosas para ello nesçesarias, e que con justiçia non les pudiese quitar de la dicha renta durante el tiempo por que la arrendaron, que asi como ellos eran e son obligados de lo tener e conplir que asi la merçet del dicho señor Rey era e es encargado de les mandar guardar la condiçion que puso que les non sea quitada la dicha renta.

P.   En quanto a los dies mill marcos de plata que disen por su escripto que daran e mas la que menester fuere para labrar la casa continuamente syn estar vaca dies años primeros siguientes e que la dicha plata sea tasada por el tiempo que bien visto fuere por presçio de quinientos e çinco mrs cada marco. Disen los dichos thesoreros que para que ellos puedan responder a ello derechamente que deuen declarar sy estos dies mill marcos de plata sy los daran de cada año labrados en moneda al dicho preçio de los dichos quinientos e çinco mrs o por que forma los han de dar, e sy obligaron de dar la dicha plata al dicho presçio en cada año de todos los dichos dies años, e asy declarados por ellos que los dichos thesoreros diran a la merçet del dicho señor Rey lo que les paresçiese que mas sea su seruiçio e prouecho.

Muy Alto Prinçipe

Poderoso Rey e Señor

P.   De parte de buestra señoria nos fue dado un escripto que se dio a vuestra altesa por algunas personas, que contiene que dando vuestra señoria el ofiçio de la thesoreria de la casa de la moneda, e non declara qual, con las condiçiones e salario que oy la tiene el thesorero, e otrosy las costas en el presçio que oy estan e con las mesmas condiçiones e ofiçiales, que daran dies mill marcos de plata e mas la que fuere menester para labrar la casa continua mente syn estar vaca dies años primeros siguientes, et que la dicha plata sea tasada por el tiempo que bien visto fuere por preçio de 505 mrs cada marco de plata, e que non sea quitada la dicha thesoreria e casa e costas en los dichos dies años. E fue nos mandado de parte de vuestra altesa que mostrasemos el dicho escripto a los vuestros thesoreros de las vuestras casas de las monedas e platicasemos con ellos sobre [2r] ello. Lo qual asy fesimos luego e los dichos thesoreros nos dixeron que querian responder a vuestra señoria. E agora muy alto señor por Diego Romero vuestro secretario nos fue dado un escripto que dixo que los dichos thesoreros avian dado a vuestra realesa e nos dixo que vuestra merçet nos mandaua que dixesemos lo que çerca dello nos paresçia. E muy esclaresçido señor non es dubda quel dicho escripto esta muy escuro alli onde disen que daran los dichos dies mill marcos de plata e mas lo que fuere menester para labrar la casa continua mente syn estar vaca los dichos dies años, ca con muy poco que labrase fenchirian la condiçion. Otrosy alli onde disen que la plata sea tasada por el tiempo que bien visto fuere por presçio de quinientos e çinco mrs cada marco, e paresçe que non se ofresçen a la dar todo el dicho tiempo, e sy la plata encaresçiese en este medio tiempo non es dubda que se deterrnian en el labrar por que non perdiesen. Por ende señor esto se deuia declarar ante de todas cosas e aquello visto diremos a vuestra merçet lo que nos paresçe çerca de todo ello.

P.   Disen las personas que dieron el escripto de la casa dela moneda que, a la primera dubda que disen contadores que non declaran quanto labrara la casa de la moneda, responden que labraran dos tanto cada año de quanto labro fasta aqui cada año o lo que a los dichos contadores bien visto fuere. A la segunda dubda que disen que non declaran sy daran la dicha plata al dicho preçio de quinientos e çinco mrs todos los dichos dies años, disen que toda via la daran al dicho presçio.

P.   Disen los thesoreros que por quanto por amos ados los escriptos que por las personas que los han dado paresçe que non hablan saluo sola mente en una casa, que ellos deuen declarar que casa es, por que declarada aquel a quien ataniere responda a ello, e sy en todas que todos responderan lo que entendieren que mas cumpla al rason señor. Otrosy disen que por que mejor puedan responder que toda via les pareçe que se deuen declarar quienes son las personas que los dichos escriptos han dado. [2v]

Muy Alto e Muy Poderoso
Prinçipe Rey e Señor

P. Los thesoreros de vuestras casas de moneda con deuida reuerençia besamos vuestras manos e nos encomendamos en la vuestra merçed. A la qual plega saber que en el vuestro muy alto conseio fue dado un escripto, por personas non declaradas, en que dixeron que dando vuestra merçed el offiçio de la thesoreria de la casa, non declarando qual, con las condiçiones e salario que oy la tiene el thesorero, e otrosi las costas de las dichas casas por el presçio que oy esta, e con aquellas mesmas condiçiones e ofiçiales, que daran dies mill marcos de plata e mas la que menester fuere para labrar la casa continuada mente syn estar vaca dies años primeros seguientes, e que labrara de la ley e manera que oy se labra, e que la dicha plata sea tasada por el tiempo que buen visto fuere por presçio de quinientos e çinco mrs cada marco, segund que por el dicho escripto se contenia.

P. Del qual dicho escrito nos fue dado el traslado e mandado de parte de vuestra altesa que respondiesemos a lo en el contenido.

P. A lo qual muy poderoso señor fue por nosotros respondido que las tales personas deuian declarar los dichos dies mill marcos de plata sy los darian de cada año labrados en moneda al dicho presçio de los dichos quinientos e çinco mrs, o por que forma los avian a dar e se obligarian de dar la dicha plata al dicho presçio en cada uno de los dichos dies años, e asi declarado que nosotros resp (*roto:* ondiesem?)os a la vuestra merçed derechamente lo que nos paresçiese.

P. A lo qual por las dichas personas fue replicado e respondido por otro segundo escripto que labrara la dicha casa dos tanto cada año de quanto labro fasta aqui, o lo que a los vuestros contadores fuese bien visto, e que en quanto al presçio de la plata que lo darian todavia al dicho presçio de los dichos quinientos e çinco mrs cada marco.

P. A lo qual por nos otros fue replicado que por quanto las dichas personas non fablauan por los dichos escriptos saluo solamente en una casa, que ellos deuian declarar qual casa era, e asy declarado que aquel a quien ataniese rresponderia a ello, e sy en todas las casas que todos responderiamos aquello que entendiesemos que a vuestro seruiçio complia.

P. E asi dado por nos otros la dicha respuesta fue nos mandado de parte de vuestra altesa por Diego Romero vuestro escriuano de camara que respondiesemos derecha mente syn embargo desto lo que nos paresçiese.

P. E muy poderoso señor por que a vuestra señora plase que syn embargo de lo que dicho es respondamos derecha mente, por ende lo que a nos otros paresçe fablando con muy omil reuerençia es esto. [3r]

P. Primera mente en quanto atane en rason del ofiçio de la thesoreria que demandan que uestra merçed les de, bien sabe vuestra señoria que syn lo nos otros procurar nin demandar plogo a la vuestra altesa mandar nos encargar de los dichos ofiçios acatando vuestra merçed ser nosotros personas de quien el Rey vuestro padre que dios de sancto parayso e vuestra merçed avia fiado otros muchos ofiçios. E como de todo ello aviamos dado e dimos buena cuenta e rason e que asy la dariamos destos mismos ofiçios los quales nos otros abcetamos, e con mucha labrança e diligençia trabajamos tanto quanto podimos asy en ordenar e assentar las dichas casas e enformar e faser enformar a los ofiçiales e obreros e monederos e mostrar les lo que avian de faser, por que como nueva mente todos venian a los dichos ofiçios non en ellos yndustros ni avisados para lo faser como conplia, como en buscar e conprar plata por forneçimiento de las dichas casas, e en enbiar por la mayor parte della fuera de los vuestros regnos asi por mar como por tierra a nuestra ventura, e aun oy dia tenemos en aventura parte de nuestras fasiendas que avemos enbiado fuera de los dichos vuestros regnos a buscar la dicha plata, que sy las dichas vuestras casas se ovieran de forneçer de plata fasta aqui de lo de vuestros regnos çierto es que se non podria aver tanta plata, e esa que se podria aver que valiera e costara a muy mayores presçios de los que agora vale, e encareçiendo la dicha plata (*roto*) era forçado de encareçer el oro, e asy en todas las otras (*roto*) de que se siguiera a la vuestra merçed muy grand deseruiçio (*roto*) dexando la administraçion de nuestras fasiendas e fasiendo sobrello muchas costas e despensas, e aun dando por la dicha plata a mayores presçios de los ordenados por la vuestra merçed por que las dichas casas contynuasen a labrar. E sy agora nos fuesen quitados los dichos ofiçios aviendo servido en ellos a vuestra merçed fiel e diligentemente syn cabsa donde esperamos merçed por aver seruido en ellos como deuemos, a nos otros seria fecho agrauio e nos vernia dende grand ynfimia e verguença por que seria entendido a muchos que algund error o fallesçimiento aviamos fecho en los dichos ofiçios por que vuestra merçed nos lo quitava. E, aun seria cosa nueva e non acostumbrada, que vuestra merçed puede saber ser çertificado que en los tiempos pasados los reyes vuestros anteçesores usando de su realesa que despues que una ves proueyan de los semejantes ofiçios non fasian mandamiento alguno syn ser fallado por que les deuiesen ser quitados, lo uno por que sy los dichos ofiçios ouieran o oviesen de ser quitados e oviesen de entre venir otros en ellos seria cabsa de no ser guardado el secreto que se deue guardar en lo que pertenesçe a las dichas casas por ser sabido por muchos, lo otro por non amenguar a los que los tenian. Nin asy mesmo vuestra merçed nunca tal fiso fasta aqui nin plega a dios que agora vuestra señoria [3v] comiençe en nos otros. Et aun señor desto se siguiria e podria seguir muchos ynconvenientes, ca dando vuestra merçed lugar a lo sobre dicho muy mejor se moveran otras algunas personas a poner condiciones e ofreçerse a poner mejor diligencia en todos los otros vuestros ofiçios de la vuestra casa e corte, pues tanta rason e seruiçio vuestro en cada uno se puede dar como se da en el caso presente, de lo qual vernia una grand confusion en todos vuestros ofiçios e deserviçio a la vuestra merçed.

P.   Otrosy muy poderoso señor en quanto atañe a lo que disen de la renta de las costas, bien sabe vuestra altesa como la dicha renta de las dichas casas se arrendo por los vuestros contadores mayores en el vuestro estrado en publica almoneda por çierto tiempo e con çiertas condiçiones, e se remato en aquellas personas que menor presçio por ellas diesen. Los quales despues aca han forneçido fasta aqui las dichas casas asy de cobre e rasuras como de las otras cosas que nesçesarias e complideras fueron e se obligaron de conplir syn fallesçimiento alguno, e asy mismo tienen conprado e forneçido para adelante de cobre e rasuras e de todas las otras cosas que para forneçimiento de las dichas casas son conplideras. E sy agora la dicha renta les fuese quitada ya vuestra merçed puede entender que a ellos seria fecho muy grand agrauio e ynjustiçia, e seria cabsa para perder lo que tienen, lo qual a vuestra altesa seria grand cargo de conçiençia. E pues vuestra merçed segund vuestras 1 (*roto:* eye?)s e ordenanças manda guardar lo que entre partes es fecha e (*roto*) mucho mas se deve guar (*roto*) merçed de (*roto*) deuen aver e han enxenplo, mayormente que seria grave que lo que es adquirido e deuido por el dicho remate e condiçiones e fuese otro resçibido apuja veniendo despues

de tiempo. E sy asi pasase no seria mas ni menos que sy vuestra
señoria mandase tornar e tomase quales quier bienes propios
de los que agora ay en la dicha renta. Por ende vuestra señoria
no deue dar lugar que tal agrauio pase.

P. Otrosy muy poderoso señor a lo que disen por el dicho
postrimero escripto que labraran dos tanto cada año de quanto
labro fasta aqui cada año la dicha casa o a lo que a los dichos
vuestros contadores fuere bien visto, toda via nos paresçe
fablando con umil reuerençia que para nos otros responder
derecha mente a vuestra merçed lo que entendieremos que
cunple a vuestro seruiçio que ellos deuen declarar si este dos
tanto que disen que labraran sy sera en todas las casas o sola
mente en una e qual sera, por que algunas de las dichas casas
labraran mucho mas quelas otras. E esto asy declarado, e otrosy
lo que bien visto fuere a los dichos vuestros contadores, entonçe
podemos responder a vuestra merçed lo que en ello nos
paresçiere e nos dispornemos por seruiçio vuestro a faser e
conplir aquello que justo e rasonable fuere e a nos otros posible
poder faser con las personas e fasiendas. [4r]

P. Otrosy muy poderoso señor en quanto atane a lo que disen que
daran çierta plata para forneçimiento de la dicha casa a rrason
de quinientos e çinco mrs el marco, a nos otros paresçe
fablando con omil reuerençia que non seria nin es vuestro
seruiçio ser sabido por publico que vuestra merçed mandaua
poner numero en la plata que en las dichas casas se ha de labrar,
nin otrosy en el presçio que se deue dar por cada marco de la
dicha plata, por quanto esto sabido seria cabsa de creçer los
presçios de la dicha plata e asy el oro e todas las otras cosas por
entender los que la dicha plata tovieran que pues de nesçesario
se rrequeria labrar la dicha suma de plata en cada año que
forçado seria cresçer los presçios della. E aun seria dubda
sy la dicha plata se podria aver, que por espirençia acaesçio
en Sevilla que algunos mercadores genoueses cabdalosos
vendieron çierta suma de plata al vuestro thesorero dela dicha
casa, e se obligaron de gela dar a çierto presçio e a
çierto tiempo. E tanto que fue sabido por otros mercadores luego
escrivieron a Flandes e a otras partes sobrello de guisa que luego
fue encareçida la dicha plata e fue cabsa por que los dichos
mercadores no podieron conplir, e estan presos agora por vuestro
mandado. E por esta misma manera se faria agora sabiendo se, et
muy poderoso señor a nos otros paresçe fablando con humil
reverençia que segund lo que avemos platicado çerca dello

112

que mucho mas vuestro seruiçio seria que este cargo fuese dado a los vuestros thesoreros para que ellos conprasen la dicha plata secretamente fasta en el dicho presçio e dende ayuso como me (*roto*: jor?) e mas conplidamente pudiesen segund fasta aqui se h (*roto*) en las dichas (*roto*) vuestro serviçio por que por espiriençia avemos visto que labran(*roto*) se mucha moneda e continuando labrar las dichas casas que luego cresçen los presçios de la dicha plata e oro, e todas las otras cosas por consegiencia, segund dicho avemos, e quando acaesçe labrarse conplidamente o que estan algunos dias que non labran luego abaxan los presçios de la dicha plata e oro de lo que vuestra señoria se puede enformar ser asy.

P. Dexando a parte los ynconvenientes e rasones que los thesoreros fasen, los quales la merçed del Rey nuestro señor deue mandar ver e proveer açerca dello como entendiere que cumple a su seruiçio, paresçe a los contadores que sy las personas que dieron el escripto o otras algunas se encargaren por la forma que se ofreçio de la casa de la moneda de Burgos o de la de Sevilla o de amas a dos, conviene a saber que labren dos tanto que aquellos e cada una dellas han labrado, que dexando a parte algunos ynconvenientes que dello se podrian seguir, en espeçial en el pujar del oro con el qual se pujaran como siempre pujaron todas las cosas, que es bien que se faga. Et sy de las otras casas de Toledo e de la Coruña se oviesen de encargar por la forma suso dicha no seria su serviçio, por que començaron a labrar tarde en ellas e no han labrado saluo muy poco en tal manera quel dos tanto seria poca quantia. [4v]

P. Alos contadores pareçe que labrando en cada año dosientos dias de lauor, quitando fiestas e pascuas e ochauas e dos meses e medio de sementera e de vendimias e aun del agosto e aun dolençias de capatases e de los otros en las fornasas o algunos de los ofiçiales o mengua de caruon que puede recresçer, que podran labrar en cada fornasa mill marcos de plata en esta manera:

		(Marcos)
P.	En Sevilla que ay dose fornas	12,000
P.	En Toledo que ay nueue fornasas	9,000
P.	En Burgos que ay siete fornasas	
7,000 mrs e en dos fornasas que se podria acreçentar 2,000 mrs que son		9,000
P.	En la Curuña que ay seys fornasas por que son pequeñas e non cabe tanta gente tornando las a çinco son	5,000
		35,000

2

Madrigal, 20 December 1439

An ordinance on the quality and circulation of blancas.

BN, MS, 13259, fos. 189v — 190v.

[189v]Ordenanças fechas en Madrigal el dicho año de 1439.

Don Juan, por la graçia de Dios Rey de Castilla, de Leon, de Toledo, de Gallisia, de Sevilla, de Cordova, de Murçia, de Jaen, del Algarbe, de Algesira, e señor de Viscaya e de Molina. A los infantes, duques, condes, ricos omes, maestres de las ordenes, priores, comendadores, subcomendadores, alcaydes de los castillos e casas fuertes e llanas, e al conçejo, alcaldes, merino, regidores, caualleros, escuderos, ofiçiales, e omes buenos de la **muy noble çibdad de Burgos, cabeça de Castilla, mi camara,** et de todas las otras çibdades e villas e logares de los mis regnos e señorios, e a todos los otros mis subditos e naturales de qual quier estado o condiçion preheminençia o dignidad que sean, e a qual quier o quales quier dellos a quien esta mi carta fuere mostrada, o el traslado della signado de escrivano publico, salut e graçia. Sepades que yo entendiendo que cumple asi a mi seruiçio e a bien comun de los dichos mis regnos e señorios, fue e es mi merçed de mandar proveer e dar orden por que sola mente anda e se use en mis regnos la buena moneda de blancas que el Rey don Enrrique mi padre e mi señor, que Dios de santo parayso, mando labrar, e asi mesmo yo despues que regne, e que non ande ni se use con ella la otra moneda que a ella dis que se ha vuelto e mesclado, la qual no fue fecha por mi mandado ante fue fecha e fabricada falsamente. Para lo qual mande faser e pregonar en la mi corte çiertos pregones, su tenor de los quales es este que se sigue.

P.   Manda el Rey nuestro señor e tiene por bien que toda la moneda que el señor Rey don Enrrique su padre de esclareçida memoria cuya anima Dios aya, mando labrar, e asi mesmo la que su señoria mando labrar, que toda vala e pase e corra e se use es a saber dos blancas un mr asi en la su corte como en todas las otras çibdades e villas e logares de los sus regnos e señorios, e que ninguno non sea osado de la desechar, e que toda la otra moneda que conosçida mente fuere mala non vala nin se use nin corre en sus regnos e señorios antes que se corre segunt que adelante dira.

P.   Pero por quanto se dise que ay alguna moneda dubdosa que clara [190r] mente non se puede conosçer ser falsa, que esta atal sea foradada e despues de foradada corra e vala por un dinero cada blanca e non mas. E por que se pueda conosçer qual es la buena e la mala e la dubdosa, manda su altesa e tiene por bien que en la su corte los sus alcaldes della, et en las çibdades e villas e logares de los sus regnos e señorios los alcaldes dellas, ayan poder, el qual su merçet les da, para ver e esaminar con las personas que ellos entiendieren que cunple la tal moneda, e la que ellos aprouaren por bueno que pase, e la otra que dieren por falsa que la fagan luego cortar e tornar a sus dueños, e la dubdosa que la fagan foradar como dicho es. E que la tal moneda foradada se pueda usar e use al dicho presçio de un dinero en la su corte e en todos los sus regnos e señorios desde el dia deste pregon fasta un año conplido primero siguiente, et non dende en adelante, et a qual quier a quien fuere fallado despues del dicho año pasado le sea cortado por malo.

P.   Otrosi que persona alguna non sea osado despues de pasados tres dias del dia deste pregon en adelante de tener nin tenga moneda falsa nin usa nin use della sopena que si le fuere fallada **que le sea tomada e cortada, et allende desto las dichas justiçias** del dicho señor rey cada unos en sus jurediçiones proçedan contra el tal como contra aquel que a sabiendas usa de moneda falsa.

P.   Por que vos mando a todos e a cada uno de vos en vuestros lugares e juredaiçiones que lo asi guardedes e cumplades e fagades guardar e conplir en todo e por todo bien e conplida mente segunt que en el se contiene e suso va encorporado et en guardandolo e cumpliendolo non vayades nin pasedes nin consyntades yr nin pasar contra el nin contra cosa alguna de lo en el contenido so las penas en el contenidas. Et por esta mi carta mando a los alcaldes desa dicha çibdad que lo fagan asi pregonar publicamente por la dicha çibdad e por todas las villas e logares de su termino tres dias uno en pos de otro dos veses cada dia uno en la mañana et otro en la tarde por manera que venga a notiçia de todos e ninguno non pueda pretender ynorançia disiendo que lo non sopieron nin vino a su notiçia, et que ellos tengan cargo para ver e esaminar con las personas que ellos entiendieren que cunpla la tal moneda, e la buena aprouar e la dubdosa faser foradar e la mala cortar como suso dicho es. Para lo qual por esta mi carta les do poder

complido e para [190v] faser todas las otras cosas e cada una
dellas que a ellos pertenesçe faser segunt el tenor e forma del
dicho pregon suso encorporado. Et los unos nin los otros non
fagades ende al por alguna manera so pena de la mi merçed e
de dies mill mrs para la mi camara et de mas por qual quier o
quales quier por quien finca de lo asi faser e conplir mando al
ome que vos esta mi carta mostrare que vos enplase que
parescades ante mi en la mi corte do quier que yo sea del dia que
vos enplasare fasta quinse dias primeros siguientes so la dicha
pena, so la qual mando a qual quier escrivano publico que para
esto fuere llamado que de ende al que vos la mostrare testimonio
signado con su signo por que yo sepa en como conplides mi
mandado. Dada enla villa de Madrigal veynte dias de disiembre
año del nasçimiento del Nuestro Señor Ihesu Xpo. de mill
e quatroçientos e treynta e nueve años.

3

29 January 1442

An ordinance on *doblas, reales* and *blancas.*

BN, MS, 13259, fos. 312R — 314R

[312r] Sobre el labrar de la moneda en las casas della.

P.   Yo el Rey fago saber a todos quantos la presente vieren por
rason que yo oue mandado e mande labrar moneda de doblas e
blancas e cornados en las mis casas de moneda de las muy
nobles çibdades de Burgos e Toledo e Seuilla e la mi villa dela
Coruna que la intençion e causa que a esto me mouio fue la
siguiente.

P.   Por quanto en el tienpo que yo mande labrar la dicha moneda de
blancas yo era en nesçesidat de dineros para conplir e dar
recabdo çerca de algunos trabajos e debates de mis regnos e
señorios, e otrosi con intençion de continuar la guerra de los
moros enemigos de nuestra santa fe catolica. Por ser socorrido
para conplir e obuiar a las tales nesçesidades e por la mengua de
moneda de blancas que en mis regnos avia, avido sobre todo mi
consejo e deliberaçion, mande que la moneda que se asi fisiese e

fiso se abaxase de la ley que el Rey don Enrrique mi señor e mi padre de esclareçida recordaçion que dios aya mando labrar esta moneda de blancas viejas que agora corre en mis regnos a respecto de veynte e quatro granos de plata por marco e çinquenta e seys mrs de talla, et yo mande labrar a los mis thesoreros en las dichas mis casas de moneda a respecto e talla de cinquenta e nueue mrs e la ley a respecto de veynte granos de plata por marco.

P. Et por quanto ha pareçido e paresçe por obra esto auer traydo e traer muchos inconuinientes e daños en mis regnos e en los subditos e naturales dellos en diversas maneras, ca lo primero las gentes començaron a sospechar e dubdar en la dicha moneda en mucha mas quantidad que ello era e devia ser en la pura verdat. Et otrosi por causa de los movimientos acaesçidos en mis regnos muchas personas non temiendo a dios nin ami nin a la mi justiçia fisieron e fabricaron en diuersas partes e por diuersas maneras falsa moneda, lo qual ha dado causa e induçion a todos los mis subditos e naturales e a otras personas quales quier que vienen fuera de los mis regnos a encareçer fuera de toda medida todas las cosas que se han de comprar e vender e asi el oro e la plata, lo qual ha redundado e redunda en grant dano de la corona real de mis regnos e de mis subditos naturales.

P. Otrosi veyendo que a mi era cargo de conçiençia que los logares pradosos e villas e castillos fronteros e todos los otros de mis regnos [312v] et señorios e de fuera dellos que han tenido e tienen de mi grandes contias de mrs de merçedes de juro de heredad e de por vida e en tierras e mantenimientos e raçiones e en otras muchas maneras, lo qual les fue puesto e asignado por **diuersos respectos e causas por los reyes donde yo vengo de** esclareçida memoria, e despues por mi, e queriendo e deseando ante de los acreçentar e onrrar en merçedes e graçias por que sean mas onrrados e ricos que non los amenguar, e considerando que aun segunt la ley de la moneda que yo asi mande labrar a cada uno viene de baxa de lo que asi de mi tiene e ha de aver la seysma parte, fue e es mi voluntad, plasiendo a nuestro señor dios, de lo restituyr e torrnar en aquel mesmo estado en que el Rey mi señor e mi padre que dios aya lo dexo, e segunt e por la mesma manera e forma e en aquel estado que estaua antes que yo mandase labrar la dicha moneda en mis regnos en la manera e forma que adelante dira.

P.   Por que mis regnos sean rasonable mente abastados de moneda mande e mando a los thesoreros de las dichas mis casas de moneda e acada uno dellos que en cada una dellas labren una fornasa de doblas de oro, e que este en cada una dellas mis armas reales, e del otro cabo la vanda, et estas doblas sean menores de çerco de las que se an fecho, e bien menodeadas, e las armas e deuisa e letras mejor tasadas. Et por quanto yo oue informaçion çierta a la sason que las buenas doblas valadies que en mis regnos e señorios se usauan e trabtauan se labrauan e auian labrado en la casa de la moneda de Malaga e en otras partes, e eran aleadas a ley de dies e nueue quirates de oro fino, e de talla de quarenta e nueue doblas al marco, e valian a la sason de moneda de blancas viejas en mis regnos ochenta o ochenta e dos mrs cada una, et estas doblas de la banda que yo mande e mando labrar son de aquella mesma ley e talla e peso.

P.   Otrosi mande e mando a los dichos mis thesoreros que labren en cada una de las dichas mis casas de la moneda reales e medios reales e quartos de reales de plata, a ley de onse dineros e quatro granos, e a la talla de sesenta e seys reales en el marco, que es a la mesma ley e talla que el Rey don Enrrique mi padre e el Rey don Juan mi avuelo e el Rey don Enrrique mi visabuelo que dios aya mandaron [313r] labrar e labraron reales de plata en sus tienpos poco mas o menos, los quales antes que yo mandase labrar la dicha moneda de blancas, en mis regnos valian a siete mrs e a siete mrs e medio e a ocho mrs de las dichas blancas viejas.

P.   Otrosi mando que todas las blancas nueuas que yo mande labrar en todas ias dichas mis casas de moneda e en cada una dellas que todos los que las tienen e tovieren las traygan a las dichas mis casas de moneda e a cada una dellas en cada parte e prouinçia donde cada una dellas esta asentada. E que la den e entreguen por ante los mis ofiçiales de cada una de las dichas casas de moneda a los dichos mis thesoreros e a cada uno dellos para que en presençia de los mis ofiçiales de cada una de las dichas casas se faga dello fundaçion e el mi ensayador faga dello ensay, e quel mi thesorero de cada una de las dichas casas sea tenudo de tornar e redusir la dicha moneda que asi le fuere leuada a las dichas mis casas de la moneda e a cada uno dellos a la mesma ley e talla que el dicho señor Rey don Enrrique mi padre mando labrar las dichas blancas viejas, conviene a saber a la dicha ley de veynte e quatro granos de plata por marco e çinquenta e seys mrs de talla. E que los que asy troxieren a fundir la dicha moneda de blancas nueuas sean tenudos de pagar al mi thesorero las costas al respecto e contia que pagauan a los dichos mis thesoreros e a cada uno dellos por faser cada marco de las dichas blancas nueuas que yo mande labrar, que es a preçio de dies mrs cada marco poco mas o menos.

P.   Et por que en fundir la dicha moneda e la aver de tornar a la pura ley e talla de las dichas blancas viejas vernia grant falta a los que la asi leuaren a fundir, mando que las tales personas que asi fueren a fundir lieuen plata en aquel numero e quantidat que fuere menester para las redusir a la dicha ley e talla de las dichas blancas viejas en tal manera que tanto numero de moneda le sea tornado como ouiere dado e entregado a los dichos mis thesoreros e a cada uno dellos.

P.   Et mando e ordeno que todas e quales quier personas de qual quier ley estado e condiçion preheminençia o dignidad que sean, e a todas otras quales quier personas que touieren e en cuyo poder fueren [313v] quales quier monedas de las dichas blancas que yo asi mande labrar como suso dicho es, que dentro de seys meses primeros siguientes del dia de la publicaçion desta mi carta las traygan a las dichas mis casas de moneda en la manera que dicha es, et les den e entreguen a los dichos mis thesoreros de las dichas mis casas de moneda, presentes los ofiçiales de las dichas mis casas de moneda, et que en este termino de los dichos seys meses toda la dicha moneda blanca que yo asi mande labrar sea fundida e tornada a la dicha ley e talla de las dichas blancas viejas como dicho es.

P.   Et por que mi merçet e voluntad es por dar verdadera ley de moneda a la republica de los dichos mis regnos e señorios, e apartar e euitar los tales daños pasados e presentes que por causa de la dicha moneda se han seguido, que del dia de la publicaçion desta mi carta en adelante la dicha moneda non vala nin se use en algunas partes de los dichos mis regnos e señorios. E si qual quier o quales quier personas dende en adelante tentaren o cometieren e de fecho usaren de la dicha moneda conprando o vendiendo o trocando o en otra qual quier manera, o non troxieren la dicha moneda a las dichas casas de moneda en el dicho termino como dicho es, que por el mesmo fecho aya perdido la dicha moneda, et demas que pierda todos sus bienes e quales quier mrs que de mi aya e tenga e aya de aver en qual quier manera e sea para la mi camara e fisco.

P. Et por que se paresca e sea conosçida la moneda que yo agora mando labrar e redusir a la ley e talla de las dichas blancas viejas, mando que del un cabo tenga un castillo e del otro una vanda en su escudo, et mando a los dichos mis thesoreros e a todos los otros offiçiales que estan enlas dichas mis casas de moneda que paren mientes e sean avisados que la dicha moneda que agora yo mando faser sea bien monedeada e redondeada e tallada por quanto las otras blancas que yo agora mando desfaser son mal menodeadas e non redondas nin bien fechas e parescan en esta el aventaja de buena moneda.

P. Et por que a todos sea manifiesto e ninguno non pueda dubdar que yo quiero dar e do ley çierta de moneda enlos dichos mis regnos e señorios a los subditos e naturales dellos, mando que qual quier persona o personas dellos que quisieren puedan faser e fagan [314r] ensay de las dichas monedas en quales quier de las dichas mis casas de la moneda, presentes los mis thesoreros e ensayadores dellas, alos quales mando que quando fueren requeridos en este caso luego lo fagan e cunplan. Fecha veynte e nueue dias de enero año del nasçimiento del nuestro señor Ihesu Xpo de mill e quatroçientos e quarenta e dos anos. Yo el Rey. Yo el doctor Fernando Dias de Toledo, oydor e referendario del Rey e su secretario la fise escrevir por su mandado. Registrada.

4

Tordesillas, 10 March 1442

An ordinance on 'old' and 'new' *blancas*

BN, MS, 13259, fos. 314R — 318R

[314r] Sobre lo de la moneda vieja e nueva.

Don Juan por la graçia de dios Rey de Castilla, de Leon, de Toledo, de Gallisia, de Seuilla, de Cordoua, de Murçia, de Jaen, del Algarbe, de Algesira, e senor de Viscaya e de Molina, a los infantes duques condes ricos omes perlados maestres do las ordenes priores comendadores subcomendadores alcaydes de los castillos e casas fuertes e llanas, e a los alcaldes

alguasiles e otras justiçias de la mi casa e corte, e al conçejo
alcaldes merino regidores cavalleros escuderos c omes buenos
de la muy noble çibdat de Burgos cabeça de Castilla e mi
camara, et a todos los otros conçejos alcalldes alguasiles
regidores cavalleros escuderos e omes buenos de todas las
çibdades e villas e logares de los mis regnos e señorios, e a
todos los otros mis subditos e naturales de qual quier estado o
condiçion preheminençia o dignidat que sean, e a qual quier o
quales quier de vos a quien esta mi carta fuere mostrada o el
traslado della signado de escrivano publico, salut e graçia. Bien
sabeys que de pocos dias pasados aca yo fise çierta ordenança
en rason de la moneda de blancas que yo oue mandado labrar en
mis regnos, la qual ordenança vos oue enbiado mandar por mis
cartas que guardasedes e fisiesedes guardar espeçial mente en
que mande e ordene que todas las blancas nueuas que yo mande
labrar en todas las mis casas de moneda fuesen traydas a las
dichas mis casas e entregadas en ellas a los mis thesoreros para
que se fundiesen, e los que la touiesen la lleuasen o enbiasen a
las dichas casas de moneda dentro de çierto termino so çiertas
penas, e que la dicha moneda blanca asi por mi mandada labrar
non valiese nin se usase dende [314v] en adelante so çiertas
penas, e que yo mandase labrar en las dichas mis casas de
moneda nueue mente moneda de blancas a la ley e talla de las
dichas blancas viejas que el Rey mi padre e mi señor auia
mandado faser e labrar, segunt que esto e otras cosas larga
mente en la dicha mi ordenança e cartas por mi sobre ello
mandadas dar se contiene, lo qual todo he aqui por espeçificado
e declarado bien asi como si de palabra a palabra aqui fuese
puesto. Et agora por quanto los procuradores de las çibdades e
villas de los mis regnos que aqui estan comigo ayuntados me
presentaron e dieron sobre esto una su petiçion su tenor de la
qual es este que se sigue. Muy alto e muy exçelente prinçipe e
muy poderoso Rey e señor, los procuradores de las vuestras
çibdades e villas de los vuestros regnos besamos vuestras manos
e nos encomendados (*sic*) en vuestra alta merçet, la qual bien
sabe como por nos otros veyendo los grandes daños que por
causa desta moneda a vuestros regnos se recresçia le fue
suplicado que vuestra señoria pluguiese mandar ver en ello e
proveer por manera que los daños e inconvinientes que dello se
seguian çesasen. E vuestra señoria lo mando ver a çiertos del
vuestro muy alto consejo, et muy esclareçido señor a nos otros
es dicho que entre otras cosas que los dichos diputados que
vuestra señoria para ello dio dispusieron ordenaron mandar
labrar moneda de villon en çierta forma, de lo qual a nuestro

paresçer seria eñadir sobre un daño otro por muchas rasones. Lo primero por que moneda de villon non se puedé labrar syn aver en ello grandes costas lo qual era nesçesario de cargar sobre ella en manera que non se podria labrar tan alta mente como convenia para correr en su valor, mayormente si vuestra señoria en ello algo quisiese ganar. Lo segundo por que segunt las gentes estan escarmentadas todas la tomarian con reçelo de lo pasado, e non se osarian atreuer a vender nin conprar saluo a preçios muy caros, lo qual seria muy dañosa cosa ca por buena que ella fuese los pueblos [315r] non sabidores de estas cosas non podrian ser çertificados del su valor, asi que seria una grant confusion peor que la pasada. Lo terçero por que non es de dubdar que luego seria falsificada asi enlos regnos comarcanos como por ventura vuestros regnos, lo qual ha paresçido asas por manifiesta espiriençia, et non sola mente en vuestro tienpo mas aun en tienpos mas antiguos, e aun que los derechos pongan en ellos muy grandes penas la cobdiçia desordenada fase a los omes atreuer e seria dar causa de error a muchos. Por ende muy excelente señor muy omill mente suplicamos a vuestra muy alta señoria que le plega mandar que non se labre la tal moneda en ninguna manera, pues ay asas de la que el senor Rey vuestro padre de gloriosa memoria mando labrar como de la vuestra, et si por aventura esta nueva non es de tanta ley como la otra, que vuestra merçet lo mande poner su preçio rasonable et con aquesto vuestros pueblos ternan con que pagar vuestros derechos e podran eso mesmo entresi negoçiar conprando e vendiendo. E si vuestra altesa acordare de mandar labrar paresçenos que deue ser de oro e de plata fina, lo qual a nuestro ver es muy grant seruiçio vuestro e onor de vuestra corona e grant provecho de vuestros regnos. Et muy alto señor dios todo poderoso ensalçe vuestro real estado a su seruiçio. Por ende yo mande ver e platicar sobre todo ello ante mi en el mi consejo, presentes la regna doña maria mi muy cara e muy amada muger, e el Rey don Juan de Navarra mi muy caro e muy amado primo, et el prinçipe don Enrrique mi muy caro e muy amado fijo primo genito heredero, e el infante don Enrrique maestre de Santiago mi muy caro e muy amado primo, e el almirante don Fadrique mi primo, et los condes e perlados e ricos omes e otros grandes e cavalleros e doctores del mi consejo que aqui comigo estan llamados, e presentes otrosi para ello los mis contadores mayores e los sobre dichos procuradores de mis regnos. E todo ello bien visto e alternado e platicado, fue acordado e concluydo en el dicho mi consejo, de acuerdo e consejo de los sobre dichos, ser muy conplidero ami seruiçio [315v] et a pro e bien publico e comun

de mis regnos e sennorios e de mis subditos e naturales, e para
quitar e evitar los escandalos e daños o otros inconvinientes que
la espirlençia ha mostrado e demuestra que se han seguido e
podrian seguir de la dicha ordenança si aquella se ouiese de
guardar e de executar, por muchas legitimas e euidentes rasones
e motivos que en el dicho mi consejo fueron dichos apuntados
tractados e platicados, que la dicha ordenança deuia e deue ser
hemendada e mejorada en quanto tanne a la moneda de blancas
por mi mandada labrar, segunt que por los dichos procuradores
me era suplicado. E esto en las cosas siguientes: lo primero que
por escusar los inconuinientes que dello se podria seguir non
conplia a mi seruiçio de mandar labrar moneda de blancas nin
otra moneda de villon en ningun tienpo syn acuerdo de los
procuradores de mis rregnos, que bastava e basta la moneda de
blancas que era mandada labrar, asi por el Rey don Enrrique mi
padre e mi señor que dios de santo parayso commo despues por
mi en uno con la moneda de oro e plata que yo avia mandado e
mandase labrar, e que para labrar la dicha moneda de plata los
dichos procuradores de mis rregnos entendian dar manera por
que mis rregnos me siruiesen e ella se labrase por mi mandado
tanta e tal e en tal manera qual cumpliese a mi seruiçio e apro e
bien comun de los dichos mis regnos. Lo segundo que se non
desfisiesen la moneda de blancas que yo mandara labrar nin se
troxiese nin leuase a las mis casas dela moneda como por la
dicha mi ordenança e cartas por mi sobre ello dadas se
contiene, mas que yo mandase faser e fuese fecho verdadero
ensay dello presentes algunos del mi consejo e los procuradores
de los dichos mis regnos por que paresçiese e fuese sabida la ley
e verdadero valor della. E que yo devia mandar e mandase que
corriese en mis regnos libre mente e syn embargo nin contrario
alguno la dicha moneda de blancas que yo asi mande labrar,
poniendola e tasandola en su justo e verdadero valor e preçio e
quantia que fuere fallado por el dicho ensay, que segunt la
verdadera ley della valia e deuia ser puesta e tasada al respecto e
egualdad de la dicha moneda vieja que el dicho Rey mi señor e
mi padre mando faser e labrar por [316r] que mis regnos e
subditos e naturales dellos non rescibiesen daño alguno, e que
aquella corriese e andouiese en los dichos mis rregnos libre
mente commo suso dicho es en uno con la moneda de blancas
que el dicho Rey mi padre e mi señor mando labrar que es de
buena e conplida ley, por que amas las dichas monedas cada
una en su grado e verdadero valor andouiesen e corriesen en los
mis regnos e ouiese abasto de buena moneda de las monedas de
oro e plata e los mantenimientos e mercadurias e cosas tornasen

a su primero estado e valor en que era antes que yo mandase labrar la dicha moneda de blancas e non se encaresçiesen nin se alçasen nin pujasen en tan grandes e desaguisados preçios commo despues aca avian pujado e subido e subian e pujauan de cada dia por causa de la dicha moneda de blancas que yo asi mande labrar non ser de tanta e tan alta ley como la moneda de blancas que el dicho Rey mi padre e mi señor mando labrar e fue labrada por su mandado como dicho es. Et que fasiendose asy non çesarian nin se enbargarian los meneos e mercadurias e el dar e el tomar e los otros contractos en mis regnos e entre mis subditos e naturales dellos et asi mesmo de los estrangeros que a ellos viniesen, como por espiriençia paresçia que cesaua e se enbargaua por la dicha causa. Otrosi que cada uno pudiese canbiar e trocar libre mente e tener canbios en la mi corte e en las çibdades e villas e logares de mis regnos asi realengos como abadengos e ordenes e behetrias e otros señorios e con quales quier personas que quisieren syn pena alguna asi moneda de oro como de plata et asi mesmo la dicha moneda de blancas, non cometiendo nin fasiendo en ello fraude nin arte nin engaño alguno mas usando dello bien e fielmente segunt los derechos quieren, non enbargantes quales quier merçedes que yo ouiese fecho de los cambios a quales quier personas asi de la mi corte e de algunas çibdades e villas e logares de mis regnos en qual quier manera, las quales yo devia revocar como aquellas que fueren fechas en mi deseruiçio e en daño de la cosa publica de mis regnos, e que syn embargo dellas todos ouiesen libertad e libre facultad de poder cambiar e trocar e tener canbios syn pena e syn enbargo alguno segund las leyes de mis regnos por mi fechas e ordenadas en este [316v] caso a petiçion de los procuradores dellos lo quieren e mandan. Por lo qual yo veyendo el dicho consejo en esta parte ser bueno e sano e muy conplidero a mi seruiçio e a mis regnos, mande faser e fue fecho por mi mandado el dicho ensay en la mi corte dentro en los mis palaçios donde yo agora esto en esta mi villa de Tordesillas por çiertos mis ensayadores de las casas de la moneda de mis regnos, presentes a ello çiertos perlados e cavalleros e docthores del mi consejo e los mis contadores mayores e los dichos procuradores. Et fue fallado que el justo valor de cada una de las dichas blancas que yo asi mande labrar segunt la verdadera ley della egualada e conparada a la dicha moneda de blancas fecha por el dicho Rey mi padre, e avido verdadero e derecho respecto e acatamiento a ella, era e es dos cornados cada blanca e aun mas. Por lo qual yo queriendo que en mis regnos corra e ande buena e verdadera moneda e en su justo e derecho e verdadero valor por que las mercadurias e mantenimientos e otras cosas que se ouiesen de vender e conprar se vendan e conpren por su derecho e justo prcçio e valor et ellas tornen e sean redusidas a los preçios que primera mente valian antes e al tienpo que yo mande faser e labrar la dicha moneda de blancas, et asi mesmo corra en mis regnos la moneda de oro e plata a los preçios que a esa sason corria e se non aya de encaresçer ni alçar nin pujar en mayores preçios la dicha moneda de oro e plata nin los mantenimientos e mercadurias nin las otras cosas, fue e es mi merçed de non mandar labrar nuevamente moneda de blancas nin entiendo mandar labrar otra moneda alguna de villon syn acuerdo de los procuradores de mis regnos, como dicho es, e de mandar e ordenar e mando e ordeno por la presente que corra e ande por mis regnos libre mente la dicha moneda de blancas fecha e mandada labrar por el dicho Rey mi señor e mi padre segunt e enel preçio e enla manera que fasta aqui ha corrido, es a saber a rason de tres cornados por una blanca e dos blancas por un mr, por quanto es çierto que segunt la verdadera ley e justo valor della deue andar e ser resçibida en mis [317r] regnos enel dicho preçio e tasaçion segunt que el dicho Rey mi Señor e mi padre la puso e ordeno, et asi mesmo que deue andar e corre e ande e corra en mis regnos la dicha mi moneda de blancas por mi mandado fecha e labrada, es a saber contando e tomando una blanca por dos cornados e tres blancas por un mr e non mas nin menos, pues se falla el dicho ensay que justa mente vale el dicho preçio e aun mas contandola e conparandola a la ley verdadera e justo valor de la dicha moneda vieja de blancas que el dicho Rey mi señor e mi padre mando labrar. E eso mesmo que cada uno pueda carmbiar e trocar e tener canbios libre e franca mente en mi corte e en las çibdades e villas e logares de mis regnos e con quales quier personas que quisieren syn pena alguna, asi moneda de oro como de plata et asi mesmo la dicha moneda de blancas asi la mandada labrar por el dicho Rey mi señor e mi padre como por mi enla manera que suso dicha es. Et que se fagan e guarden e cumplan todas las otras cosas sobre dichas asi acordadas e concluidas en el mi consejo e con los procuradores de mis regnos como susodicho es, non embargante la dicha mi ordenança e cartas sobre ello dadas e las penas en ellas contenidas nin las dichas merçedes nin quales quier mis cartas e previllejos sobre ello dadas nin otras quales quier que en contrario sean o ser puedan. Lo qual todo yo de mi çierta çiençia e propio motu e poderio real absoluto revoco e anullo en quanto es o podria ser contra lo suso dicho por mi agora ordenado e mandado por que asi cumple a mi seruiçio e al bien comun de mis regnos e para quitar e evitar dellos muchos escandalos e inconuinientes que fasiendose de otra guisa se podria seguir. Por que vos mando a todos e a cada uno de vos que lo guardades et cumplades e fagades guardar e conplir en todo e por todo segunt que en esta mi carta se contiene. Et non vayades nin pasedes nin consyntades yr nin pasar contra ello nin contra cosa alguna nin parte dello so pena de la mi merçet e de priuaçion de los ofiçios e de confiscaçion de los bienes [317v] de los que lo contrario fisieredes para la mi camara. Otrosi pues fue e es mi merçed de revocar e tornar la dicha mi moneda de blancas a su justo e verdadero valor por manera que la dicha moneda de blancas asi por mi mandado fecha e labrada es e deve ser avida por esa mesma moneda e desa mesma ley que la moneda de blancas quel dicho Rey mi padre e mi señor mando labrar, contando tres blancas de las que yo mande labrar por seys cornados que son un mr, las quales tres blancas corresponden en la ley e verdadero valor a dos blancas de la moneda de blancas fecha e mandada labrar por el dicho Rey mi señor e mi padre, e estas dos blancas valen seys cornados que son un mr como suso dicho es. Mi merçet es e mando que asi la moneda de oro e plata como los mantenimientos e mercadurias e todas las otras cosas que por causa de la mi moneda de blancas non ser de tan alta ley como la del dicho Rey mi padre se encaresçieron e subieron e pujaron despues que la yo mande labrar aca a mayores preçios de lo que valian antes e al tienpo que yo mande labrar la dicha moneda de blancas sean tornadas e redusidas e se tornen e reduscan e las fagades tornar e redusir a los mesmos preçios e valor en que andauan e corrian e valian antes e al tiempo que yo mandase labrar la dicha mi moneda de blancas, pues por la provision por mi fecha en rason de la dicha moneda çesa e deue çesar la cabsa de la dicha carestia e puja. Lo qual todo suso dicho mando a vos las dichas justiçias e a cada uno de vos que lo fagades asy pregonar por las plaças e mercados e otros logares acostumbrados de la mi corte e de todas las çibdades e villas e logares de mis regnos por pregonero e ante escriuano publico, por que venga a notiçia de todos e dello non podades nin puedan pretender ynorançia. Et mando a vos las dichas mis justiçias e a cada uno de vos que lo fagades asi guardar e conplir et a cada uno de vos que proçedades contra los que non quisieren tomar e resçebir la dicha mi moneda en el preçio e valor e tasaçion suso dicho e contra todos los otros que non quisieren guardar e conpiir lo suso dicho e cada cosa dello como contra aquellos que non obedesçen nin cunplen los mandamientos e ordenanças de [318r] su Rey e señor natural. Et mando sopena de la mi merçet e de dies mill mrs para la mi camara a quel quier escriuano publico que para esto fuere llamado que de ende al que vos la mostrare testimonio signado con su signo por que yo sepa como complides mi mandado. Dada en la villa de Tordesillas dies dias de março año del nasçimiento del nuestro señor Ihesu Xpo. de mill e quatroçientos e quarenta e dos años. Yo el Rey. Yo el docthor Fernan Dias de Toledo oydor e referendario del Rey e su secretario la fise escrevir por su mandado. Registrada.

5

Valladolid, 6 April 1442

An ordinance on the prices of gold coins and silver.

BN, MS, 13259, fos. 318R — 319R.

P. Del valor de la moneda de oro.
[318r] Don Juan por la graçia de dios Rey de Castilla de Leon de Toledo de Gallisia de Seuilla de Cordoua de Murçia de Jaen del Algarbe de Algesira e señor de Viscaya e de Molina. A los infantes duques condes perlados ricos omes maestres de las ordenes priores comendadores subcomendadores alcaydes de los castillos e casas fuertes e llanas, et a los alcaldes alguasiles e otras justiçias quales quier de la mi casa e corte e chançelleria, et a los mis adelantados e merinos, et al conçejo alcaldes merino regidores cavalleros escuderos e omes buenos de la muy noble çibdad de Burgos cabeça de Castilla mi camara, et a todos los otros conçejos alcaldes alguasiles merinos regidores cavalleros escuderos oficiales e omes buenos de todas las çibdades e villas e logares de los mis regnos e señorios asi realengos como abadengos e ordenes e behetrias et otros quales quier, e a todos los otros mis subditos e naturales de qual quier ley e estado o condiçion preheminençia o dignidad que sean, e a qual quier o quales quier de vos a quien esta mi carta fuere mostrada o el traslado della signado de escriuano publico, salut e gracia. Bien sabeys que por otra mi carta vos enbie notificar en como yo auia mandado faser ensay en la mi corte presentes çiertos del mi consejo, e los mis contadores mayores, e çiertos procuradores de las çibdades e villas de mis regnos que conmigo estan, de la mi

moneda de blancas que yo mande labrar. Et por que aquella non era de tanta ley como la moneda de blancas que el Rey don Enrrique mi padre e mi señor que dios de santo parayso mando labrar, yo queriendo redusir la dicha mi moneda a su justo valor della, auido respecto a la verdadera ley e justo valor de la moneda de blancas [318v] que agora corre en mis rregnos de la que el dicho Rey mi padre e mi señor mando labrar como dicho es, mande que valiesen tres blancas de la moneda mia que yo asy mande labrar como dos blancas de la moneda del dicho Rey mi padre, que son las dichas dos blancas un mr et que non valiesen mas nin menos, e vos enbie mandar que lo usasedes e guardasedes asy segunt mas largamente se contiene en çiertas mis cartas que en esta rason mande dar. Et agora por quanto a mi es fecha relaçion que despues de las dichas mis cartas se ha alçado la moneda del oro asy de doblas como de florines en mayores preçios de lo que de rason deue ser, de lo qual a mi viene deseruiçio e a mis regnos grant daño, por ende yo queriendo proueer sobre ello mande e encomende a çiertos del mi consejo que platicasen sobre ello con los mis contadores mayores e con los procuradores de las çibdades e villas de mis regnos que comigo estan porque yo pusiese e ordenase çierto e justo preçio e valor a la dicha moneda de oro e aquel fuese guardado e non variado. Los quales lo fisieron asy e ello bien visto e platicado yo con acuerdo de los sobre dichos, es mi merçet de mandar e ordenar e mando e ordeno por la presente que de aqui adelante las dichas mis doblas de la banda que yo mande labrar vala cada una dellas çient mrs e non mas, es a saber contando dos blancas por un mr de la moneda blanca del dicho Rey mi padre e tres blancas por un mr de la mi moneda de blancas. Et asy mesmo que vala el floryn de oro de aragon sesenta e çinco mrs e non mas, contando dos blancas por un mr de la moneda de blancas del dicho Rey mi padre e tres blancas por un mr de la dicha mi moneda de blancas. E quales quier que cambiaren las dichas monedas de oro sean tenudos de las tomar e resçebir a los dichos preçios e non mas nin menos, pero quando las ouieren ellos a dar es mi merçet que puedan ganar en cada dobla un mr e medio e en cada floryn un mr allende de los sobre dichos preçios, asi que puedan canbiar e dar la dobla a çiento e un mrs e medio e el floryn a sesenta e seys mrs e non menos. Otrosi que sean resçebidas las dichas doblas e florines en pago de qual quier debda a rason de los dichos çiento e un mrs e medio cada [319r] dobla e a rason de sesenta e seys mrs cada floryn segunt que los cambiadores las pueden dar segunt dicho es e non mas. Et otrosy que el marco de la plata de marcar de honse dineros e

seys granos de ley que non vala mas de quinientos e sesenta mrs.
E quales quier mercadores e cambiadores e otras quales quier
personas que ouieren de canbiar o tomar o dar en pago las
dichas monedas de oro e las tractar et asi mesmo conprar e
vender la dicha plata o la dar o tomar en pago sean tenudos de
guardar e guarden las dichas tasas e preçios en la manera que
suso dicha es, et de las non pasar nin quebrantar so pena que los
que lo contrario fisieren pierdan todas las monedas de oro e
plata que trocaren e cambiaren o tractaren o dieren en pago o
vendieren que paguen quatro tanto de lo suyo por cada ves que
lo contrario fesieren, de lo qual sea la meytad para la mi camara
e la otra meytad para el acusador. Por que vos mando que lo
guardedes e cumplades e fagades guardar e conplir asi en todo e
por todo segunt que en esta mi carta se contiene, e non vayades
nin pasedes nin consyntades yr nin pasar contre ello nin contra
parte dello en alguna manera, e que lo fagades asi pregonar en
la mi corte e en las plaças e logares acostumbrados de las
çibdades e villas e logares de mis rregnos e señorios por
pregonero e por escriuano publico por que venga a notiçia de
todos e dello non podades nin puedan pretender ynorançia, e
que vos las dichas justiçias executedes, e fagades executar las
dichas penas en aquellos que en ellas incurriesen, e fagades
poner de manifiesto lo que pertenesçe a la mi camara para
recudir con ello a quien vos yo enbiare mandar. Et los unos nin
los otros non fagades ende al por alguna manera so pena de la mi
merçet e de privaçion de los ofiçios e de confiscaçion de los
bienes de los que lo contrario fisieredes para la mi camara. Et
mando so la dicha pena a qual quier escrivano publico que para
esto fuere llamado que de ende al que la mostrare testimonio
signado con su signo por que yo sepa en como complides mi
mandado. Dada en la villa de Valladolid seys dias de abril año
del nasçimiento del nuestro señor Ihesu Xpo. de mill e
quatroçientos e quarenta e dos años. Yo el Rey. Yo el doctor
Fernando Dias de Toledo ref *(termina aqui sin dar las últimas*
palabras de la fórmula acostumbrada: referendario del rey e su
secretario la fize escrevir por su mandado. Registrada.)

6

Arevalo, 16 February 1468

The farm of the mint of Murcia for one year from 1 January 1468.

AGS, EMR, Leg. 519

[1r] Casa de moneda Murcia.

Los derechos pertenesçientes al Rey nuestro señor de la casa de la moneda de Murçia deste año que començo primero dia de enero de 1468 años.

P. Arrendaronse estos dichos derechos pertenesçientes al dicho señor Rey de la dicha casa de la moneda de Murçia a bueltas de las otras casas del reyno por un año que començo primero dia de enero deste año de 1468 años a Alfonso Gonsales de Guadalajara thesorero de la casa de la moneda de Avila en çierto presçio con ciertas condiciones, entre las quales se contiene que diese rrepartimiento de las dichas casas. El qual dicho Alfonso Gonzalez dio el dicho rrepartimiento firmado de su nombre et señalado de los contadores del dicho señor Rey que tyene el escrivano de las rrentas, por el qual paresçe que rrepartio en esta dicha casa de moneda de Murcia çiento e dies mill mrs, segund mas largamente se contiene en la postura de las dichas casas que esta antes desto.

P. Et despues Termo Doria genoues abitante en la çibdad de Toledo fiso çierta puja en todas las dichas casas con las dichas condiçiones e con condiçion que diese rrepartimiento de la dicha puja sobre las dichas casas o sobre qual quier o quales quier dellas quel quisyese el qual dicho Termo Doria dio cl dicho rrepartimiento firmado de su nombre et senalado de los dichos contadores por el qual paresçe que en esta dicha casa non rrepartio cosa alguna et asy quedo la dicha casa en el dicho presçio de los dichos 110,000 mrs.

P. Et despues desto en la villa de Areualo 16 dias del mes de febrero [1v] del dicho año de 1468 años ante Alfonso de Quintanilla e Luys de Mesa e Françisco Ferrandes de Sevilla e Juan Rodrigues de Baeça contadores en logar de Juan de Bivero et Pedrarias de Avila e Pedro de Fuentiveros e Alvar Gomes de Çibdad Real contadores mayores del dicho señor Rey e de su consejo estando presente el thesorero Alfonso

Sanchez de Logroño asentados en el estrado de las rrentas del
dicho señor Rey paresçio presente don Yuda Bienveniste
vesino de la çibdad de Segovia et dixo quel por faser
seruiçio al dicho señor Rey que pujaua e pujo mas en esta
dicha casa quarenta mill mrs çerrados por que le sean dados
de prometido el quarto dellos et los dichos contadores dixeron
que le rreçebian e rreçibieron la dicha puja con las dichas
condiçiones e prometido. Et cargados los dichos 40,000 mrs
de la dicha puja esta la dicha casa en 150,000 mrs.

7

Segovia, 26 October 1469
*Copy of Henry IV's grant of the treasureship of the mint of
Toro to Rodrigo de Ulloa, given in Madrid on 20 March 1469.*
AGS, EMR, Leg. 519.

[1r] Casa de moneda Çibdad de Toro.

Rodrigo de Ulloa contador mayor del Rey nuestro señor e del su consejo e su tesorero mayor de la casa de la moneda de la çibdad de Toro.

Mostro una carta del dicho señor Rey escripta en papel e
firmada de su nombre fecha en esta guisa.

Este es traslado de una carta del Rey nuestro señor escripta en
papel e firmada de su nombre su thenor de la qual es este que se
sigue. Don Enrrique por la graçia de dios Rey de Castilla de
Leon de Toledo de Gallisia de Sevilla de Cordova de Murçia
de Jahen del Algarbe de Algesiras de Gibraltar e señor de
Viscaya e de Molina, por algunas justas legitimas cabsas que a
ello me mueuven complideras ami seruiçio e al pro e bien
comun de mis rregnos e subditos e naturales dellos e
acresentamiento de mis rrentas e derechos e para nobleçer e
acreçentar la noble çibdad de Toro, es mi merçed e por
esta mi carta ordeno e mando e quiero que de aqui adelante para
sempre jamas aya una mi casa de moneda en la dicha çibdad
de Toro en la qual se pueda labrar e labren quales quier
monedas de oro e plata e vellon de la ley e talla e segund e en la

manera que yo he mandado e ordenado e mandare o ordenare
que se labren en las dichas mis casas de monedas, e que aya en
ella un thesorero e alcaldes e alguasil e escriuano e guardas e
ensayador e fundidor e tallador e blanqueador e capatases, e los
otros oficiales e obreros e monederos que yo tengo hordenado e
mandado que aya en las otras mis casas de monedas, los quales
puedan usar e gosen de los priuillejos e franquesas e libertades e
jurediçion e esençiones de que gosan e pueden e deuen gosar
los ofiçiales e obreros e monederos de las otras mis casas de
moneda, espeçialmente los de la mi casa de la noble çibdad
de Segouia. E por esta mi carta mando al conçejo alcaldes
alguasil rregidores caualleros e escuderos ofiçiales e omes
buenos dela dicha çibdad de Toro, asy a los que agora son
como a los que seran de aqui adelante, que fagan e den logar que
sea fecha en ella la dicha casa de moneda e se puedan labrar e
labren en ella las dichas mis monedas e ayan en ellas los dichos
mis oficiales e obreros e monederos en la forma susodicha. E
por faser bien e merçed a Rodrigo de Ulloa mi contador mayor
e del mi consejo por los muchos e buenos e leales e señalados
seruiçios que me ha fecho e fase de cada dia, espeçial mente
en los escandalos e movimientos de mis rregnos en los quales yo
he fallado en el mucha lealtad e fidelidad, e en alguna emienda e
satysfaçion dellos e de los peligros [1v] e gastos e costas que
ha padesçido en mi seruiçio, por esta mi carta le fago
merçed que sea mi tesorero de la dicha mi casa de moneda de
la dicha çibdad de Toro para en toda su vida, e que el en mi
nombre e por mi abtoridad pueda poner e nombrar e ponga e
nombre los dichos alcaldes e alguasil e escrivano e guardas e
ensayador e entallador e fundidor e blancario (sic) e capatases,
e los otros ofiçiales e obreros e monederos que oviere de aver
en la dicha mi casa de la moneda, los quel quisiere e entendiere
que cumple ami seruiçio tanto que aquello sea fasta en
numero de (blank) oficiales obreros e monederos. E que cada
que aquellos que por el o por su logar a mi me fueren nombrados
pasaren desta presente vida pueda poner e nombrar e ponga e
nombre otros en su logar, e sy algunos delinquieren en los dichos
officios e fallaren non ser sufiçientes para ellos los pueda
quitar e mudar e poner otros en su logar fasta quel dicho numero
de los dichos (blank) ofiçiales, los quales obreros e monederos
pueda tomar e nombrar e tomen e nombren en la dicha çibdad
de Toro e su tierra e en otras quales quier çibdades e villas e
logares e señorios de mis rregnos e señorios e en sus tierras
quel mas quisiere e entendiere que cumple a mi serviçio, los
quales todos es mi merçed que gosen de todos los previllejos e

otras esençiones e otras libertades e franquesas e ymmunidades
de que pueden e han de e deuen gosar los ofiçiales e obreros e
monederos de las otras mis casas de moneda de las çibdades
de Burgos e Segouia e de las otras mis casas de moneda, e que
los dichos alcaldes e alguasil e ofiçiales de la dicha mi casa de
moneda de la dicha çibdad de Toro tenga otra tanta juridiçion
e poderio segund e por la forma e manera que lo tiene los
alcaldes e alguasil e oficiales de las dichas casas de Burgos e
Segouia, e asy mesmo todos los dichos ofiçiales de la dicha
casa tengan su cabildo e todas las otras preheminençias que
tienen los dichos ofiçiales de las dichas casas de Burgos e
Segouia de todo bien e conplidamente en guisa que les non
menguan ende cosa alguna. E por faser mas bien e merçed al
dicho Rodrigo de Ulloa mi contador mayor e del mi consejo por
los muchos e buenos e leales seruiçios que me ha fecho e fase
de cada dia e en alguna emienda e rremuneraçion dellos e de
todo lo suso dicho, por esta dicha mi carta desde agora le fago
merçed graçia e donaçion de todos los derechos que a mi
pertenesçieren e pertenesçer devieren de todas las dichas
monedas de oro e plata e vellon que se labrare en la dicha mi
casa de moneda de la dicha çibdad de Toro para que los aya e
lieua por suyos e como suyos e para sy e para en toda su vida
bien e complidamente e que non sean tenudos de dar nin den
cuenta nin rrason dellos a mi nin a mis contadores mayores nin a
otra persona alguna. E mando e do liçençia e facultad al
dicho Rodrigo de Ulloa mi contador mayor e del mi consejo
para que pueda labrar e faser labrar en la dicha mi casa de
moneda todas las monedas de oro e plata e vellon e cada una
dellas a la ley e talla e con aquellos señales e figuras e letras
que yo he mandado e mandare que se labren en las otras mis
casas, las quales mando que valan en todos mis rregnos e
señorios a los presçios e segund e en la manera que valen e
valieren las otras monedas que se han labrado e labraren en las
otras dichas mis casas de monedas, e mando a los dichos
ofiçiales e obreros e monederos [2r] que por el dicho Rodrigo
de Ulloa en mi nombre fueren nombrados e puestos en la dicha
mi casa que labren en ella las dichas monedas e cada una dellas
de la dicha ley e talla e señales e figuras e letras e rrecudan e
fagan rrecodir con todos los dichos derechos que a mi
pertenesçen de las dichas monedas al dicho Rodrigo de Ulloa
mi contador mayor e del mi consejo para en toda su vida commo
dicho es bien e complidamente, pues que yo le fago merçed
dellos. E seguro e prometo en mi fe rreal de non rreuocar esta
merçed que yo fago al dicho Rodrigo de Ulloa de la dicha

tesoreria e de los dichos ofiçios e asy mismo de los dichos
derechos mas que le sea firme e valedera para en toda su vida
como dicho es. E mando a los ynfantes duques condes
marqueses rricos omes maestres de las ordenes priores e a los
del mi consejo e oydores de la mi audiencia e al mi justiçia
mayor e a los mis adelantados e merinos e a los alcaldes e
alguasiles e otros jueses de la mi casa e corte e chancilleria e a
los comendadores e subcomendadores alcaydes de los castillos
e casas fuertes e llanas, e a todos los conçejos corregidores e
alcaldes e alguasiles rregidores caualleros escuderos e
ofiçiales e omes buenos de la dicha çibdad de Toro e de
todas las otras çibdades e villas e logares de los mis rregnos e
señorios, e a quales quier mis vasallos subditos e naturales de
qual quier ley estado o condiçion preheminençia o dignidad
que sean que guarden e cumplan e fagan guardar e complir todo
lo en esta mi carta contenido e cada cosa e parte dello en todo e
por todo segund que en ella se contiene, e non vayan nin pasen
nin consientan yr nin pasar contra ello nin contra parte dello
agora nin de aqui adelante en alguna manera, e traten las dichas
monedas que se labraren en la dicha mi casa de moneda de la
dicha çibdad de Toro en dar e en tomar a los presçios e
segund e en la manera que trataren las dichas monedas labradas
en las dichas mis casas de monedas, e fagan guardar e guarden a
todos los dichos ofiçiales o obreros e monederos que por el
dicho Rodrigo de Ulloa fueren nombrados e puestos en la dicha
casa fasta en el numero susodicho todas las graçias e
merçedes franquesas e libertades e esençiones e preuillejos
e preeminençias e perrogativas que son e deven ser guardadas
a los dichos ofiçiales e obreros e monederos de las dichas
casas de Burgos e Segouia e de las otras dichas mis casas de
moneda, e dexen e consientan a los dichos alcaldes e alguasil de
la dicha casa usar de la dicha su juvediçion. A los quales por
esta dicha mi carta do poder e facultad para ello e mando a los
mis contadores mayores que en sy (sic) el traslado desta mi
carta e lo pongan e asientan en los mis libros e den e tornnen el
original sobre escripto dellos al dicho Rodrigo de Ulloa, e
pongan e asientan en los dichos mis libros por ofiçiales e
obrreros e monederos de la dicha mi casa a las personas quel
dicho Rodrigo de Ulloa nombrare e el enbiare desir por sus
copias e çedulas firmadas de su nombre, e otrosy den e libren a
los dichos ofiçiales e obreros e monederos mi carta de
preuillojo sobre la dicha rrason en el thenor e segund e por la
forma que lo tienen los ofiçiales e obreros e monederos de las
dichas casas de monedas de las dichas çibdades de Burgos e

Segovia, e les den e librȩn las dichas mis cartas et sobrecartas que sobrȩllo les complieren e menester ouieren para que les [2v] sean guardadas todas las dichas cosas susodichas e cada una dellas. El qual previllejo mando al mi chançeller e notarios e a los otros mis ofiçiales que estan a la tabla de los mis sellos que libren e pasen e sellen et los unos nin los otros non fagades nin fagan ende al por alguna manera so pena de la mi merçed e de priuaçion de los ofiçios e de confiscaçion de los bienes de los que lo contrario fisieren para la mi camara e demas por qual quier o quales quier por quien fincare de lo asy faser e complir mando al ome que les esta mi carta mostrare o su traslado signado de escrivano publico que los enplase que parescan ante mi en la mi corte do quier que yo sea del dia que los enplasare fasta quinse dias primeros siguientes so la dicha pena, so la qual mando a qual quier escrivano publico que para esto fuere llamado que de ende al que la mostrare testimonio signado con su signo por que yo sepa en como se cumple mi mandado. Dada en la noble e leal villa de Madrid a veynte dias de março año del nasçimiento de nuestro señor Ihesu Xpo. de mill e quatroçientos e sesenta e nueue años. Yo el Rey. Yo Juan de Ouiedo secretario del Rey nuestro señor la fise escreuir por su mandado. Fecho e sacado fue este traslado de la dicha carta del dicho señor Rey en la çibdad de Segouia veynte e seys dias del mes de otubre año del nasçimiento de nuestro señor Ihesu Xpo. de mill e quatroçientos e sesenta e nueue años.

8

Alcalá de Guadaira, 9 August 1469

Henry IV orders the resumption of the minting of gold and billon coins.

AGS, EMR, Leg. 519.

[1r] Para que labren todas las casas de moneda del rregno.

Traslado de la carta del Rey que se dio para que todas las casas de moneda del regno labren moneda de oro e vellon e blancas en çierta forma e manera en esta carta contenida.

Don Enrrique por la gracia de dios Rey de Castilla de Leon de
Toledo de Gallisia de Seuilla de Cordoua de Murçia de Iahen
del Algarbe de Algesira de Gibraltar et señor de Viscaya e de
Molina, al conçejo alcaldes alguasil rregidores caualleros
escuderos ofiçiales e omes buenos de la muy noble çibdad
de Burgos cabeça de Castilla mi camara, e de todas las otras
çibdades e villas e logares de los mis rregnos e señorios, e a
los mis thesoreros e ensayadores e otros ofiçiales de las mis
casas de moneda salud e graçia. Bien sabedes como por otras
mis cartas vos enbie faser saber que por la grand confusion que
avia en la lauor de la moneda que se fasia en las mis casas a
suplicaçion de los procuradores de mis rregnos yo avia
mandado çesar toda la lauor de las dichas mis casas de
moneda fasta tanto que yo con acuerdo de los del mi consejo e de
los procuradores diese orden de la forma en que se devia labrar
la dicha moneda. Et agora sabed que por muchas de las
çibdades de mis rregnos me es suplicado que yo mande labrar
moneda en las dichas casas, por que disen que se pierde todo el
trabto de las mercadorias de las dichas çibdades, por lo qual
yo mande a los del mi consejo e a los dichos procuradores de los
dichos mis rregnos que conmigo estauan que fablasen e
platicasen sobresto. Por los quales ha seydo fablado e platicado
por muchas e diversas veses sobrello, e para lo platicar fueron
llamados thesoreros de las dichas casas e ensayadores e
ofiçiales de la dicha moneda, e senaladamente agora en esta
dicha çibdad de Sevilla fue mucho visto e platicado con las
personas que dello mas podian saber. E fallose que segund el
estado que en mis rregnos por agora esta no se podia luego a se
dar complidamente orden alguna en la lauor de la dicha
moneda, pero que por el presente para euitar mayores males se
deuia tomar alguna media via como la dicha moneda se labrase
con el menor daño que se pudiese. Lo qual todo visto e
platicado [1v] como quier que en ello ovo algunas diversidades
pero por la mayor e mas sana parte fue determinado e acordado
que la dicha moneda se devia labrar por el presente fasta tanto
que mejor e mas complidamente se podiese tomar en la forma
siguiente. Que se labren enrriques de ley de veynte e tres
quilates un grano mas o otro menos e de çinquenta pieças un
tomin mas o otro menos en marco. E otrosy que se labren
quartos de a çinquenta e quatro granos e de talla de setenta
pieças el marco. Otrosy fue acordado por que la gente pobre
padesçia grand trabajo por mengua de moneda menuda et por
esto se devia labrar moneda de blancas de ley de honse granos e
de talla de çiento e sesenta pieças el marco, o que de la una

parte tenga un castillo e de la otra un leon, e diga en las letras de
enderredor lo que dise en las blancas que agora corren en mis
rregnos que cada uno vale tres cornados, et que en la lauor desta
moneda de blancas yo no aya de aver derecho ninguno et que
desta moneda menuda se labre el diesmo de los marcos que se
labrase de quartos en non mas nin menos de manera que
ninguno pueda labrar quartos que non labre el diesmo de lo que
labrare de quartos de moneda menuda e non mas nin menos, por
que en la lauor desta moneda menuda se fallan muchos
ynconvenientes et solamente se sufre de faser por la nesçesidad
de los pobres. Et que en el labrar de lo suso dicho se guarde las
leyes e formas que por mis ordenamientos que para labrar las
monedas pasadas yo he dado a la dicha casa. Lo qual todo por
mi visto mande que se fisiese e cumpliese como de suso es
contenido. Por que vos mando a todos e a cada uno de vos que
en todas esas çibdades e villas e logares donde ay casas que
labrades e fagades labrar las dichas monedas de la ley e talla en
la forma suso contenida. E es mi merçed que sy en qual quier
tiempo yo mandare çesar de labrar las dichas monedas e
algund oro o villon estouiere en la dicha casa de moneda para
labrar que todavia non enbargante el dicho mandamiento se
labre e fasta ser labrado non se entienda aver efecto el dicho
çeso. Et non consintades que persona nin personas algunas
labren las dichas monedas de oro e metal de menor ley e talla de
la de suso contenida. Et por esta mi carta mando que vos las
dichas mis justicias proçedades contra las tales personas con
aquellas penas en que caen e incurren los que fasen moneda
falsa, e non lo dexades [2r] de asi faser e conplir e executar. Et
por que mejor pueda ser guardado todo lo suso dicho e en la
dicha moneda non se pueda faser fraude nin baxa alguna mi
merçed e voluntad es que en cada una de las dichas mis casas
de moneda sea puesta una persona fiel sabia e discreta en el
dicho ofiçio de la dicha moneda, e tenga cargo de ver
rrequeryr e rreconosçer la ley e talla de la dicha moneda que
en las dichas casas se fisiere, e de orden e rremedio como en ella
non se faga fraude nin colusion alguna nin baxa de la dicha ley e
talla e fasta que la tal presona la delibre de ley e talla non se
pueda labrar ni delibrar la dicha moneda. Pero si no quisiere ser
presente a ello seyendo rrequerido que se pueda faser e fagan
syn el. Las quales dichas personas mando que sean nombradas e
diputadas por Rodrigo de Ulloa e el liçençiado de Cibdad
Rodrigo mis contadores mayores e del mi consejo que son de los
procuradores de mis rregnos, et por el dottor de Madrid asi
mismo mi procurador e del mi consejo. Et mando a los dichos

mis thesoreros que fagan dar lo que fuere menester para orquilla
e para los otros rreparos de las dichas casas e les sea
rresçebido en cuenta por los mis contadores segund se gastare
por ante los mis escriuanos de las dichas casas segund se
acostumbro faser en los tiempos pasados. Et otrosy mando que
los dichos mis thesoreros e ofiçiales de las dichas mis casas de
moneda ayan e lieuen los derechos e salarios acostumbrados,
segund que lo tengo mandado e ordenado por mis cartas e
ordenamientos lo qual mando a los dichos mis thesoreros que lo
den e paguen segund que lo han de uso e de costumbre. E mando
questa mi carta sea pregonada e publicada en la mi corte con
trompetas por que todas las personas lo sepan e non puedan
pretender ynorançia. Et los unos nin los otros non fagades nin
fagan ende al por alguna manera so pena de la mi merçed e de
privaçion de los ofiçios e de confiscaçion de los bienes de
los que lo contrario fisieren para la mi camara e fisco, e demas
mando al ome que lo esta mi carta mostrare que los enplase que
parescan ante mi en la mi corte do quier que yo sea del dia que
les enplasare fasta quinse dias pasados siguientes so la dicha
pena. Sobre lo qual mando a qual quier escribano publico que
para esto fuere llamado que de ende al que gela mostrare
testimonio sygnado con su sygno por que yo sepa [2v] en como
se cumple mi mandado. Dada en la villa de Alcala de Guadayra
a nueve dias de agosto año del nasçimiento del nuestro
señor Ihesu Xpo. de mill e quatrocientos e sesenta e nueve
años. Yo el Rey. Yo Juan de Ouiedo secretario del Rey
nuestro señor la fise escrevir por su mandado. Registrada.

9

25 August 1469

A secret directive from Henry IV to the officials of the mint at Seville.

AGS, EMR, Leg. 519

Casa de moneda   Traslado del aluala del Rey que se dio
de Sevilla.   para que la casa de moneda de Sevilla
                        labre secretamente moneda de oro e

villon segund que se ha labrado en las
casas de Segovia e Jaen.

Yo el Rey fago saber a vos el mi thesorero e ensayadores e
escrivano e maestro de valança e otros ofiçiales de la mi
casa de la moneda de la muy noble et muy leal çibdad de
Sevilla, e a cada uno de vos, como por otra mi carta firmada de
mi nombre e sellada con mi sello e sobre escripta e librada de los
mis contadores mayores vos enbie mandar que labrasedes en
esa dicha mi casa de moneda moneda de enrriques de ley de
veynte e tres quilates un grano mas o menos e de çinquenta
pieças un tomin mas o otro menos en marco, e moneda de
quartos de ley de çinquenta e quatro granos e de setenta
pieças al marco, e moneda de blancas de onse granos e de
çiento e sesenta pieças en talla, segund que esto e otras
cosas mas largamente se contiene e es contenido en la dicha mi
carta. Et agora sabed que por algunas cabsas que a ello me
mueven conplideras a mi serviçio, mande dar este mi aluala
para vos e para cada uno de vos, por el qual vos mando que luego
que con ella fueredes rrequeridos secretamente, syn que ninguno
de vos lo diga nin descubra a persona alguna so pena de
privacion de los ofiçios e de confiscaçion de los bienes,
tengades en el labrar de las dichas monedas de oro e vellon la
forma syguiente. Que fagades ante todas cosas notificar e
publicar en las çibdades de Jahen e de Segouia o en qual quier
dellas la mi carta general que de suso fase mençio por donde
yo mando labrar la dicha moneda, e asy fecha la dicha
notefiçaçion que vos los dichos mis ensayadores o qual quier
de vos por ante escrivano de la dicha mi casa de moneda fagades
cada dos meses un ensay de la ley de las monedas de oro e villon
que se labrare en las mis casas de la moneda de las [1v] dichas
çibdades de Jahen e Segovia o de qual quier dellas, e despues
que fuere fecha la primera labrança de moneda de oro e vellon
que se fisiere despues de la notificaçion de la dicha carta et asy
mesmo el mi maestro e guardas de la dicha mi casa por ante
dicho mi escrivano fagan leuada de la talla de la dicha moneda
de oro e vellon que se labrare en las dichas mis casas de moneda
de Jahen e Segovia o qual quier dellas despues de la
publiçaçion e notefiçaçion de la dicha carta segund dicho
es, e de la ley e talla que por el dicho ensay e leuada fallardes que
se labrare la dicha moneda de oro e vellon vos los dichos mis
thesoreros e ofiçiales labresedes e fagades labrar las dichas
monedas de oro e vellon que asy por la dicha mi carta vos yo
enbio mandar que labrasedes. E esto se entienda que de la ley e

talla que la fallardes de dos en dos meses la labredes los dichos
dos meses, e asy cada dos meses fecho el dicho ensay e leuada
por la tal ley e leuada labredes los dichos dos meses. Lo qual vos
mando que asy fagades e cumplades non embargante la dicha mi
carta e todo lo en ella contenido, nin embargante los
ordenamentos nin otros quales quier cartas nin alualaes que yo
aya dado, nin otras quales quier cosas que en contrario de lo
suso dicho sean o ser puedan, nin de las penas en los dichos
ordenamientos e cartas e alualaes contenidas, las quales vos yo
por este mi aluala alço e quito e vos do liçencia e abtoridad
para labrar e faser labrar las dichas monedas de oro e vellon de
la dicha ley e talla e segund e por lo forma e manera que en este
dicho mi aluala se contiene, por que asy entiendo que cumple a
mi seruiçio e al bien comun e trabto de la dicha çibdad de
Sevilla, pero es mi merçed e mando que fecho por vosotros
cada dos meses el dicho ensay e leuada por donde asy avedes de
labrar como dicho es e pase por fee antel dicho mi escriuano de
la dicha mi casa e los otros mis ofiçiales della segund que por
mi antes desto esta ordenado e mandado. Lo qual todo vos
mando que fagades e [2r] cumplades segund e en la manera que
vos lo embio mandar so las penas en la dicha mi carta
contenidas, las quales mando que sean esecutadas en quales
quier personas que lo contrario fisieren et non fagades ende al.
Fecha veynte e çinco dias de agosto año del nasçimiento
del nuestro señor Ihesu Xpo. de mill e quatroçientos e
sesenta e nueve años. Yo el Rey.

P. Fue sobre escripto para el dicho thesorero e ofiçiales que lo
vean e cumplan en esta guisa. Thesorero e ensayadores e
maestro de balança e otros ofiçiales de la casa de la moneda
de la muy noble e leal çibdad de Sevilla, e a cada uno de vos, e
las otras personas a quienes este aluala del Rey nuestro señor
desta otra parte escripto atanne o atanner puede en qual quier
manera, ved este dicho aluala desta otra parte escripto e
guardadlo e complidlo en todo e por todo segund que en el se
contiene e su señoria por el vos lo embia mandar.

APPENDIX B: TABLES

General Notes

1. Fifteenth-century Castilian accounts express monetary data in *maravedíes* and, where necessary, in 'fractional' moneys such as *dineros* and *cornados*. In order to avoid confusions arising from the averaging out of data and from the use of such fractional moneys, figures in the appendices are given in *maravedíes* and the decimal parts thereof.

2. Figures given in italics are in *maravedíes viejos;* all others are in *maravedíes nuevos.*

3. Unless otherwise stated, all data are from accounts in the cathedral archive of Burgos.

1. COMMODITY PRICES

Column 1:   Price per pound *(libra)* of wax

Column 2:   Price per pound *(libra)* of plaster

Column 3:   Price per *cántara* of red wine

Column 4:   Price per *cántara* of white wine

Column 5:   Price per ream *(resma)* of paper

Column 6:   Price per large sheet of parchment

Column 7:   Price per rabbit

Column 8:   Price per *vara* of Bruges cloth

Column 9:   Price per *vara* of Courtrai cloth

Notes: Prices in columns 8-9 are from the accounts of the *mayordomos* in the municipal archive of Seville. Prices in brackets refer to wax which, according to the Burgos accounts, was bought in Medina del Campo.

	(1)	(2)	(3)	(4)	(5)	(6)	(7)	(8)	(9)
1390	5		8.8	19.2	62		1.75		
1391	4.7	0.75	16	17	62.5	4			
1392									
1393	5.93	1	8.5	18	51.4	4	1.75		
1394	6.17	1.2	9.6	27	52	3.75	1.15		
1395	5.65	1.2	11.5	19	48	3.75	1.65		
1396	5.07	1.2	19.2	25	59.4	3.5	1.65		
1397	5.45	1.2	14.4	21	71	3.6	2		
1398		1.2							
1399									
1400								81.83	70
1401									70
1402	10	1.8	23	40	180	8	3		
1403									
1404								107.5	
1405								115	
1406								115	
1407	9.5	1.9	19.2	40	175	9.2	3.5	140	120
1408								160	120
1409								150	110
1410								125	102.5
1411								130	110
1412	11	2.2	21.33	32	180	12	4	125	85
1413								107.5	80
1414								120	85
1415								115	90
1416	11	2.3	24	48	176.4	9	4	127.5	85
1417								125.75	90
1418	9	2.3	24.3	32	175	7.45	4		
1419		2.5	24	40	172	9	4.5	127.5	90
1420								125	90
1421	7.5	2.5	25.33	40	174	9.5	5		
1422	8	2.5	21.33	40	195	9.5	4	100	75
1423	8	2.5	26.66	40	185	8.5	4	100	80
1424	8	2.5	24	44	175	7	5	100	85
1425	8	2.5	24	40	180	7		110	80
1426								100	75
1427	10.2	2.5	26.66	40	180	7	5		
1428	10.75	2.5	21.33	40	180	6.5	5	100	75
1429	10.1	2.5	24	38	180	6	5	100	77
1430	9.53	2.5	24	40	180	7	4		
1431	9.27	2.5			180	7	3.5		

	(1)	(2)	(3)	(4)	(5)	(6)	(7)	(8)	(9)
1432	9.1	2.5	26	38	180	7	3	123	100
1433	8.85		24	48	180	7.9		126	
1434	9.83		22.66	48	180	7.9			
1435	9.5	3.5	24	40	180	7.5	5	130	110
1436	9.5	3.5	24	36	180	10	6		
1437	10	3	26.66	48	175	9	5		
1438	11	3	34.66	56	175	8.5	6		
1439	12		28	48	170	10			
1440	20	3.5	36	56	200	10.5			
1441	16		28	48	180	10	6		
1442	17.5		40	56	200	11.5			
1443	15		32	64	180	11.15	7		
1444			36	48	190	11	10		
1445	19		28	48	190	12	7	180	130
1446	18.83		36	66.5	190	11	7	180	130
1447	17.5				190	9	8	180	120
1448	(14)				195	11	7	180	123.5
1449					200	12			
1450					180	11	8		
1451			44	60	180	10.3	9		
1452	(14)				215	9	9		
1453					180	8.2	8		
1454	15				180	10.5	10	210	155
1455	17				180	11	9	210	160
1456	19				200	12	7	216	
1457	17				180		8.5	220	170
1458	17				195	8.8	10	220	175
1459	17				190		8	250	175
1460	18.5		60	72	195	9			
1461	20					12	12	250	190
1462	25						10		
1463						20	9		
1464							10		
1465	39.5								
1466	(38.5)	4							
1467	39.5	9.5	50	78			15		
1468	43	6					15		
1469							25	300	240
1470	50						15		
1471									
1472		6						355	270
1473	42	7					15	360	280

	(1)	(2)	(3)	(4)	(5)	(6)	(7)	(8)	(9)
1474	42						18	400	280
1475	44	8					18		
1476	40						16		
1477	40						18		
1478		7					18		
1479	45						20		
1480	43						20		

2. COIN PRICES

Column 1: Silver *real*.

Column 2: Aragonese florin.

Column 3: Castilian *dobla*.

Column 4: *Dobla de la banda*.

Column 5: *Enrique*.

Column 6: *Franco de oro*.

Column 7: *Corona de oro*.

Column 7: *Ducado*.

Note: Figures in brackets are possible interpolations.

	(1)	(2)	(3)	(4)	(5)	(6)	(7)	(8)
1390	3.2	23	40					
1391	3.1	22.5	38.5			33.75		
1392		[45]						
1393		[45]						
1394		[45]						
1395	3	[45]						
1396		[45]						
1397		22.25						
1398		[46]						
1399		[47]						
1400		[48]						
1401		[49]						
1402		[50.5]						
1403		[50.5]						
1404	6	50	45					
1405		[50.5]						
1406		[50.5]						
1407	3	51	45					
1408		[50.5]						
1409		[50.5]						
1410		[50.5]						
1411		[50.5]						
1412	3	52	40					
1413		[50.5]						

	(1)	(2)	(3)	(4)	(5)	(6)	(7)	(8)
1414		[50.5]						
1415		[50.5]						
1416	*3*	50	*40*					
1417		[50.5]						
1418		51	90					
1419	7	51	90					
1420		[51.5]						
1421	7	52	90					
1422	7	52	90					
1423	7	52	90					
1424	7	52.25	90					
1425	7	52	90					
1426		[52.25]						
1427	7	52.5	90					
1428	7	53	90					
1429	7	53.5	98					
1430		55	100				82	
1431	7	54.5	110				80	
1432	7	55.5	110				80	
1433	7	59.5	115				90	
1434	7.25	62.62	118				94	
1435	8	67	120				100	
1436	8	67.5	128				105	
1437	8.75	69.67	130				108	
1438	8.75	70.83	135				106	
1439	8.75	75	135	110			108	
1440	10	88.33	140	112.5			100	
1441	9.75	77.5	180	136			140	
1442	9.5	68.67	140				105	
1443	10.5	68.17	150				115	110
1444	10.75	77.5	140					110
1445	10.5	80	140	125				
1446	11.5	84.33	150					
1447	12.17	87.17	180	130				
1448	12.67	95.83	180	137				
1449	13	101.37	187.5	143				
1450	13	101	190	150				
1451	14.5	106.67	200					160
1452	14.5	106.67	200					165
1453	14.5	106.67	200					
1454	14.5	106.67	200	152				
1455	14	106.67	200	153				

	(1)	(2)	(3)	(4)	(5)	(6)	(7)	(8)
1456	14.5	113.6	200					
1457	15	118.67	200	165				
1458	18	125	200	168				
1459	19.5	129	200	173				
1460	18.5	125	200					
1461	18	140	200					
1462	16	103	200					
1463	16	130			215			
1464	17.75	147.5	205					
1465	17	155	250					
1466	18.67	170	250		340	245		
1467	19.25	173.33	270		340	245		
1468	20.5	180	300			250		
1469	19	190	300		340	260		
1470	28	200	400					
1471	26.75	210	400			300		
1472	24	210						
1473	26.25	210	365			300		
1474	26.67	216.67	330			200		
1475	29	235	370					
1476	30	245	350			300		
1477	30	245						
1478	30	260						
1479	30.67		375					
1480	31		350			360		

3. MONEY OF ACCOUNT, SILVER, AND GOLD

Column 1: Price per ounce of silver in *mrs.*

Column 2: Value of *maravedí* in grams of standard silver (270 grains).

Column 3: Value of *maravedí* in Aragonese florins.

Note: Figures in brackets are possible interpolations.

	(1)	(2)	(3)
1390			.02174
1391			.02222
1392			[.02222]
1393			[.02222]
1394			[.02222]
1395			[.02222]
1396			[.02222]
1397			.02247
1398			[.02174]
1399			[.02128]
1400			[.02083]
1401			[.02041]
1402			[.01980]
1403			[.01980]
1404	24	.59896	.02
1405	[49.5]	[.58075]	[.01980]
1406	[49.5]	[.58075]	[.01980]
1407	24	.59896	.01961
1408	[49.5]	[.58075]	[.01980]
1409	[49.5]	[.58075]	[.01980]
1410	[49.5]	[.58075]	[.01980]
1411	[49.5]	[.58075]	[.01980]
1412	26	.55288	.01923
1413	[49.5]	[.58075]	[.01980]
1414	[49.5]	[.58075]	[.01980]
1415	[49.5]	[.58075]	[.01980]
1416	25	.575	.02

	(1)	(2)	(3)
1417	[49.5]	[.58075]	[.01980]
1418	50	.575	.01961
1419	[50]	[.575]	.01961
1420	[52]	[.55288]	[.01942]
1421	55	.52273	.01923
1422	52	.55288	.01923
1423	[52]	[.55288]	.01923
1424	52	.55288	.01914
1425	56	.51339	.01923
1426	[56]	[.51339]	[.01914]
1427	56	.51339	.01905
1428	56	.51339	.01887
1429	56	.51339	.01869
1430	55	.52273	.01818
1431	53.3	.53940	.01835
1432	58	.49569	.01802
1433	62.5	.46	.01681
1434	63	.45635	.01597
1435	65	.44231	.01492
1436	65	.44231	.01481
1437	65	.44231	.01435
1438	70	.41071	.01412
1439	75	.38333	.01333
1440	80	.35937	.01132
1441	90	.31944	.01290
1442	80	.35937	.01456
1443	80	.35937	.01467
1444	80	.35937	.01290
1445	80	.35937	.0125
1446	90	.31944	.01186
1447	100	.2875	.01147
1448	100	.2875	.01043
1449	100	.2875	.00986
1450	110	.26136	.00990
1451	110	.26136	.00937

	(1)	(2)	(3)
1452	110	.26136	.00937
1453	110	.26136	.00937
1454	110	.26136	.00937
1455	110	.26136	.00937
1456	110	.26136	.0088
1457	110	.26136	.00843
1458	110	.26136	.008
1459	110	.26136	.00775
1460	125	.23	.008
1461	125	.23	.00714
1462	126	.22817	.00971
1463	125	.23	.00769
1464	125	.23	.00678
1465	160	.17969	.00645
1466	165	.17424	.00588
1467	165	.17424	.00577
1468	180	.15972	.00555
1469	190	.15131	.00523
1470	230	.125	.005
1471	230	.125	.00476
1472	250	.115	.00476
1473	230	.125	.00476
1474	230	.125	.00461
1475			.00425
1476			.00408
1477			.00408
1478			.00385

4. WAGES

Column 1: Wage per day, *obrero.*
Column 2: Wage per day, *retejador.*
Column 3: Wage per day, *carpintero.*
Column 4: Wage per day, *obrera.*

	(1)	(2)	(3)	(4)
1390	3.15	4		
1391	2.75	4		1.8
1392	3.17			
1393	2.83	4.25		2
1394	3.33	4.25		
1395	2.75	4.5		
1396	3.5	4.5		
1397	3.42	4.5		
1398		5	5	1.4
1399				
1400				
1401				
1402	6	11	8	3.5
1403				
1404				
1405				
1406				
1407	8.83	12	11.33	5.5
1408				
1409				
1410				
1411				
1412	7.2	12	11	
1413				
1414				
1415				
1416	9.75	12		
1417				
1418	8.12	12	13	

	(1)	(2)	(3)	(4)
1419	10.5	12	12.5	
1420				
1421	8.12	12	13	
1422	8.75	12	14	
1423	8.14	12	14	
1424	8	12	13.33	
1425	8	12	14	
1426				
1427	9.29	13	13	
1428	9.67	13	13	
1429	7.75	13	13	
1430	9.5		13	
1431	11	14	13.5	
1432	8.25	14	13	
1433	9.5	13	12	
1434	8	13	14.5	
1435	10	14	12	
1436	10	12.83	15	
1437		13	16.5	
1438				
1439		14		
1440	14			
1441		14		
1442				
1443	12	16		
1444	13	14.4		
1445		15.5		
1468	20.25	25		10.5
1469	20		25	
1470				
1471		30		
14/2	25	35	33.5	
1473				
1474				

	(1)	(2)	(3)	(4)
1475				
1476				
1477	21	35		
1478	20			
1479				
1480		37.5		

5. ANNUAL SALARIES — OFFICIALS OF THE CATHEDRAL CHAPTER, BURGOS.

In the statistical data that follow it is important to note that salary figures represent the amounts paid with respect to a particular task and do not necessarily indicate the income of an individual official. Thus, to cite a typical example, whereas the 500 *mrs* salary for the *contadores del cabildo* in 1445 was shared by *two* such officials, the following year the same salary was shared by *three* officals. This fact by itself would make it extraordinarily difficult to calculate the fate of individuals' salaries during this period, but there are other problems which make the task almost insuperable. In the first place it must have been the case that the criteria for calculating salary totals varied over the years. For example, the data on the salaries of the *escribanos del cabildo* seem to point conclusively to a change from a 'calculated' to a 'notional' salary, and in some cases (the salaries of the *escribanos del consistorio* and the *reparador del cabildo*) conversions of income in kind into cash in the early 1450s obtrude into the salary calculations. Secondly, it was often the case that an individual performed more than one official chore. Indeed, in the case of the canons some of the salaries listed below would merely be 'additional perks'. It is within the context of these difficulties and the more specific observations given below, that the comments in the text (above) must be judged.

Lacunae in data on salaries are more easily made good by interpolations because of a greater degree of stability and lack of variations. However, interpolations have only been used when terminal entries were identical.

Abogado or *letrado del cabildo* (lawyer)

1444-1456	:	1,000 *mrs*
1457-1462	:	1,500 *mrs*
*1463-1470	:	2,500 *mrs*
1471-1472	:	1,500 *mrs*
*1475	:	3,000 *mrs*
*1478-1479	:	3,000 *mrs*

During the years marked with an asterisk *two* men were paid as *letrados* or *abogados* — from 1463 one was paid 1,500 *mrs* and the other 1,000 *mrs*, but the entry for 1475 makes it clear that from this point on each was paid 1,500 *mrs*.

Carpintero (carpenter)

1453-1480   .   100 *mrs*

For an explanation of the change from daily wage rates to annual salary payments see above p. 45. In several *Libros Redondos* the salaried *carpintero del cabildo* is described simply as *moro* (1453, 1456-8) or as *moro-carpintero* (1460-3).

Contadores del cabildo (accountants)

1396-1416	:	300 *mrs*
1418-1421	:	400 *mrs*
1422-1453	:	500 *mrs*
1454-1471	:	1,000 *mrs*
1472-1476	:	1,500 *mrs*
1477	:	2,000 *mrs*
1478-1480	:	1,500 *mrs*

This is a good example of the way in which salaries were often paid *for the job* and irrespective of the number of persons involved. Normally there were two *contadores,* but not infrequently the same salary was given to three *contadores* (1446-7, 1465, 1478, 1480). The year 1477 was exceptional — four *contadores* were given 500 *mrs* each and the total salary payment rose to 2,000 *mrs.* The use of 'old' *maravedíes* as late as 1453 is remarkable, and the change to 'new' *maravedíes* in the following year did not of course entail any increase in the salary. The *contadores* were usually cathedral dignitaries. In 1407, for example, the *contadores* were the *capiscol* and Anton Martines, *canonigo,* and in 1450 the *capiscol* and Pedro Gutierrez de Bibar, *canonigo.*

Echaperro (dog-ejector)

1427-1451	:	200 *mrs*
1455-1462	:	500 *mrs*

This rather oddly named salaried official also acted as a bell-ringer, and not infrequently he was described as the *campanero echaperros.*

Escribanos del cabildo (chapter scribes or secretaries)

1402-1449	:	465 *mrs*
1450-1461	:	2,465 *mrs*
1462-1480	:	2,460 *mrs*

With one exception all salary payments were for one *escribano* (in 1412 the *Libro Redondo* refers to two *escribanos*). This example is a good illustration of the difficulties involved in trying to make any sense from data on salaries. It is clear from the entries during the first decade of the fifteenth century that the 'salary' of the *escribano* was originally calculated on an 'upkeep' or 'maintenance' basis. Thus the entries for 1402, 1404 and 1407 arrive at a total salary of 465 *mrs* by allowing one *maravedí* per day for meat and wine (365 *mrs*) and adding on 100 *mrs* per year for clothing. Thereafter, however, the rationale behind the salary payment was never again repeated. Moreover, if we assume that the bizarre drop of five *mrs* in the yearly salary from 1462 onwards can only be explained by an uncorrected and careless clerical error, then the change from a 'calculated' to a 'notional' salary is complete. The *escribano del cabildo* was sometimes referred to as the *notario de los señores*.

Escribanos del consistorio (consistory scribes or secretaries)

1402-1451	:	200 *mrs*
1452	:	680 *mrs*
1453-1455	:	650 *mrs*
1456	:	400 *mrs*
1457-1480	:	200 *mrs*

With one exception all entries which refer to the specific number of *escribanos* make it clear that there were two (in 1412 there were three). The cash salary remained constant at 200 *mrs* throughout the whole period. The exceptional payments during the years 1452-1456 were due to the fact that some of the grain income which the *escribanos* were supposed to receive was paid to them in cash instead of in kind. Thus, in addition to their salary of 200 *mrs*, the *escribanos* were paid 480 *mrs* '*por la meytad del trigo que les fallescio*' (1452), 450 *mrs* '*por la meytad del trigo que les fallescio este año*' (1453), and 450 *mrs* '*de su salario e por el trigo que les quitaron*' (1454, 1455).

Mayordomo del cabildo (chief financial official of the chapter)

1396-1418	:	*400 mrs*
1419-1422	:	*500 mrs*
1423	:	2,500 *mrs*
1424-1437	:	2,000 *mrs*
1438-1441	:	4,500 *mrs*
1442-1443	:	4,000 *mrs*
1444	:	5,000 *mrs*
1445	:	4,000 *mrs*
1446-1450	:	3,000 *mrs*
1451	:	4,500 *mrs*
1452	:	4,000 *mrs*
1453	:	4,500 *mrs*
1454-1457	:	5,000 *mrs*
1458	:	8,000 *mrs*
1459	:	7,000 *mrs*
1460-1464	:	6,000 *mrs*
1465	:	7,000 *mrs*
1466-1468	:	8,000 *mrs*
1469	:	10,000 *mrs*
1470-1472	:	15,000 *mrs*
1473	:	20,000 *mrs*
1474-1475	:	11,000 *mrs*
1476-1478	:	20,000 *mrs*
1479	:	13,000 *mrs*
1480	:	30,000 *mrs*

There was only one *mayordomo* and he was invariably a member of the chathedral chapter. He was sometimes referred to as the *'mayordomo de la bolsa'*.

Mayordomos del Libro Redondo (financial officials in charge of the *Libro Redondo* accounts)

1396-1418	:	*100 mrs*
1419-1422	:	*300 mrs*
1423-1480	:	1,000 *mrs*

The data in this case provide a good example of the impossibility of obtaining an accurate picture of salaries as the income of individuals rather than as the remuneration for a specific task. In the first place, although the salary for the job was divided between the two *mayordomos* who did the work, there were exceptional years: in 1440, for example, there were three *mayordomos* for the same salary. Secondly, the terminology and payments changed from 1468 onwards — salary payments of 1,300 *mrs* were given to these officials as *mayordomos* and *contadores* (or *puntadores*) *delas raciones*. This was, in effect, *pluriempleo,* and the accounts made notional distinctions between the two tasks — that is, the officials continued to be paid 1,000 *mrs* as *mayordomos* and an additional 300 *mrs* as *puntadores*. These *mayordomos* were invariably canons.

Pregoneros ('Announcers' or 'criers')

1395-1396	:	*30 mrs*
1412-1419	:	100 *mrs*
1421	:	120 *mrs*
1423	:	100 *mrs*
1424	:	120 *mrs*
1425	:	150 *mrs*
1427-1428	:	110 *mrs*
1429	:	70 *mrs*
1432-1435	:	120 *mrs*
1436-1437	:	150 *mrs*
1438	:	180 *mrs*
1442	:	200 *mrs*
1443	:	230 *mrs*
1444	:	300 *mrs*
1445-1451	:	200 *mrs*
1452-1453	:	500 *mrs*
1454-1457	:	400 *mrs*
1459	:	320 *mrs*
1461-1480	:	400 *mrs*

Portero mayor (chief porter)

1402-1480	:	70 *mrs*

158

Procuradores del cabildo (procurators)

1402-1407	:	200 *mrs*
1428-1441	:	500 *mrs*
1442	:	600 *mrs*
1443	:	500 *mrs*
1444-1446	:	1,000 *mrs*
1448	:	500 *mrs*
1449-1450	:	600 *mrs*
1451	:	800 *mrs*
1452-1471	:	1,000 *mrs*
1472	:	1,500 *mrs*
1473	:	2,000 *mrs*
1474-1478	:	3,000 *mrs*
1479	:	8,000 *mrs*
1480	:	2,000 *mrs*

Usually there was only one *procurador,* but on occasion the yearly salary had to be divided between two *procuradores* (1402, 1404, 1407, 1428, 1436, 1466-8).

Raedor or rasero (granary cleaner)

1402-1480	:	70 *mrs*

Apart from 1452, when the salary was shared between two *raedores,* there was only one such official throughout the century.

Reparador del cabildo ('Repairer' of chapter property)

1428	:	500 *mrs*
1437-1438	:	300 *mrs*
1440-1450	:	500 *mrs*
1451	:	1,300 *mrs*
1452	:	1,040 *mrs*
1453	:	1,025 *mrs*
1454	:	800 *mrs*
1455-1464	:	500 *mrs*
1467-1478	:	600 *mrs*

There was only one *reparador*. The inflated payments for 1451-3 were due to some wheat income in kind being converted into cash. Thus in 1453, in addition to the salary of 800 *mrs*, the *reparador* was given 225 *mrs 'por la meytad del trigo quele fallescio de su salario'*.

Troxeros (granary supervisors)

1402-1422	:	200 *mrs*
1423-1451	:	400 *mrs*
1452	:	300 *mrs*
1453	:	200 *mrs*
1454-1474	:	300 *mrs*
1475-1480	:	600 *mrs*

In 1453 and from 1468 to 1480 there was only one *troxero;* from 1402 to 1452 and from 1454 to 1467 there were two *troxeros*.

6. BIMETALLIC RATIOS

The ratios have been established from the Burgos data on coined money by dividing the price of pure gold (calculated from Aragonese florins) by the price of pure silver (calculated from *reales*). The ratios are approximate only because the calculations fail to take into account the alloy content of the coins and because quotations for *reales* and florins in any one year may, for obvious reasons, be incongruous. In general terms, however, the ratios are accurate enough to support the arguments propounded in this study (above pp. 28-30, 40-1).

Year	Ratio	Year	Ratio	Year	Ratio
1404	10.65	1431	9.95	1458	8.88
1405		1432	10.13	1459	8.46
1406		1433	10.87	1460	8.64
1407	10.87	1434	11.04	1461	9.94
1408		1435	10.71	1462	8.23
1409		1436	10.77	1463	10.39
1410		1437	10.18	1464	10.62
1411		1438	10.35	1465	11.65
1412	11.08	1439	10.96	1466	11.64
1413		1440	11.29	1467	11.51
1414		1441	10.16	1468	11.06
1415		1442	9.24	1469	12.59
1416	10.65	1443	8.30	1470	8.99
1417		1444	9.21	1471	9.87
1418		1445	9.74	1472	11.02
1419	9.31	1446	9.37	1473	10.07
1420		1447	9.16	1474	10.23
1421	9.50	1448	9.67		
1422	9.50	1449	9.97		
1423	9.50	1450	9.93		
1424	9.54	1451	9.40		
1425	9.50	1452	9.40		
1426		1453	9.40		
1427	9.59	1454	9.40		
1428	9.68	1455	9.74		
1429	9.77	1456	10.01		
1430		1457	10.11		

APPENDIX C: GRAPHS

1. — The Devaluation of the Money of Account
The Maravedi in terms of Silver & Aragonese Florins
1435=100

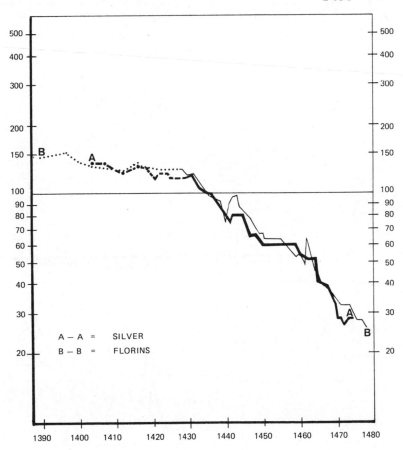

A — A = SILVER
B — B = FLORINS

2. — Index Numbers of Commodity Prices in Money of Account
1435=100

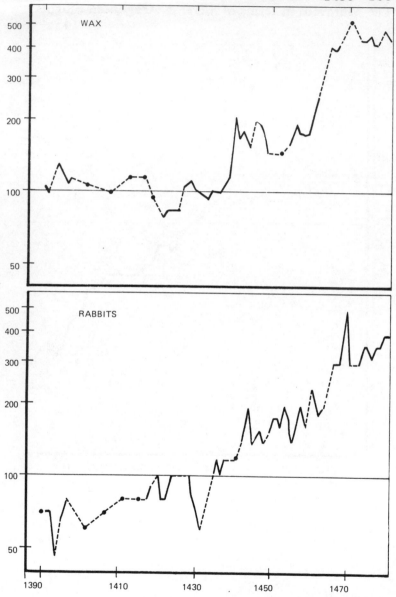

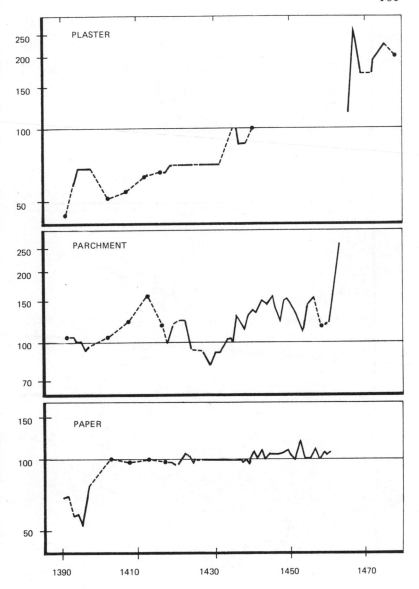

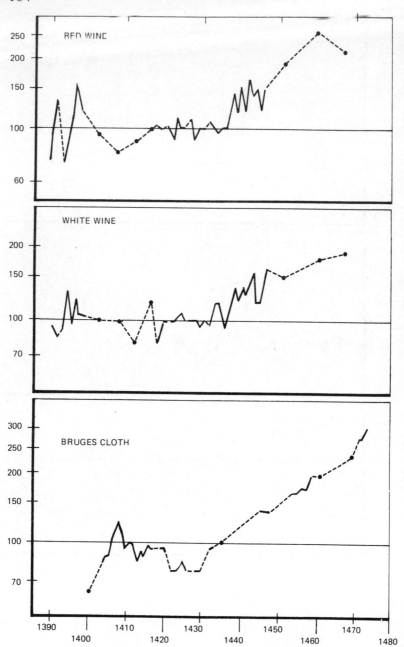

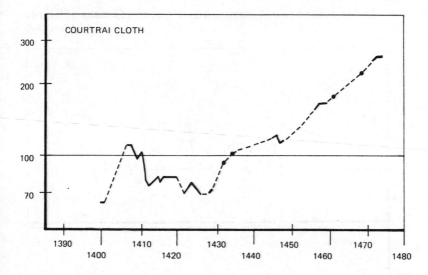

COURTRAI CLOTH

3. — Index Number of Commodity Prices in Grams of Silver
1435=100

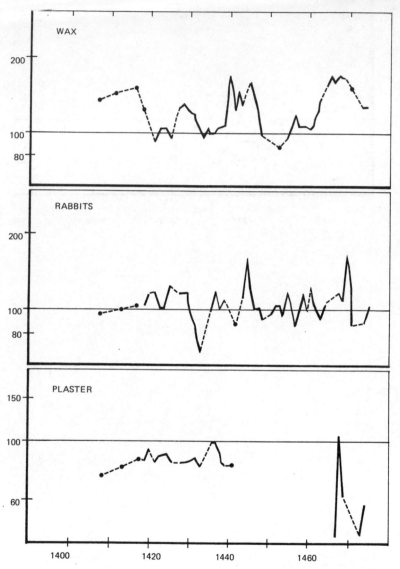

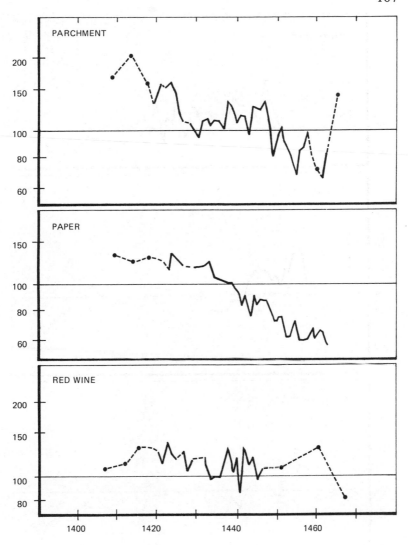

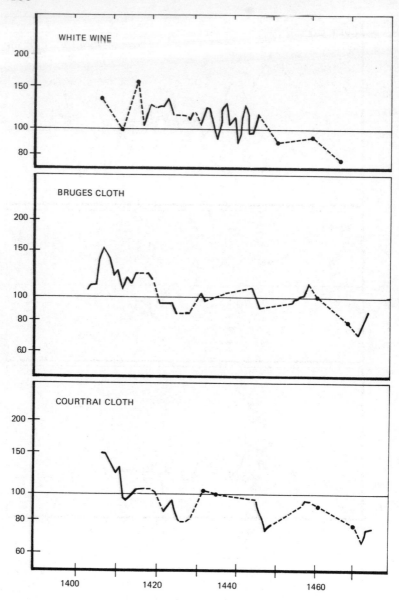

4. — Index Numbers of Coin & Silver Prices in Money of Account   1435=100

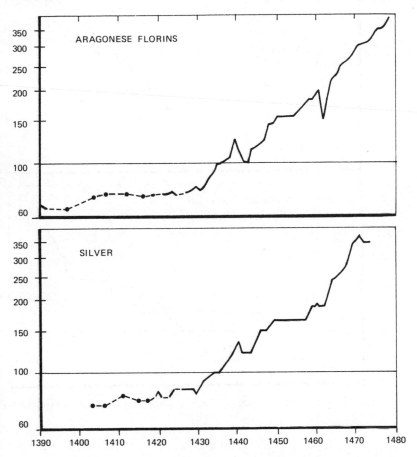

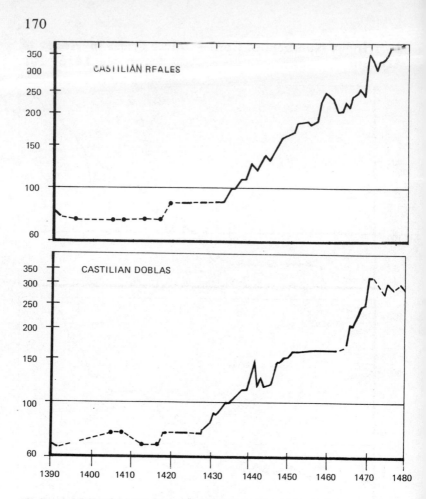

5. — Index Numbers of Wages in MRS and Grams of Silver
1435=100

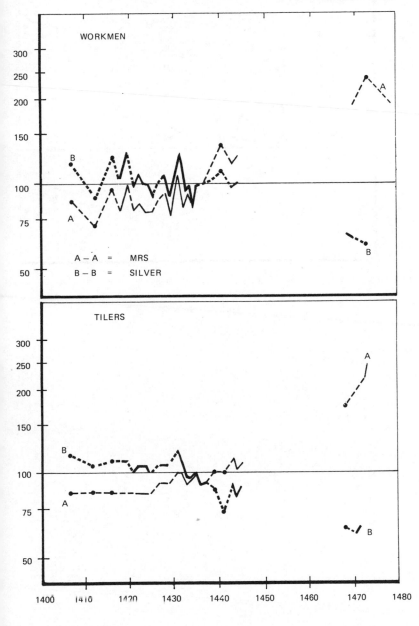

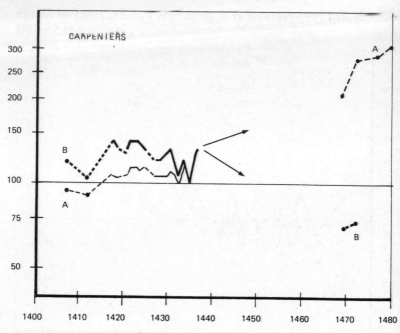

CARPENTERS

BIBLIOGRAPHY

The intention of this short bibliography is merely to give a list of the works cited in this study. It is not a detailed survey of all the manuscript and printed works consulted. The archival records which have been examined are listed in the Abbreviations on p. xi.

Amador de los Ríos, J., *Memoria histórico-critica sobre las treguas celebradas en 1439 entre los reyes de Castilla y de Granada* (Madrid, n.d.)

Anes Alvarez, G., *Las crisis agrarias en la España moderna* (Madrid, 1970)

Basas Fernández, M., *El consulado de Burgos en el siglo XVI* (Madrid, 1963)

Braudel, F., and Spooner, F., 'Prices in Europe from 1450 to 1750', in E.E. Rich and C.H. Wilson, eds., *Cambridge Economic History of Europe*, IV, *The Economy of Expanding Europe in the sixteenth and seventeenth centuries* (Cambridge, 1967), 374-486

Colección de documentos inéditos para la historia de Guipúzcoa (San Sebastian, 1958) I.

Collantes de Terán, A., *Sevilla en la baja edad media: la ciudad y sus hombres* (Seville, 1977)

Cortes de los antiguos reinos de León y Castilla (Real Academia de la Historia, 7 vols. Madrid, 1861-1903)

Crone, G.R. (ed.), *The Voyages of Cadamosto and other documents on Western Africa in the second half of the Fifteenth Century* (Hakluyt Society, 1937)

Crónica de Juan II (Biblioteca de Autores Españoles, LXX. Madrid, 1878)

Day, John, 'The Great Bullion Famine of the Fifteenth Century', *Past and Present,* no. 79 (1978), 3-54

Enríquez del Castillo, Diego, *Crónica del rey don Enrique el Cuarto* (Biblioteca de Autores Españoles, LXX. Madrid, 1878)

Escavias, Pedro de, *Hechos del condestable don Miguel Lucas de Iranzo,* ed. Juan de Mata Carriazo (Madrid, 1940)

García de Cortazar, J.A., *Vizcaya en el siglo XV. Aspectos económicos y sociales* (Bilbao, 1966)

Gautier-Dalché, J., 'L'histoire monetaire de l'Espagne septentrionale et centrale du XIᵉ au XIIᵉ siècles: Quelques réflexions sur diverses problèmes', *Anuario de Estudios Medievales,* VI (1969), 43-95

Gil Farres, O., *Historia de la moneda española* (Madrid, 1959)

174

González, Tomás (ed.), *Colección de cédulas, cartas patentes, provisiones, reales ordenes y documentos concernientes a las Provincias Vascongadas*, 6 vols. (Madrid, 1829-33)

Grice-Hutchinson, M., *The School of Salamanca. Readings in Spanish Monetary Theory, 1544-1605* (Oxford, 1952)

Grice-Hutchinson, M., *Early Economic Thought in Spain, 1177-1740* (London, 1978)

Hamilton, Earl J., *American Treasure and the Price Revolution in Spain, 1501-1650* (Cambridge, Mass., 1934)

Hamilton, Earl J., *Money, Prices and Wages in Valencia, Aragon and Navarre, 1351-1500* (Cambridge, Mass., 1936)

Hamilton, Earl J., *War and Prices in Spain, 1651-1800* (Cambridge, Mass., 1947)

Hamilton, Earl J., *El florecimiento del capitalismo y otros ensayos de historia económica* (Madrid, 1948)

Heers, J., 'Le commerce des basques en Mediterranée', *Bulletin Hispanique*, LVII (1955), 292-324.

Heers, J., *Gênes au XV*^{e}*siècle* (Paris, 1961)

Iradiel Murugarren, P., *Evolución de la industria textil castellana en los siglos XII-XVI* (Salamanca, 1974)

Jago, Charles, 'The Influence of Debt on the Relations between Crown and Aristocracy in seventeenth-century Castile', *Economic History Review*, 2nd ser. XXVI (1973), 218-36

Lacarra, J.M., 'Aspectos económicos de la sumisión de los reinos de taifas (1010-1102)', in *Homenaje a Jaime Vicens Vives*, I (Barcelona, 1965), 255-77

Ladero Quesada, Miguel Angel, *Granada. Historia de un país islámico* (Madrid, 1969)

Ladero Quesada, Miguel Angel, 'Las aduanas de Castilla en el siglo XV', *Revue internationale d'histoire de la banque*, no. 7 (1973), 83-110

Ladero Quesada, M.A., *La Hacienda Real de Castilla en el siglo XV*(La Laguna, 1973)

Ladero Quesada, M.A., 'Moneda y tasa de precios en 1462: Un episodio ignorado en la política económica de Enrique IV de Castilla', *Moneda y Crédito*, no. 129 (1974), 91-115

Ladero Quesada, Miguel Angel, 'Para una imagen de Castilla: 1429-1504', in *Homenaje al Dr. Juan Reglà Campistol* Valencia, I, 201-15

Ladero Quesada, Miguel Angel (ed.), *Andalucía, de la Edad Media a la Moderna* (Anexos de la revista 'Hispania', 7: Madrid, 1977)

Ladero Quesada, Miguel Angel, and González Jiménez, Manuel, *Diezmo eclesiástico y producción de cereales en el reino de Sevilla (1408-1503)* (Seville, 1979)

Lóper de Ayala, Pedro, *Crónica de Enrique II de Castilla* (Biblioteca de Autores Españoles, LXVIII. Madrid, 1878)

MacKay, Angus, 'Popular Movements and Pogroms in fifteenth-century Castile', *Past and Present,* no. 55 (1972), 33-67

MacKay, Angus, 'The ballad and the frontier in late medieval Spain', *Bulletin of Hispanic Studies,* LIII (1976), 15-33

MacKay, Angus, *Spain in the Middle Ages: From Frontier to Empire, 1000-1500* (London, 1977)

MacKay, Angus, 'Recent Literature on Spanish Economic History', *Economic History Review,* 2nd ser. XXXI (1978), 129-45

Magalhães-Godinho, V., *L'Economie de l'Empire Portugais aux XVᵉ et XVIᵉ siècles* (Paris, 1969)

Malowist, M., 'The Western Sudan in the Middle Ages', *Past and Present,* no. 33 (1966)

Memorias de Don Enrique IV de Castilla (Real Academia de la Historia. Madrid, 1835-1913), II

Mitre Fernández, Emilio, 'La frontière de Grenade aux environs de 1400', *Le Moyen Age,* LXXVIII (1972), 489-522

Molenat, J.-P., 'Chemins et ports du nord de la Castille au temps des Rois Catholiques', *Mélanges de la Casa de Velázquez,* VII (1971), 115-62

Oresme, Nicholas, *De Moneta,* ed. and trans. Charles Johnson (London, 1956)

Pike, R., *Enterprise and adventure. The Genoese in Seville and the Opening up of the New World* (New York, 1967)

Pulgar, Fernando del, *Claros varones de Castilla,* ed. R.B. Tate (Oxford, 1971)

Ruiz, Juan, *Libro de Buen Amor,* ed. R.S. Willis (Princeton, 1972)

Ruiz, T.F., 'The Transformation of the Castilian Municipalities: The Case of Burgos, 1248-1350', *Past and Present,* no. 77 (1977), 3-32

Russell, P.E., *The English Intervention in Spain and Portugal in the time of Edward III and Richard II* (Oxford, 1955)

Sáez, Liciniano, *Demostración histórica del verdadero valor de todas las monedas que corrían en Castilla durante el reynado del Señor Don Enrique IV, y de su correspondencia con las del Señor Don Carlos IV* (Madrid, 1805)

Sánchez, Garci, *Los Anales de Garci Sánchez, jurado de Sevilla,* ed. Juan de Mata Carriazo (Seville, 1953)

Smith, R.S., *The Spanish Guild Merchant. A History of the Consulado, 1250-1700* (Durham, 1940)

Spooner, Frank C., *The International Economy and Monetary Movements in France, 1493-1725* (Cambridge, Mass., 1972)

Spufford, Peter, and Wilkinson, Wendy, *Interim Listing of the*

Exchange Rates of Medieval Europe (Keele, 1977)

Suárez Fernández, Luis, *Juan II y la frontera de Granada* (Valladolid, 1954)

Suárez Fernández, L., *Navegación y comercio en el golfo de Vizcaya* (Madrid, 1959)

Suárez Fernández, Luis, 'Un libro de asientos de Juan II', *Hispania,* XVII (1957), 323-68

Suárez Fernández, L., 'España cristiana, crisis de la reconquista, luchas civiles: Pedro I, Enrique II, Juan I y Enrique II de Castilla', in R. Menéndez Pidal ed., *Historia de España,* XIV (Madrid, 1964)

Suárez Fernández, L., 'Los Trastámaras de Castilla y Aragón en el siglo XV', in R. Menéndez Pidal ed., *Historia de España,* XV (Madrid, 1964)

Torres Fontes, Juan (ed.), *Estudio sobre la "Crónica de Enrique IV" del Dr. Galíndez de Carvajal* (Murcia, 1946)

Torres Fontes, Juan, *Don Pedro Fajardo, adelantado mayor del reino de Murcia* (Madrid, 1953)

Torres Fontes, Juan, 'La vida en la ciudad de Murcia en 1442-1444: Precios y salarios', *Anuario de historia económica y social,* I (1968), 691-714

Valdeón Baruque, J., 'Las reformas monetarias de Enrique II de Castilla', in *Homenaje al Prof. Alarcos* (Valladolid, 1966) II, 829-45

Valera, Mosén Diego de, *Memorial de diversas hazañas,* ed. Juan de Mata Carriazo (Madrid, 1941)

Vilar, Pierre, 'Problems of the Formation of Capitalism', *Past and Present,* no. 10 (1956), 15-38

Vilar, Pierre, *Oro y moneda en la historia (1450-1920)* (3rd ed., Barcelona, 1974)

Wilson, Sir Thomas, 'The State of England (1600)', ed. F.J. Fisher, in *Camden Miscellany,* vol. XVI (Camden Society, 3rd ser. LII, 1936)

Wolff, P., 'The 1391 Pogrom in Spain. Social Crisis or not?', *Past and Present,* no. 50 (1971), 4-18

INDEX

Other volumes in this series

Copies obtainable on order from
Swift Printers (Sales) Ltd., 1-7 Albion Place, Britton Street, London EC1M 5RE